At Standing Rock and Wounded Knee

At Standing Rock and Wounded Knee

The Journals and Papers of Father Francis M. Craft, 1888–1890

Edited and Annotated
by
Thomas W. Foley

Foreword by Michael F. Steltenkamp

THE ARTHUR H. CLARK COMPANY
An imprint of the University of Oklahoma Press
Norman, Oklahoma
2009

ALSO BY THOMAS W. FOLEY

Father Francis M. Craft, Missionary to the Sioux (Lincoln, 2002)
Faces of Faith: A History of the First Order of Indian Sisters (Baltimore, 2008)

Library of Congress Cataloging-in-Publication Data

Craft, Francis M.

At Standing Rock and Wounded Knee : the journals and papers of Father Francis M. Craft, 1888–1890 / edited and annotated by Thomas W. Foley ; foreword by Michael F. Steltenkamp.

p. cm.

Includes bibliographical references and index.

ISBN 978-0-87062-372-1 (hardcover : alk. paper) 1. Craft, Francis M.—Diaries. 2. Craft, Francis M.—Correspondence. 3. Hunkpapa Indians—Missions—Standing Rock Indian Reservation (N.D. and S.D.) 4. Standing Rock Indian Reservation (N.D. and S.D.)—Religious life and customs. 5. Standing Rock Indian Reservation (N.D. and S.D.)—Social life and customs. 6. Wounded

Knee Massacre, S.D., 1890—Personal narratives. I. Foley, Thomas W., 1931– II. Title.

E99.H79C73 2009

266'.2'092—dc22

2008040617

The paper in this book meets the guidelines for permanence and durability of the Committee on Production Guidelines for Book Longevity of the Council on Library Resources, Inc. ∞

---

1 2 3 4 5 6 7 8 9 10

Few of us are given a voice after 120 years.

This is Father Craft's opportunity to be heard.

Contents

Illustrations

Figures

Maps

Foreword

Anyone familiar with the Ghost Dance religion is aware of a "Father Craft" who witnessed the tragic bloodletting that occurred on Wounded Knee Creek in 1890. There for seemingly unknown reasons, Craft comes across in the historical literature as a kind of itinerant Irish Catholic priest who incurred a near-fatal wound at the hands of an angry Sioux warrior.

Nothing was known of the man's very unconventional, inspiring, and perplexing ways until Thomas Foley produced in 2002 the biography *Father Francis M. Craft: Missionary to the Sioux*. When I read this biography, my curiosity about the priest and his era was stirred enough to visit East Stroudsburg, Pennsylvania, and walk paths that were well known to Craft. It was there that he died in obscurity as the dedicated and beloved pastor of a Catholic church.

In order to write Craft's biography, Foley conducted extensive research that helped illuminate the priest's journals. Foley revealed to readers a figure substantially more complex than previously thought. Through Foley, we learn that Craft also bore the titles of soldier, physician, convert to Catholicism, and, of special significance, priest of Mohawk descent. In the Jesuit Order for six years, Craft was later ordained for the Vicariate of Dakota Territory, where he served as a "missionary to the Sioux" (now properly referred to as "Lakotas") of North and South Dakota. He was even adopted by the family of Spotted Tail and fluently spoke their language.

Through Foley, we learn that Craft's presence at Wounded Knee was a presence to people among whom he once served as priest. Since he happened to be visiting the Pine Ridge reservation at the time, and since this group of Ghost Dancers was there under military arrest, he chose to visit with them and serve as a pacifying presence for both army personnel and Indians. Unlike many later commentators, Craft commended the soldiers for their restraint when bullets began to fly. At the same time, if his wound proved to be fatal, he asked to be buried with the Lakotas who died there and who were placed in a mass grave that now marks the site.

Foley revealed a late-nineteenth-century world of religious sectarianism that influenced the actions of many who converged upon the American frontier. What also becomes clear in Craft's journals is that he was at odds with many persons when he worked as an Indian missionary. Outspoken when advancing a position, he contended with Protestant government officials and regularly confronted the hierarchy of his own church. It seemed they focused more on Katherine Drexel's well-funded evangelistic efforts than on his founding of a devout, but penniless, congregation of Indian sisters. A veteran of five wars and a missionary to several Lakota agencies, the once controversial Craft eventually found respite as a beloved parish pastor in Pennsylvania.

Craft's journals capture an "edge" to his personality that probably helped bring him into conflict with an array of people. However, a greater testimony to the man took place symbolically and was not reported in anyone's memoirs or history books. Namely, hundreds attended the priest's funeral to mourn their heartfelt loss.

The journals that Foley presents in this volume are Craft's diary-like report of day-to-day activities as a missionary in the years before he acquired notoriety as a priest at Wounded Knee. Most missionaries of this period recorded their experience in such journals, and many of these unpublished documents are available to researchers at Marquette University's Catholic Mission Archives. With the publication of Craft's reflections, readers acquire a very personal glimpse of a man whose identity was little more than a footnote. Because of Foley's efforts, we probably now know more about this priest than is known of anyone present on the killing field that day in 1890.

Readers should know that Craft's journals are not typical of missionary diaries. The priest did not provide the "thick description" of Lakota culture that other priests often reported. Others were also generally not as critical as Craft in their evaluation of individuals. However, like other journals of the period, they do convey a sense of the nineteenth-century reservation world that no longer exists. As a result, readers can appreciate some experiences that are universal and transcendent. On the other hand, there is material that elicits consternation.

As for his social relationships, Craft had admirers and detractors. Perhaps he was the sort of person whom people either really liked or really disliked, and perhaps Craft simply wrote about these same sentiments that he, also, felt toward others. Perhaps it was cathartic for Craft to criticize people on paper and so be less combative in real life.

These musings come to mind when reading about a time and place far removed from contemporary experience. However, combined with Foley's earlier biography, Craft's journal produces the portrait of a man whose life seems tailor-made for the movie screen.

MICHAEL F. STELTENKAMP
Wheeling Jesuit University

Acknowledgments

I am grateful to Father Regis Probstfield, Order of Saint Benedict (OSB), pastor of the Catholic Indian Mission at Standing Rock Reservation, Ft. Yates, North Dakota, for translating the Latin entries in Father Craft's journals and to Harvey Markowitz, a scholar with the D'Arcy McNickle Center for the History of the American Indian at the Newberry Library, Chicago, for his translations of the Lakota entries. Mark Thiel, archivist at Marquette University, was most helpful in identifying some of the more obscure religious associates of Father Craft; and years ago, Anita S. Tilden of the U.S. Department of Interior had a wonderful idea when she began assembling the eight-volume *Biographical and Historical Index of American Indians and Persons Involved in Indian Affairs*. Together with several *Who's Who* reference books, some contemporary histories included in the bibliography, and the *Annual Reports of the Commissioner of Indian Affairs, 1881–1900*, these volumes greatly assisted me in identifying the individuals Father Craft mentions in his journals.

Finally, I am especially grateful to Father Michael F. Steltenkamp, Society of Jesus (SJ), of the Religious Studies Department at Wheeling Jesuit University for his careful review and thoughtful recommendations, which contributed substantially to a more thorough understanding of Father Craft's observations and reactions to the cultural events he encountered and described in his missionary work among the Sioux.

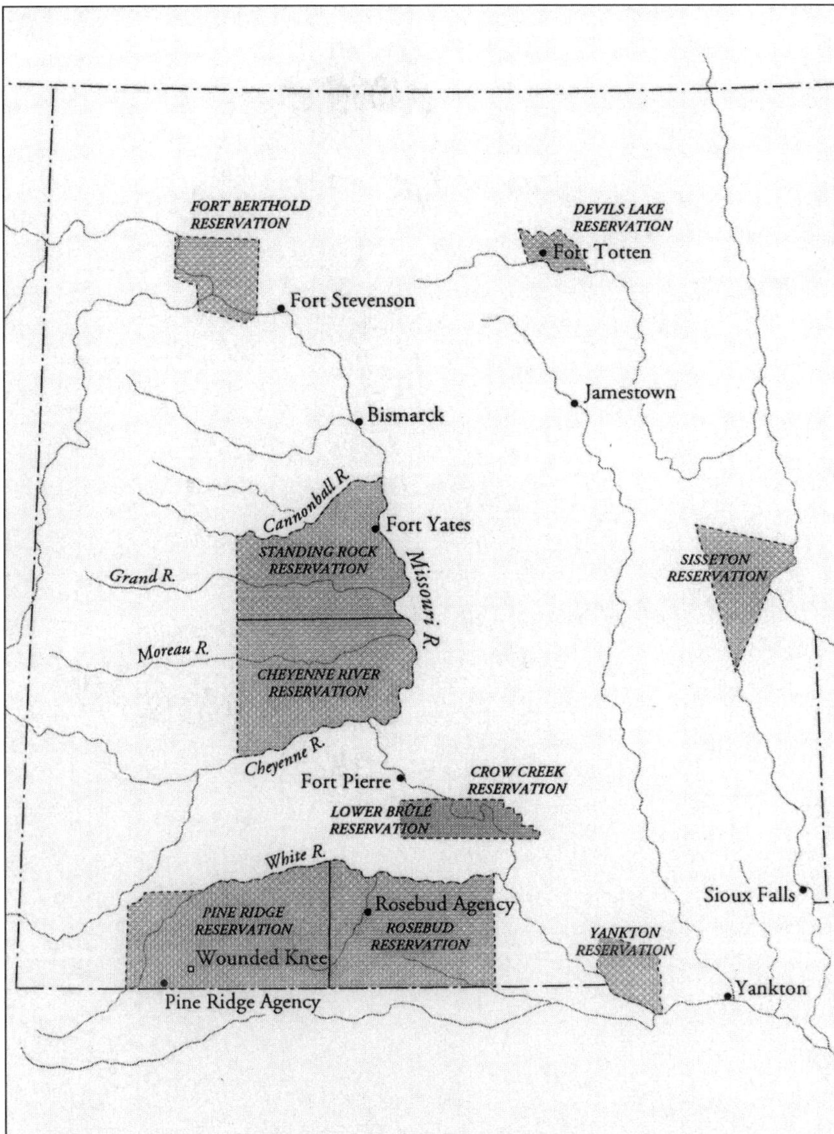

MAP 1. Dakota Territory reservations, late nineteenth century. *Based on map in* Father Francis M. Craft: Missionary to the Sioux, *by Thomas W. Foley, by permission of the University of Nebraska Press. © 2002 by the University of Nebraska Press.*

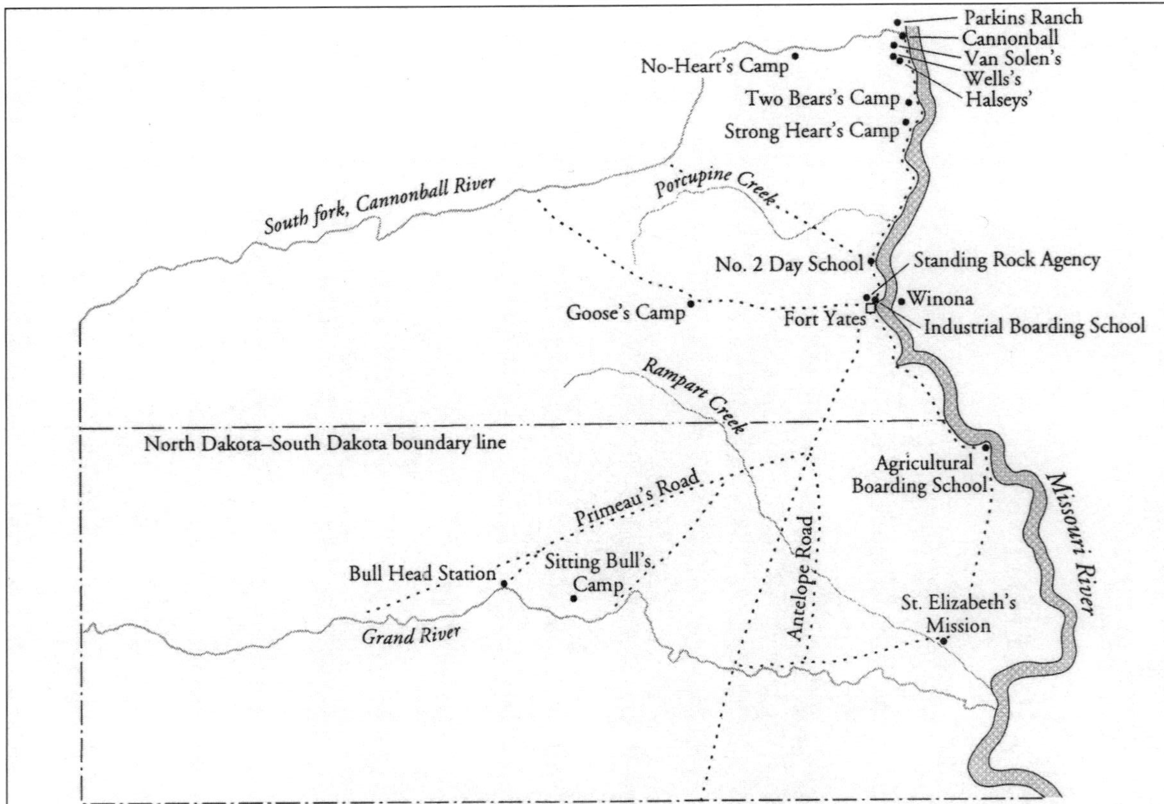

MAP 2. Standing Rock Indian Reservation, late nineteenth century.
Based on map in Father Francis M. Craft: Missionary to the Sioux, *by Thomas W. Foley, by permission of the University of Nebraska Press. © 2002 by the University of Nebraska Press.*

Introduction

The journals of Father Francis M. Craft cover a twenty-six-month period and were primarily written on Standing Rock Reservation in Dakota Territory, beginning March 21, 1888, and ending May 28, 1890. They provide fascinating insights into reservation life from the federal acquisition of Sioux lands during the Dawes Commission of 1888–89 to events preceding the tragedy at Wounded Knee in December 1890. They also reflect the dramatic competition among religious denominations that quarreled over the salvation of Indian souls, secular groups and settlers who squabbled over Indian lands, and all sides as they sought to profit from government funds, programs, and provisions designed to facilitate the acculturation of Native Americans. Other correspondence from Father Craft's papers, which came into my possession in 1944, reveals how a missionary priest came to be in the middle of the last conflict of the Indian Wars.

The journals reveal the deeply intimate and eloquent personal expressions of a classically educated, erudite eastern white man in the midst of a Sioux Nation in the final stages of collapse. Father Craft's musings include Lakota epithets, Latin dictums, a few French phrases, a lone Welsh slogan, and a smattering of Shakespeare laced with quotes from Lord Byron and the Roman poet Juvenal. Most of this book, though, is uniquely his.

His writings vividly reflect his elation at a rare success, his profound sense of loss at failure and defeat, and his fierce determination in between these extremes. Frustrated by Indian obstinacy toward civilization and secular opposition to his methodology, thwarted repeatedly by his own hierarchy, Craft nevertheless met the daily challenges of missionary work with charity, reverence, and humor.

Father Craft's missionary style placed him at odds with almost everyone on the reservations. A disciple of Roberto De Nobili, a nineteenth-century Jesuit who pioneered the method of missionary adaptation in southern India, Father Craft immersed himself into the Native culture to gain the trust and friendship of his flock. He wore feathers in his hat and learned the Lakota language, often defending Indian culture and customs as he railed against the corruptive and abusive influence of white settlers and government bureaucrats. At the same time, he condemned Indian practices such as polygamy and gambling, and he encouraged the young to learn the white man's ways in both government and religious schools. He assimilated enough of the Indian culture to offend the white establishment even as he worked diligently for the acculturation of the Indian into the white world. His demands that students have limited or no vacations from boarding schools, for example, were understandably opposed by the close-knit Indian families he served. His willingness to criticize powerful Indian agents such as James McLaughlin, as well as U.S. Commissioner of Indian Affairs Thomas Morgan, compromised his religious superiors' diplomatic efforts to maintain the federally financed contract school system in the face of secular demands to finally separate church and state on the reservations. All of this, complicated by a fiercely independent streak of Americanism he displayed as he traveled a three-hundred-mile circuit among the camps of the Sioux, worried and dismayed his Benedictine and Jesuit contemporaries. Steeped in centuries of European and religious traditions, these devoted missionaries, who conducted their activities from established churches and schools on the reservations, were often baffled by the freewheeling autonomy exhibited by Father Craft.

Of all the western missionaries, perhaps none was more complex or controversial. Father Craft was a challenge to everyone, regardless of rank or status. Often arrogant and confrontational with others, he drew allegations from some quarters of being an eccentric crank at best, a lunatic at worst. Beset with his own prejudices, he was nevertheless a visionary—a century ahead of his time in some respects, a hundred years behind in others. In an earlier age, he would have been a knight; to Black Elk, he was a "good man, and not like the other *wasichus*" (white men). Of this we can be sure. He was like no other on the western frontier.

A full appreciation of his journals requires an awareness of Father Craft's origins as well as the events and characters affecting his experiences on Standing Rock Agency.[1] Francis Craft was born in New York City on September 23, 1852, the first son of Isaac and Sarah (Phillips) Craft. From his paternal grandmother, Rebecca Basset, he acquired the Indian blood that would eventually bring him to the field at Wounded Knee. Rebecca's parents (his great-grandparents) were an immigrant Welshman named Basset and the full-blood daughter of a Mohawk chief who had fought on the winning side in the Revolutionary War. Rebecca married William Craft, who had also served his new country in the same war. Isaac, Francis's father, was the second son of William and Rebecca. A medical doctor, Isaac practiced surgery at Bellevue Hospital in New York City. In 1851, Isaac married Sarah Phillips, who was descended from Revolutionary War hero Nathanael Greene. From this lineage, Francis acquired the Sons of the Revolution Medal that he proudly wore on his chest at Wounded Knee. This mix of Native blood, military heritage, and a medical legacy would profoundly affect the course of his adventurous career.

The Craft family home was located at 495 Hudson Street in New York City. They were members of the Episcopal Church of St. Luke, and Francis's early education was at a local public elementary school. When Francis was ten, his father gave him written permission to join the Union Army as General Lee's Confederate Army approached Gettysburg, Pennsylvania. He took the note—written on the back of his father's commission as a captain of the

[1] For a complete biography, see Foley, *Father Francis M. Craft, Missionary to the Sioux.*

Second Regiment of Artillery and signed by New York governor DeWitt Clinton—and reached Gettysburg in time for the epic battle of the Civil War. Recruited as a messenger boy, Francis was knocked unconscious by a bayonet blow to the head on the first day of the battle. Troops of a Massachusetts regiment rescued him.[2] And so ended Francis Craft's first, albeit brief, attempt to emulate the military exploits of his forebears.

At age twelve, he enrolled in the College of Physicians and Surgeons at Columbia University to follow in the path of his father.[3] From there he transferred to the University of Louvain in Belgium for advanced studies in surgical methods. Conveniently, another war broke out, immediately attracting the attention of a recently graduated eighteen-year-old surgeon who was still too young to practice medicine. It was July 1870, and the Franco–Prussian War was about to be quickly ended at the Battle of Sedan. A mercenary for France, Craft served with the Marquis de Gallifet's "mixed squadron" in the final, desperate charge of the conflict that brought an end to the Second Empire in France.[4]

Toward the end of the Civil War, Craft's father had moved the family and his medical practice to an area in northeast Pennsylvania called Red Ridge, just outside the town of Milford. It was to that bucolic setting that the now veteran of two wars returned to join his father in the practice of medicine. However, the young man seemed always to have a propensity to seek out the next adventure, and the one that caught his interest lay in Cuba, where Cuban rebels had begun their own revolution against Spanish rule back in 1868. The Cuban War for Independence would become known in history as the "Ten Years War." Craft became a part of it in 1871, when he recruited 250 Civil War veterans (from both sides)—"all Irishmen but four"—and sailed with them from Tampa, Florida, to

[2] Kelley [*sic*], "Rev. Francis J. [*sic*] Craft Served Many Countries," 39.

[3] *East Stroudsburg (Pa.) Morning Press*, "Father Craft, Hero of Many Wounds, Quietly Dies Here," September 13, 1920.

[4] Craft to James Edward Kelly, 16 and 26 January 1917, James Edward Kelly Papers, New-York Historical Society (hereafter cited as Kelly Papers).

Cuba, where they fought a guerrilla action as mercenaries for the Cuban flag. His Cuban cohorts included "Maceo, [Antonio] Gomez, Garcia, and Bandera," and he himself rose to the rank of brigadier general, earning the sobriquet "the American devil" as leader of the "American Division of the Cuban Army."[5]

Exactly when Craft returned from this first Cuban adventure (he later would serve there again in the Spanish–American War) is unknown. However, he noted in his journal as he visited Our Lady of Mercy Church in Brooklyn, New York, on April 10, 1890, that it was the "first [Catholic church] I ever entered as a Protestant in 1874." From that entry one can speculate that his return from the Ten Years War and his conversion to Catholicism occurred during that same general time frame: 1872–74. He may well have been exposed to a Jesuit influence during his study at Louvain some four years earlier, or perhaps he was swayed by those 246 Irishmen in Cuba. A housekeeper of his reportedly said that he had become "interested in the Catholic faith through a group of Irish soldiers that he knew."[6]

Whatever the cause for his conversion, he entered the Society of Jesus (the Jesuits) in January 1876 at West Park, New York. Twenty-three years old, a veteran of three wars, and a practicing physician, Craft hardly fit the mold of entry-level candidates for a religious profession. In a sense, though, it was his status as a convert that caused him the most difficulty as he tried to adhere to the Jesuit pursuit of perfection. As a convert, Craft felt forced to reach by trial and error many truths and practices that others simply took on faith. In a letter to a Jesuit adviser at West Point, New York, Craft explained as follows:

> Those born and educated in the Church, grasp, and even put in practice, truths which I can reach only by painful and long-continued efforts. Not, as I would be compelled to do, by reflection, and step by step, but

[5] *Stroudsburg (Pa.) Daily Times*, "Doctor, Soldier, Priest," November 1, 1902; and Craft to James Edward Kelly, 12 May 1910, Kelly Papers.

[6] Rev. Harold G. Durkin to Dr. Dolan, 5 October 1945, Diocese of Sioux Falls. Durkin was pastor at St. Matthew's Catholic Church in East Stroudsburg, Penn., from 1943–61, and Craft had served as its first pastor from 1902–20.

> at once and almost instinctively. . . . They have an infallible guide, who, unless resisted, will lead them safely. I have *not,*—at least in the same way—and yet I must reach the same end as they. We both fight our way; but they strike surely, while I often "beat the air." I am placed as it were between two fires; on one side is the obligation to aim at perfection, and on the other is obedience. If I stand, which means, of course, falling back, I am guilty; if I advance it is without orders, and is in some way against obedience, and again I am guilty. It's the old story. "You shall and you shan't, you will and you won't, you'll be damned if you do and damned if you don't." *N'importe* [It's no matter], I can't help it. All I can do, is, to study my position as well as I can, and try to find the most vulnerable point in the enemy's lines. If I can cut my way out, so much the better; if I can't, "*non omni moriar*" ["I shall not wholly die"], I hope.[7]

For almost four years, he plunged into the classically based Jesuit curriculum, making his nonbinding "vows of devotion," more an informal pledge to persevere in the novitiate, on April 12, 1877. In the fourth year, he returned to the College of Louvain in Belgium, this time for additional studies in philosophy. Late in 1879, he was transferred to Woodstock College, a Jesuit seminary outside Baltimore, Maryland.

It was here that Craft crossed paths with Martin Marty, OSB, who in 1880 was appointed the first bishop of the newly established Diocese of Dakota Territory. Marty had brought Swiss Benedictine priests and brothers to Standing Rock Reservation in the mid-1870s, establishing a mission and an agricultural boarding school among the Lakota Sioux. Priests and other missionary aspirants were in short supply for such an ambitious undertaking, and Marty turned to Woodstock College to recruit additional candidates. There he found Francis M. Craft, headstrong, far too independent and challenging for a religious order, but also of Indian descent and medical skill, who would later write that he "became an Indian to save the Indian," and that he would not have endured the trials of priesthood for any other purpose.[8]

---

[7] Craft to Isadore Daubresse, 25 November 1879, Lauinger Library, Georgetown University Archives.

[8] Craft journal, 21 March 1888.

Marty sent Craft as a catechist among the Kalispel tribes in Montana, probably at St. Ignatius Mission, in 1880 or 1881. In 1883 he was ordained by Bishop Marty in Omaha, Nebraska, as a secular (or diocesan) priest for the Vicariate of Dakota Territory. The bishop then assigned him immediately to the Rosebud Indian Reservation in the Dakota Territory.

In 1870, President Ulysses S. Grant had introduced the so-called Peace Policy, which designated various Indian reservations to specific religious groups in the hope of fostering better relations with the tribes and improving efforts at assimilation. Rosebud Reservation was assigned exclusively to the Episcopal Church, and Standing Rock (also located in the Dakota Territory) to the Catholic Church. By the early 1880s, however, the Peace Policy had lost what little beneficent effect it may have had, and the reservations were opened to proselytizing by any and all religious faiths. Still, the exclusivity of the previous decade echoed and reverberated on most reservations.

As the first Black Robe[9] assigned to Rosebud, Father Craft was not long in alienating the Reverend William J. Cleveland, an Episcopalian missionary, and James G. Wright, the U.S. Indian agent in charge of the reservation. Craft had been warmly received by the Rosebud Sioux and was adopted into the family of Spotted Tail, a noted Sicangu chief who had been assassinated for fostering progressive ways back in 1881. The Rosebud Sioux had been unable to settle on a successor to Spotted Tail, who reportedly had told his people that in the event of his death, the first Black Robe to serve permanently on the reservation should be named chief in his place. The Sicangu gave Craft the name Wanbli cinca aglahpaya (The Eagle Covers Its Young, or Hovering Eagle), and the priest promptly moved into Spotted Tail's abandoned house on Rosebud.

Cleveland and Wright brought charges against the interloper, alleging that Craft had "held himself and his church above all civil

[9] "Black Robe" (*sina sapa*) was the Indians' name for Catholic missionary priests, after the black cassocks they wore.

law or the authority, wishes, or other instructions of the President, honorable Secretary of the Interior, or any other constituted authority."[10] Without a hearing of any sort, Craft was expelled from Indian Country by the U.S. Commissioner of Indian Affairs. He was later reinstated, but Bishop Marty arranged a compromise that led to his reassignment to Standing Rock rather than Rosebud Reservation. In November 1884, Craft arrived at Standing Rock Reservation—a reservation firmly founded in a Catholic history dating back to the assignment of another Catholic priest, Father Joseph A. Stephan, who had served as its first agent from 1878 to 1881. Father Stephan would later become the director of the Bureau of Catholic Indian Missions (BCIM), a role in which he would also serve as Craft's immediate supervisor.

Father Craft would now bring his unique style to assist the Benedictines in their work on the agency, home to two of the more notable names in the annals of reservation life: Sitting Bull and Agent James McLaughlin.

Father Craft leveraged his adoption into the family of Spotted Tail by claiming kinship with tribal members throughout the Dakota reservations. Spotted Tail's wife was his "mother," the slain Sicangu leader his "father," their children were his brothers and sisters, the next generation his nieces and nephews, and so on. Consequently, the journals often convey confusing references to this assumed genealogical relationship with the people he met on Rosebud, Standing Rock, and Fort Berthold Reservations. Adoption into the family was a sacred rite of Sioux beliefs—*hukapi*—creating a bond between people that is stronger than a biological kinship; those connected by this relationship are obliged to die for each other should the need arise. It was a matter of considerable significance to both Father Craft *and* his extended family throughout the Dakota reservations.

---

[10] James G. Wright to Commissioner of Indian Affairs, 16 January 1884, Bureau of Catholic Indian Missions (BCIM) Records, Marquette University Archives (hereafter cited as BCIM Records).

Figure 1. James E. Kelly's sketch of Father Craft in full regalia as Hovering Eagle. *Department of Special Collections, Marquette University Libraries.*

FIGURE 2.
Father Joseph A. Stephan, first agent at Standing Rock Reservation; later he would become director of the Bureau of Catholic Indian Missions. *Department of Special Collections and University Archives, Marquette University Libraries.*

A cautionary note: portions of Craft's journals will be found offensive by today's more enlightened standards. However, they reflect the racial, ethnic, and religious prejudices of his times and are offered unchanged in the interest of historical accuracy.

The first volume is a leather-bound notebook approximately 7¼" high by 4¾" wide. There are three volumes in all, the other two being about the same size with stiff cardboard covers. The small size was convenient for carrying in a coat pocket or saddlebag. The journals cover a period of 798 days—about twenty-six months without missing a day. Rarely in that span did he scratch out or erase what he had penned and then only to change a word or insert a line or two. He wrote in ink with a steel-tipped pen. Quill pens, he complained, blotted too much. "The hardness & acuteness of

FIGURE 3.
Sitting Bull, famous Hunkpapa leader, on Standing Rock Reservation, ca. 1888. Photograph by D. F. Barry. *Denver Public Library, Western History Collection, Call No. B-77.*

the new ideas requires sharp steel to commit them properly to paper," he wrote on a November day in 1888.

Father Craft filled his three ledger books with approximately 105,000 words, averaging about 130 words for each daily entry. Some of the longer commentaries, which generally occur earlier on in the journals, total more than 1,500 words each. As his creative outlets shifted to other venues in May 1890, later entries waned to only ten words or so. To better manage and present such a long journal to the reader, I focus in this book on the entries Father Craft wrote during those periods when he was located on Standing Rock Reservation. For the sake of brevity, I have summarized the entries Craft wrote at Fort Berthold and during his sundry visits to St. Paul, Chicago, and other locations as they occur chronologically in the course of the journals. I have omitted short, repetitive entries, often relating to the time he celebrated morning mass, and have so indicated by ellipses. In addition, I have inserted paragraph breaks to facilitate readability (paper was a precious commodity on the frontier, and every line was used). I have added translations of Latin, Lakota, and foreign phrases in brackets and have also added the days of the week where Craft had not already provided them. In the footnotes, I have added commentary to provide the reader with a fuller cultural context for Craft's observations or to identify relevant people, places, and events wherever possible. Finally, I have briefly related Craft's journal references to other existing correspondence, such as his letters to associates.

Craft ceased writing a journal in May 1890. His travels and lectures that summer, however, would eventually bring him into contact with high government officials as they considered how best to respond to the Ghost Dance Movement that swept across the Dakota reservations. These events would find him once again in Indian country, on the field at Wounded Knee, on December 29, 1890.

The Standing Rock journal entries total some 87,000 words that thoroughly reflect the unique character that was Father Craft. They also reveal the competing religious and secular interests in the Dakotas as well as his relationships with such well-known reservation figures as Agent James McLaughlin, Sitting Bull, and other Lakota leaders.

The question can be asked, Why, after five years on the reservations, did he choose to begin a journal? Part of the answer certainly was a need to document his actions in order to protect himself against further charges and slanderous accusations. The pending summer visit by the Dawes Commission likely entered into his decision as did a realization that what he was about to do was historically and religiously significant: God had called him to establish a congregation of Sioux Indian sisters. Thus, on a cold and blustery day in March 1888, Father Craft picked up his pen and began his journal.

Abbreviations

A M D G	ad maiorem Dei gloriam (for the greater glory of God [the Jesuit motto])
BCIM	Bureau of Catholic Indian Missions
BVM	Blessed Virgin Mary
BS	Blessed Sacrament
CSsR	Congregatio Sanctissimi Redemptons (Congregation of the Most Holy Redeemer)
DT	Dakota Territory
M	meridies (noon)
OSB	Order of Saint Benedict
OSF	Order of Saint Francis
RIP	rest in peace
SHCJ	Sisters of the Holy Child Jesus
SJ	Society of Jesus
Ven	venerable

Part I
The First Standing Rock Journal
March–August 1888

Acta et agenda
memoranda
&
inquirenda
et alia varia diligentissime
observanda et studenda
*A M D G**

[Translation]
Acts done and to be done
to be remembered
&
searched after
and other various things to be most diligently
observed and studied
For the Greater Glory of God

* A M D G, as written by Craft, stands for the Latin *ad maiorem Dei gloriam*, the Jesuit motto.

[Frontispiece]

✝

Thoughts in the saddle
On the general beauty & rectitude of things as they ought to be, & as we would like to have them,
and
The general yellowness & utter undesirability & misery of things as they are, & as we don't like to have them,
by
An Indian Missionary

	[Translation]
Tolle, lege, et si vere	Take, read, and if you think
Scripsi putas, miserere	I have truly written, have mercy
Sacerdoti misero.	On a wretched priest.
Bonum semen seminavit,	He sowed good seed,
Suo sanguine origavit,	He watered it with his blood,
Pro hoc gente barbaro.	For this barbarous nation.
Si non crescit terram crede	If it does not grow, consider
Aridam et malam esse.	The land arid and evil,
Et datam diabolo.	And given to the devil.

At Standing Rock Reservation, Dakota Territory, 1888

O Maria sis mihi propitia
[O Mary, be merciful to me]

March 21st 1888 [Wednesday, Feast of St. Benedict, Abbot]

"Infandum Tamaheca jubes venorare dolorem" ["You bid Tamaheca[1] to renew his unspeakable sorrow"] squeaks the pen as

[1] Tamaheca (The Lean Chief) was the Lakota name given to Craft's superior, Bishop Martin Marty, OSB. Buechel's *Dictionary* defines the word as "poor, lean, not fat." The Sioux evidently thought it aptly described the bishop's stature: 5'10" and about 140 pounds (see Karolevitz, *Bishop Martin Marty*, 5). Craft may have begun his journal at the suggestion of Bishop Marty.

it commences the daily record of an Indian Missionary's labors & annoyances, & his thoughts regarding them. Had I commenced this while at Rosebud [Indian Reservation], I might have been able now to judge of the present & future by the lights of the past, & from past happiness to draw consolation in present troubles. What's the use of recalling & writing down the annoyances of each day when they are hard enough to bear & already too hard to forget without recording them.

Here I have annihilated my former life, & been born again among these savages, & am one of them. "I've taught myself strange tongues, & in strange eyes have made me not a stranger." What Indian blood [Mohawk] I have is not from these, & when with the Kalispels,[2] I never thought to claim it. When the Sicangus[3] adopted me into their nation & into the family of their head chief, & made me their chief in his place, it seemed to be the will of God that I should be a savage among savages to win the savages to Christ, & really, the affection & manly loyalty of my new nation & kindred left me nothing to regret.

The devil could not see so many souls saved without a sharp fight. He urged on Protestant persecution, &, through it, roused the Government against me, & worst of all, blinded my Commanding Officer [Bishop Marty] to such an extent that he left me to fight alone. I conquered the Protestants & the Government, but the Bishop's eyes were not yet open, & I was ordered here. N'importes,—a soldier must obey.

Here I have to deal with savages corrupted, & wishing to be left to rot in peace, & corrupt Government officials who seek to rule or ruin, & daily lay snares for, & rouse up the violent kind of opposition against any priest who dare do his duty. I *dare*, & through "pity for my people" even though they take part against me, & even though my own self-respect should compel me to discard them as

---

[2] The Kalispels were a Salish tribe located in Idaho and western Montana.

[3] The Sicangus were Spotted Tail's tribe, located on Rosebud Indian Reservation, where Craft had served in 1883. The French called them the *Brulé*, which means "burnt thighs."

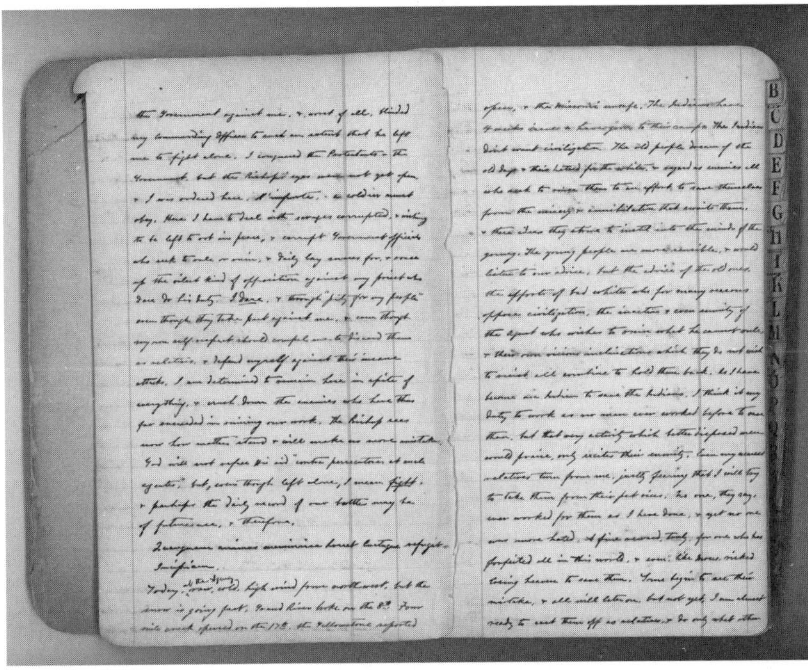

relatives & defend myself against their insane attacks, I am determined to remain here in spite of everything, & crush down the enemies who have thus far succeeded in ruining our work. The Bishop sees now how matters stand & will make no more mistakes. God will not refuse His aid "contra persecutores et male agentes" [against persecutors and those acting evilly], but, even though left alone, I mean <u>fight</u>, & perhaps the daily record of our battles may be of future use, & therefore—

> Quamguam animus meminisse horret luctugue refugit, Incipiam. [Although the soul (mind) shudders at remembering and takes refuge in sorrow, I will begin.]

Today, at the Agency, raw, cold, high wind from northwest, but the snow is going fast. Grand River broke on the 8th. Four Mile Creek[4] opened on the 17th, the Yellowstone [River] reported open, & the Missouri [River] unsafe. The Indians have four weeks issue & have gone to their camps.

The Indians don't want civilization. The old people dream of the old days & their hatred for the whites, & regard as enemies all who seek to rouse them to an effort to save themselves from the misery & annihilation that awaits them, & these ideas they strive to instill into the minds of the young. The young people are more sensible, & would listen to our advice, but the advice of the old ones, the efforts of the bad whites who for many reasons oppose civilization, the inaction & even the enmity of the Agent who wishes to ruin what he cannot rule, & their own vicious inclinations which they do not wish to resist all combine to hold them back.

As I have become an Indian to save the Indians, I think it my duty to work as no man ever worked before to save them, but that activity which better disposed men would praise, only excites their enmity. Even my nearest relatives turn from me, justly fearing that I will try to take them from their pet vices. No one, they say, ever worked for them as I have done, & yet no one was more hated. A fine reward, truly, for one who has forfeited all in this world, & even, like Moses, risked losing heaven to save them. Some begin to see this mistake, & all will later on, but not yet.

I am almost ready to cast them off as relatives, & do only what other priests are willing to do, but the ties of a relationship are too sacred, & too deeply rooted into the heart & all belonging to it, to be torn away without leaving a terrible wreck. It is necessary that I should love them sincerely, in order to be able to undergo the labors & trials necessary to save them; bread & meat feed & strengthen the body but love & charity alone can feed and strengthen the heart, & if my heart weakens, I will not have courage to do what must be done. Besides, it seems mean & dishonorable

[4] A creek entering the Missouri River four miles below Fort Yates.

to lose courage & retreat after I have advanced to the enemies centre, & the battle is about to be turned. When they were in less trouble I did not abandon them; why should I now? The Son of God made Himself man to save man, & bore the consequences to the death, & still does not desert them. I became as Indian to save the Indians, & I should stand by the consequences of my act to the end. I have Christ's example, & right reason to justify me, & by God's grace, I hope to conquer. Vive la guerre. [Long live the war.]

. . . Tonight write to the Bishop.[5] Tomorrow start for Cannonball,[6] if weather permits. Thoroughly exhausted from last Grand River trip.[7] Fever still troublesome. Must spare my strength for better times & more fruitful work.

March 22d 1888 [Thursday]

. . . Saddled up and rode to Mrs. Van Solen's[8] at Cannonball. Horse mean and yellow, & bucked beautifully. Road execrable. Stopped at Charles Halsey's,[9] smoked, talked, & persuaded two Indians that I was the younger brother of Father Craft, their Wanbli-cinca-aglahpaya [The eagle covers its young; i.e., Craft's Indian name, Hovering Eagle]. Truly, I *am* changed, & these poor fools will find it out to their cost.

Reached Mrs Van Solen's in good time, before dark, & will say mass & bless palms (cedar) tomorrow. I can't decide yet which is the greatest "onus diei" [burden of the day],—to put off my starting or stop on the road long enough to say the Office,[10] or to say the Rosary on my fingers while the horse is bucking like a demon, & thoughts

[5] Bishop Martin Marty.

[6] A settlement located at the confluence of the Cannonball and Missouri Rivers about twenty-five miles north of the Agency.

[7] Indian camps situated along the Grand River, about 30 miles below Fort Yates. A Grand River trip involved round trip travel exceeding 100 miles.

[8] Marie Van Solen, the first teacher of the Sioux at Standing Rock Agency, was the daughter of Honore Picotte, an early fur trader, and his wife, Alma, a full-blood Sioux (Hinton, *South of the Cannonball*, p. 59).

[9] Charles Halsey, a mixed-blood, was a local trader and interpreter.

[10] A formal selection of psalms, hymns, prayers, and readings for daily recitation required of all priests and religious.

anything but prayerful & pious try to sneak in among pious aspirations. Wahtesni telo! Gnaska cincapi! [Worthless children of frogs!] etc. etc. etc.

March 23d [Friday]

. . . Said Mass (high mass) at Mrs. Van Solen's & blessed the palms. Got through at noon. Saddled up & rode to Wells'.[11] Stopped at High Bear's. The Indians are trying to have him broken as chief because he carried out the Agent's orders by announcing Saturday as the only dance day. I will tell the District Farmer & let him settle it.

Ahewanka [Frosted], a son of old Red Fish,[12] claims to have power from the Devil to cure sickness, find things lost, etc. etc. Sent him a challenge & denounced the whole affair as a humbug.

A fine Catholic Agency, this. I could make such affairs supremely ridiculous, but the Agent & all the whites stand ready to oppose all done to civilize or convert. If any noise is made, they all blame the priest. A Priest must do his duty, & if Satan opposes him, Catholic Pharisees all unite to misrepresent his conduct, & injure his work. A fine time I am having. God's herder, riding day & night on the range, rounding up the best ones of the herd of Israel. Wild cattle they are: stampedes, charges of mad bulls, obstinate brutal yellowness[13] of Sitting Bull, wheeling, plunging & bellowing like demons around me. "Circumdederunt me vituli multi; tauri pingues obsiderunt me." [Many bulls have surrounded me; strong bulls have besieged me (Psalm 22.13).]

I have to defend myself against the wolves that attack my herd, against my mad herd that join the wolves against me, & against the hirelings who draw pay for watching God's herd, & at the same

---

[11] Aaron C. Wells and his wife, Josephine, who conducted a school just below Parkin's Ranch (see footnote 17 regarding Parkin's Ranch).

[12] Red Fish (Ho-gan-du-ta) was a Lower Yanktonai Sioux (Kingsbury, *History of Dakota Territory*, 1:950).

[13] "Yellowness" is an idiom often used by Craft as a synonym for malevolence, undesirability, stubbornness, cowardice, and so forth.

time try to help the wolves devour it, & kill or drive away the herder who is too active & vigilant in guarding it.

I am in the Agent's way. He can no longer set priests at variance, or misrepresent them to the Bishop, or make them fear him & worship him, & neglect their duty to serve him, & he looks to me as the cause of his failure. He is right. We now have peace & unity. I have worked hard to get it & I have got it. I tried to win the Agent over too, by showing him how much we could aid him in keeping his position, but he wanted to rule the priests & degrade them as he had always done, & that, of course, could not be allowed. It is the old story. False brethren, low born & low bred; incapable of understanding the work of God & His priests, desirous of gratifying their "stinking pride" or vanity by ruling & degrading beneath them those to whose standard they will not try to rise, turn against the Church that gave them all they have & hope for, & try to bend it to suit their depraved & worldly tastes. James the blacksmith is a worthy successor to Alexander the coppersmith.[14]

A fine thing, truly, if priests—who have in the world stood high above such reptiles, & who have forsaken the world & its honors, & trampled upon its false teachings, for the sake of gaining the eternal glories of heaven by following & teaching here the truth of Christ,—should be found so mad, & so blinded, & so wretchedly & foolishly base as to fall down & worship a creature of their own making, & after eating unlimited mud & swallowing unlimited insults, find in the end that they had "Forfeited to be his slave," "All here, & all beyond the grave."

I have fully determined that this must end here & now. The history of our failures here, since McLaughlin became Agent, is exceedingly mortifying. I have checked the stampede of our herds, & mean to turn them back to the ranges of the Church, &, of course, this

[14] Craft's verbal jab about James the blacksmith being a worthy successor to Alexander the coppersmith (Alexander was St. Paul the Apostle's accuser in 2 Tim. 4:14) was aimed at James McLaughlin, the U. S. Indian Agent in charge of Standing Rock. McLaughlin began his career with the Indian Service as a blacksmith ten years earlier at Devils Lake Agency in Dakota Territory (DT).

hireling tries to drive them over me. Now comes the crises,—such as it must be in every mission managed as this has been. If the Bishop & my brother priests do not turn against me, I shall succeed, & I am sure that they see the case in its true light now. McLaughlin has the cunning of Satan. He has tried in every way to misrepresent me to Bishop, priests, & seculars since he found I was determined to do my duty. Failing in this, he tries now to turn the Indians against me, beginning with Sitting Bull & the bad element, & extending his efforts to others who are not so bad. Some he tries to move by open means; others by quietly letting them see that their allegiance to me will be regarded as treason to him. He thinks to cause some disturbance which he can lay to my charge, or so annoy me that I will yield or leave. He has sadly mistaken his man. He could not possibly do worse than he has now done without giving me a legal hold, which I would at once take up. When he, either by active instigation or silent consent, caused the outrageous accusations of Sitting Bull to be brought against me,[15] I laid out my course and, Deo volente [God willing], I shall carry it out to the end. I will not yield my principles, & I will not leave to give the enemies of the Church a triumph. I will remain here & fight it out until the last enemy of our faith has been crushed & the mission is at peace.

I have informed the Bishop of his designs & have now so arranged matters here that he is placed in the dilemma of either undoing the evil he has done, & letting the Church alone or being crushed down under the stampede he has raised.

I have temporarily, & perhaps, if necessary, permanently changed my plan of action with the Indians, withdrawing from aiding them in any way that could divert my attention from the enemy's movements. I have notified the Agent to control Sitting Bull & other opponents, & seldom go near their camp,—never, except when absolutely necessary, so as to give no chance to anyone to accuse me of beginning a fight. The Indians deserve, for their cowardly supine-

[15] Sitting Bull brought charges against Craft with Inspector Bannister of the Department of Indian Affairs. I could find no record of these charges, but they probably concerned Craft's recruitment of postulants for the Benedictine sisterhood.

ness, that I should neglect them awhile. I avoid, carefully, doing anything different from what is done by other priests, except, of course, the care of distant missions, & even that not too actively, & in the meantime, both here & at Washington, I put in motion every possible means to discover the enemy's plans & to defeat them. I will soon, I think, succeed & then I may without danger begin my active work again. I have just discovered that the Agent, while abusing the Bishop & priests, & especially F.[ather] Stephan,[16] openly, is secretly availing himself of their aid, & crediting it to other parties.

Met Ignatius Catch-the-bear, & Agnes Comes-last, my cousins, at Mrs. Wells. Good children, my converts, & penitents, & Ignatius a communicant. Most of those I vaccinated here 3 weeks ago took well. I fear that many of the baptisms do not "take." For instance, there's old Antelope, baptized 3 times, so he says. It certainly didn't take either time. "Quemadmodum desiderat cervus ad fontes aquarum" ["As a deer pants after the fountains of waters" (Psalm 42:1)], even so did this Antelope *not* desire the water of life, & though brought to it he wouldn't drink."

March 24th [Saturday]

"Ego domini et soporatus sum" ["I slept and was sound asleep" (Psalm 42:6)] on a table, well rolled up in blankets, & woke this morning to hear Dakota's gentle zephyrs sweetly sighing, in advance of a "blazing blue blizzard" just from the southeast. Blizzard increased during the day. Mrs. Van Solen left my vestments here & went on to Parkins[17] in time to escape the worst of the storm. No travel today. Curried my horse, & prepared for mass tomorrow.

Few Indians come here. Mr. Wells won't feed them, or encourage their idleness & vice. The time has surely come when they must decide between giving up Indian ways, & adopting civilized habits, or perishing miserably. The Church does not condemn what is either

[16] Father Stephan at this time was director of BCIM, located in Washington, D.C.

[17] Parkin's Ranch was owned by Henry S. Parkin and his wife Alma (Picotte), a sister of Marie Van Solen. Located near the Missouri River on the north bank of the Cannonball River, just beyond the boundary of the reservation, the ranch evolved into a way-stop for travelers en route from Fort Yates to Bismarck, N.Dak. (Hinton, *South of the Cannonball*, 29).

good or indifferent, & when at Rosebud I told them that, though their customs required for their integrity the freedom of the old life, & must necessarily deteriorate when brought into contact with civilization, still I would not condemn them in toto, but would encourage what was good, as long as it remained so, but when I should tell them that the time had come when it had become injurious to them they must abandon it. They agreed, & kept their word. I acted in the same way here, but these are differently disposed, & while they might be willing to exchange their customs for those of the whites, they are not willing to give up the vices which they hope to conceal under cover of their old customs, which now exist only in name, & serve only to conceal vices that will not bear the light.

The old chiefs, especially, & bad whites, who, for their own purposes do not desire a change, & employees who could not make a living elsewhere, & to whom the dawn of religion & civilization would mean the banishment of their & other deeds of darkness, are the chief obstacles to advancement. The worst of all, for many reasons, is Agent McLaughlin. N'importe. Though this is a work requiring great sanctity, & indomitable energy, & requiring another Xavier,[18] still I should not be discouraged & abandon it. Far as I am from anything like sanctity, still I am a soldier of the Church, here under orders, & expected to do my best. I have the blood of a fighting race in me, & while it is in me I must remember that it is consecrated to God, & must be shed freely for His sake.

When I came here from Rosebud, I had the history of this mission to teach me the cause of past failures, & I determined to succeed if it was in the power of men to do so. Unity & energy were needed. I worked hard until I saw unity established, & will still work & suffer to the end to maintain it. As for energy, I determined to work as none here ever worked before, that all might see & feel that there was no excuse for not following God's law, & when I took for myself all that was hard & bitter, & left for my spiritual children only what was easy & sweet.

My Indian relatives were not what they were at Rosebud, & their

[18] St. Francis Xavier, Spanish Jesuit missionary, 1506–1552.

misconduct gave me many a bitter experience, but my relationship with them was, & still is, a powerful means to win them to Christ, & I did not disown it, hard as it was. All interested in ruining our work tried to get me to give it up, even going so far as to misrepresent it to those, who, they thought, might influence me. But I remark that all who wish us to succeed, maintain that I have taken the proper course, & that hereafter, even more than now, I will be able to use it to advantage. God's ways are not the world's ways. Pantaenus, De Nobili, Brebeuf, & many others whose course the Church has approved did just what I did, for the same reasons, & even to a greater extent. They were blamed & persecuted, as I have been, & they triumphed, as I <u>will</u> by God's aid.

Fine consolation it would be at the moment of death if I should have to remember that the last of my line had weakened after advancing to the enemy's centre, & feared to do for God & Our Lady's sake what my fathers did for more worldly glory. Amice, ut quid venisti? [Friend, for what purpose have you come? (Matt. 26:50)] To fail, perhaps, because other failed, & to run, because I saw others run. The deuce I did. <u>Not much</u>. Besides, as everybody has run away & left me, if I run too I shall be the hindmost, & as tradition hath it, "The devil takes the hindmost."[19] I guess I won't sneak into his grip. Better first in the charge, than last in the retreat, so here goes for the "divil av a foight" [devil of a fight (written with an Irish brogue)].

I don't think, however, that the enemies of the Church will have much time to think about plotting against me. The deuce is to pay in their ranks, & I can afford to rest on my arms, & enjoy my cigarette & a comfortable laugh at their expense. I happen to know of a beautiful political breeze, just foretold by one politically weatherwise, that will make a sharp rustling among certain "sore & yellow leaves," now just hanging by the merest thread to the tree of office.

The noble "Lo"[20] too is going to have his unwashed paws just "too,

[19] Francis Beaumont and John Fletcher, *Philaster* (1620), 5.3.137. References are to act, scene, and line.

[20] A reference to Alexander Pope's *An Essay on Man*, 1773: "Lo the poor Indian!" (epistle 1, line 99). It became a term of derision in frontier journalism.

too utterly" full "for anything out" of a "heap big bizness." The land-shark joyfully gambols westward, with dorsal fin "taninyon" [apparent], & his starboard "eye in a fine phrensy rolling," his capacious jaws sweetly smiling with an openness & expectancy born of well grounded hope, & quivering with joy, from the tip of his Israelitish nose to the end of his lively dorsal appendage. From afar he scents the odor of old moccasins & stale canšaša,[21] & the music of his Easter greeting to his red brother of similar "undoubted veracity"—echoes sweetly along the hills where the "Ho-bu" [a wild young man] dwelleth, & the coffee-cooler cooleth,[22] & dies away sweetly & gently along the winding valley of the Mini-šo-še [Missouri River].

"We'll open the Sioux Reservation,
And boom the great alkali plains,
There's money in civilization,
And the tenderfoot pays for our pains."

All ye who dream of the return of the gay & festive buffalo, & think my prophecy has a fishy odor, draw near, I pray you, light an "ilegunpapi wašteruna" [a burning, sweet smelling thing; i.e. "light up a cigarette"], veil your doubting visage with the morning paper, & meditate, if aural length interferes not in your case with cerebral activity,—upon the indubitable signs of the times. Alas poor Lo. Hater of the "Wašicun Wakitešne" [evil white man]. Toki la ye ye? Toki la ye ye? Tehan nikta ya ya. Nope mayuzaye. Tehan nikta la la ka ya ya. [Where are you going? Where are you going? You are going far. Shake my hand. You are going far away.][23]

This evening the blizzard seems tired, but the sky has a bad look, & I fear that my church tomorrow won't be very full. No matter.

---

[21] The bark that the Lakota mixed with tobacco.

[22] "Coffee-coolers" was a name given to those Indians who loitered around the military forts, scraping a subsistence from the white military rather than relying on traditional Indian ways. They were also called "loafers."

[23] Father Craft chronicles the early rumors surrounding the pending visit of the Dawes Commission, which would arrive on Standing Rock Reservation in July 1888 to negotiate the purchase of eleven million acres of Sioux land. Speculation called for the potential relocation of the Sioux to Indian Country in Oklahoma Territory, echoing the removal of the Cherokees and other tribes from the southeast forty years earlier.

So much more grace left for those who come. That beast of a horse "Pinch" has jolted & bucked for some days, until I am sore, bruised, & bad tempered. I must do some more riding on Monday, I suppose, but I need rest more than the Indians need grace,—at least, I would appreciate the rest, but they don't care much about the grace.

Once, at Grand River, an old woman sent for me. I got there after a lively contest with a bucking horse, bad roads, & several execrable snow drifts. The old lady was very sick, but "yellowness" of the Government mule type squinted & glittered in her eye, & "Satan's mother-in-law" was stamped in big letters on every line of her wrinkled phiz. I had seen such imps before, but she was very low, & divine pity getting the better of disgust, I laid myself out to save her miserable soul.

> Charitable Missionary: "My daughter, did you send for me?"
> Satan's Mother-in-law: "Yes."
> C.M.: "Well, as you are very sick, I will instruct & baptize you & —"
> S.M.: "Oh the devil! I know all about that. Won't have it. Onions. Onions."
> C.M.: "But my daughter, think of your soul first. God's grace —"
> S.M.: "I don't want any grace. I want onions, onions, onions."
> C.M.: "Alas daughter, I have no onions, but I will give you the grace of God,—&—"
> S.M.: "Don't I tell you I won't have it! *Onions*!"

No use. After gravely informing her that her son-in-law below was better able than I to satisfy those who preferred onions to grace, I departed, venting my disappointment in a good solid kick on the paunch of a worthless, vicious yellow cur that came to take leave. He left, "par levibus ventis, volucrique simillima somno" ["like the swift winds, and most like a fleeting dream"], for the shelter of the nearest tipi, & I left to rustle something to eat, & to make brand-new resolutions concerning sick calls.

March 25th 1888 [Palm Sunday]

Got up late, blizzard, of course, this time from the north-east, & not as bad as it might be if it tried. About 100 Indians at mass.

Blessed the palms. They come for the Hante-wakan [Holy cedar, which Craft substituted for palms] if for nothing else. Sang high mass. Announced the Easter communions for Tuesday.

Gave it to Ahewanka [Frosted] & his devils in the neck. Sent a challenge to Satan, couched in opprobrious language, & spit in his face with hearty good will. Explained demons & demonology. Poor wretches, trembling at their own shadows, & yet fearing still more the one who, they well know, has the power & the will to protect them. May God reward according to their works the incarnate demons, whether in the form of coppersmiths or blacksmiths, who have caused this.

These poor creatures call me "The-eagle-hovers-over-its-young," & yet my poor little eagles fly from the nest, where the eagles wings would shelter them, his blood nourish them, & his beak & talons defend them. How often would I have gathered them, as the bird gathers its young, under my wings, but they would not.[24] It is hard, very hard, cruelly bitter, to see them perish because they have listened to bad advises, but what can I do? I cannot force their will. I have done all that man can do. I have labored & taught unceasingly,—defied men, demons, & the elements; borne heat, cold, hunger, thirst, poverty,—spent days & nights in the saddle while my body was racked with pain, & my brain & heart with anxiety & misery, until blind & dizzy, & fainting, sheer force of habit held me in the saddle, while my horse wandered from the trail, & I, only half conscious, had no power to check or guide. I can truly say that my blood has sprinkled every trail on the reserve. The superstitious savages call me often the "storm spirit," because the wildest blizzard could not stop me. I rode it as I rode my horse to reach a sick Indian. Again & again, when alone on the prairie, freezing in a blizzard, or lying crushed & bleeding under a fallen horse, when it seemed certain that my moments of life were very few, I have felt grateful to God for allowing me to die in harness for my people. May God refuse me justice & mercy at my death if I did not sincerely love them. I

[24] As he often did in his journals, Craft is paraphrasing scripture, specifically Matt. 23:37.

have tried to storm heaven for them, & compel God to help them. I begged, like Moses, to be blotted out of the book of life if they were to be lost, & when, on Jan. 1st, I resigned the chieftainship, & made the Sacred Heart of Jesus Head Chief of the Dakotas, & signed with my blood the formula of conferring the chieftainship, the oath of allegiance, & the consecration to the Sacred Heart, I hoped to bind our Lord in honor to use His power & mercy for their especial benefit, retaining for myself only the privilege of working, fighting, & suffering for them as before, as Christ's lieutenant. What more can I do? They all know this, for they say it, & yet— & yet, they are—what their folly has made them. I have been called a "crank" by the enemies of the Church, because my actions were not in accord with "worldly wisdom," which God calls folly, & avoided & doubted & feared by those who knew better, because they feared to incur the world's resentment by seeming to sympathize with one at variance with the world.

So all agree that I am a very odd fish. It is beautiful to see such oneness of sentiment,—such fraternal concord, in one point, at least, between friends & enemies. But what wonder that there should be neutral ground where fool & knave can meet;—the "damned rascal" with the "damned coward."

That I am a "confirmed crank" I doubt, since the principles upon which my acts are based have been pronounced sound by competent authorities; but that I shall be a confirmed misanthropist, I verily believe. "Damned villainy" is not lovable. "Damned cowardice" is simply nauseating. "Damned ingratitude" is as golden in hue as the combined yellowness of both,—& where do I meet aught else? Deuce take it. I am too much provoked to think further just now, & besides, I am tired & sleepy.

Tobed [*sic*], to sleep, perchance to dream,—& wake with a headache. Waga [Cottonwood][25] says that Cannonball [River] has

[25] Wa-ha (Cottonwood) was a Lower Yanktonai Sioux (Kingsbury, *History of Dakota Territory*, 1:950). Please note that the spelling of Indian names often varies depending on the source; hence, for example, Kingsbury spells Cottonwood's name "Wa-ha," whereas Craft and a Lakota dictionary spell it "Waga."

broken,—water too deep to cross. Waga is a humbug, but a pleasant one, & is it not more pleasant to deal with a hypocrite than with a hog? Besides, is he not a Chief cooler, go to?[26] & a fellow that can smile away back to his collar button, go to? & a fellow that has three wives, & two fat dogs, & a dance-hall, & everything handsome about him?

March 26th [Monday]

Wind N.W. Clear, but cold & blowing. Very few scholars came ["scholars" equates to current day usage of "student" or "pupil"]. High Bear[27] came to complain about the Indians trying to get him broken as chief. His boy does not come to school. Half measures won't do. He risks offending the Indians by carrying out the Agent's order in one matter, & risks offending the Agent & school-teacher by keeping his boy at home to please the old-time element. That is just the plan pursued by all the best of them. They would like to get the priests to help them, & therefore do just enough good to excite the anger of the enemies of the Church, & to keep in with the enemies of the Church they do enough dirty contemptible yellowness to make priests doubt & despise them.

If a few of them would only make a start, & muster up courage enough to do all I tell them, & disregard the threats of the bad element, I could easily protect them, & others, seeing how well they would prosper, would soon join them, & I could soon have everything in good order. "What fools these mortals be."[28] "So sings the fairy, & he sings in sooth." They try to "kiyugata" [his hand spread out; i.e., "serve"] God with one hand, & the devil with the other, & they can't be made to see that it's no use to try to serve both God & Mammon. An ancient error, by the bye, in which poor Lo is by no means alone.

[26] "Go to" may be a Lakota idiom for "also."

[27] Eugene Highbear (Ma-to-wau-kan-tyu) was a Brulé who served as a district farmer on Standing Rock Reservation (*Annual Report of the Commissioner*, 1892, p. 833, hereafter cited as *Annual Report*; see also Kingsbury, *History of Dakota Territory*, 1:950).

[28] Shakespeare, *Midsummer Night's Dream*, 3.2.115.

Through policy, I have to encourage them to obey & trust the Agent. He represents the Government, and, consequently, law & order, but it's rather risky, & he is imprudent enough to let the Indians see his malice towards me, &, besides, I am afraid that, when I tell them that he will maintain them in carrying out his orders, they may blame me when he "crawfishes,"—as we always have reason to fear that he will. Never was he known to stand by a friend, & all who are foolish enough to aid or believe & trust him are sure to get badly "left," & pay sweetly "through the nose" for their credulity.

Mr. Wells went to Parkins but could not cross Cannonball. Water too high. All Back water. Mrs. Parkins sent a note around by an Indian, enclosing one from Annie Tarvasarna. F.X. [Francis Xavier?] No-heart dying. 15 miles up Cannonball. Start tomorrow early.

March 27th [Tuesday]

Warm, light wind from south-east. Went to No Hearts,[29] about 15 miles up Cannonball. Snow deep, no road. To avoid the drifted prairie, I had to follow the lines of ridges, using the field-glass to mark out my course. In crossing from ridge to ridge I had to walk & lead the horse over the drifts. Reached Spotted Crow's, tired, bruised, sore, faint, dizzy, & snow-blind. Got something to eat.

Red-fox[30] the policeman came up following my trail, on his way to No-Hearts'. Went on with him, after we had smoked, & duly execrated snow, bad roads, etc. It took me 7 or 8 hours from Wells to No Hearts'. Attended to No Heart & gave him a scapular.[31] He had been bleeding terribly from the lungs, but is now better. The family received me splendidly, & the children almost smothered me with kisses & deafened me with noisy congratulations on my safe arrival.

[29] No Heart (Cante-wan-ica) was a Minneconjoux chief. In 1893, he was an assistant carpenter on Standing Rock Reservation (*Annual Reports*, 1893, 559).

[30] Red Fox performed in Buffalo Bill's Wild West Shows for fifteen years, starting in 1893 (Hinton, *South of the Cannonball*, 90).

[31] An emblem of devotion worn about the neck.

I went to see the child of a Gros Ventre,[32] Zatela's son-in-law. Dying. Tubercles in the brain. The boy is one I baptized 2 years ago. Gave him the blessing puer. regrot [for a sick child] & gave the father a paper to get from Parkins material for a coffin, & a black dress for his wife (my eldest sister) who says she wishes to mourn like the whites, & with the hope of a good Catholic. They have more faith than the other Indians, & treat me as a relative whom they love & respect. Such a reception as they gave me did much to take the pain out of sore bones & bruised muscles, & made me look back over the steep hills & drifted prairies I had just crossed with much satisfaction. I felt at peace with bad roads, sore bones, bucking horse, & everything & everybody.

I laid off during the evening in "the bosom of my family," among father, mother, sisters & brothers, & gave forth clouds of perfumed cigarette smoke & much good advice, all of which was received by appreciative noses & well disposed minds. If they don't do all I tell them, it is surely not through malice, but through weakness. After duly admiring the working of my field-glass at night, eating a big supper, & taking care of our horses, we turned in, rolled in blankets, with feet to the stove, & slept the sleep of very just & very tired men, while the feet of many little mice beat tattoo, & Dakota winds blew our taps.

March 28th [Wednesday]

Wind South-east. Clouds thin & broken, but much snow in the air. Thermometer last night registered 18° below zero, but it don't seem so very cold. Got up early, washed in snow to prepare for a ride facing the wind. Ate breakfast, after giving Pinch his corn. Baptized Peter Mato-sabiciye [Bear Who Blackens Himself] & Paul Hehaka-piya-nazin [Elk Who Stands Renewed], the twin babies of my big brother George Long-beard.

Saddled up, & after parting blessings to everyone, & parting handshaking, hugs, kisses, & good wishes & thanks from all, mounted

[32] French for "big bellies."

Pinch who pranced beautifully, but out of regard for the children didn't buck,—more common-sense than I ever gave him credit for, & with cigarette lighted in lieu of stirrup-cup, plunged through the last night's drifts to the top of the hill. After taking an observation with the glass, I found a line of ridges leading to the place where my yesterdays trail left the hills beyond Spotted Crows'. I followed it, & found much better footing than yesterday, & a great saving of distance by cutting off the angle formed by my trail from the hills to Spotted Crows, & thence to No Hearts'.

As I struck my old trail at the point I aimed for, I found the track of 2 ponies going from Spotted Crows' to Zatela's camp. Track now well marked. Made very fair time. Reached Zatela's. Left word with Long Dog's wife that No Heart was better. Followed the line of ridge towards Two Bears' camp. Found the road there towards Parkins' ranch & Mr. Wells' school well broken. Struck a lope & soon got in. Time from No Heart's to Wells' 6 hours.

Announced Easter duties for tomorrow to the school-children. Sat down to smoke, after unsaddling Pinch,—that rascal is tough as steel, came back fresh as a daisy, & golden with "yellowness." Ate supper, kicked off chaparejos & boots, lit a cigarette & philosophized. Thought of Zatela's & No Heart's camps, peace—rest—contentment, etc. Martin Catka came to ask about the hour for mass tomorrow. Very good,—seems to have a soul, and, even to *know* it. Saw a fair cousin of mine, who seems to prefer the serpent's den to the eagle's nest, & the white blanket of the "ho-bu" to the white robe of innocence I gave her in baptism. In fact, she won't prepare for confession & communion, goes much in bad company, & to night dances, & likes to be courted at night. Got mad, & disgusted, & began to feel tired. Thought of new expletives,—something deep, long, bitter, loud, & filling & rasping to the throat, & soothing to a ruffled temper. "Gnaška cincapi!" [Frog children!] might, I think, be <u>broadened</u> <u>&</u> <u>deepened</u>. How would "Natapeha cincapi!" [Toad children!] fill the bill. "Excellent well in faith." Mem. Employ it for the future.

Cigarette needs relighting. Just like an Indian. Won't go, if not watched. Lit it again, smoked, meditated on the sedative & curative effects of a consciousness of Indian conscientiousness, & the proneness of the reverse to bring on a relapse of fatigue, soreness, crossness, etc.—execrated, in most choice & elegant Sioux, the general yellowness of things in general. Went to bed & slept the sleep of the tired, vexed, & thoroughly bad tempered man.—At least that's what I'm now going to do, so I may as well consider it done.

March 29th [Thursday]

Holy Thursday. Sang high mass. 8 made their Easter communions. Confession before mass. All school-children except Mrs. Wells. I did not urge the older Indians very strongly to go to their Easter Duties, since Easter 1886 when over 50 presented themselves for communion after a substantial breakfast, & tried to deceive me up to the last moment. I luckily found out in time. Sheer malice & diabolic "yellowness."

Some were noisy during mass, & I remarked that they all belonged to the devil-dreaming outfit. The communicants behaved well. Spoke sharply to the noisy ones, & when one boy spoke again I promptly ordered him out.

After mass took breakfast with the communicants. Ignatius Catch-the-bear, Paul Tašunkalizahan [Fast Horse], Joseph Canwape [Leaf], Martin Catka [Left Hand], Boniface Buya-inyanka [Noisey Runner], Mary Agnes Black-horse, & Mary Aniwin. My little sister Ada Mary Sweeney (half-blood) who so long refused to be baptized, asked for baptism after mass, & rounded up 5 more neophytes. Baptized them, after repeating in toto their former instructions, & blessed a crucifix for my little sister-missionary Ada.

Mary Zuya-win [War Woman] sent for me from Two Bear's camp. Case of dysentery, aggravated by improper food, & then starvation. Rode on to Parkins ranch. Ice on Cannonball dangerous. Water backed up from Missouri. About 10 feet deep. Tied Pinch to a bush under the bank, & crossed on foot. "Cooled" on Mr. Parkins for bread, meat, & tea for Mary. Left the provisions for her, & threatened yellow vengeance against anyone else who should venture to eat any of it. Had a sweet time finding the road back. Dark. Snow blowing in my face, had left my night-glass at Mr. Wells. After the customary remarks concerning gnaškas & natapehas [frogs and toads], & their genealogical record, I managed to strike the right trail, & got in safely. One who travels here after sunset in the winter, ought to be caught, heavily ironed, & tied up in a straight jacket, & sent to some asylum for the insane, or else be punished for an attempt at suicide. It is more than dangerous,—it is almost certain to be fatal. Ate supper, smoked, wrote this much, & now,—"Come gentle sleep, attend thy votary's prayer."[33]

March 30th [Good Friday]

Warm. Wind south-east. Prepared to go to the Agency, but worked so long helping Mr. Wells with his quarterly school reports, that I thought it better to start early tomorrow morning, so as not to cross creeks after dark. I would like to be at the Agency, as the young men of St. Mary's Society will probably meet this evening, but perhaps it is better to neglect them for a time. Kind treatment does not work well with the Hunkpapas & Sihasapas.[34] Cold, distant, careless, haughty behavior,—orders given sharply & sternly, & rigidly enforced, would seem to be, for the present, the best plan. & yet, is it at all surprising? They say that they were born & reared as brutes, & wish to live & die as brutes, &, if such is the case, (and it would seem so, from their brutal ways) then the chain & the lash will govern them better than the gentle means suitable for those who have still some relics of human nature left. It is a question how far I can succeed in bringing this people up to the commonly received standard of humanity, morality, decency, & christianity.

I often take a look through the lenses of these things, just as I look over a country with my field-glass to mark out the best course, & avoid too dangerous ground, & viewed in this way the difficulties seem almost insurmountable. It would seem as if this race of corrupted, brutal savages, must totally rot, or be swept from the

[33] Thomas Warton, *Latin Epigram on Sleep* (John Wolcot, trans.), quoted in Stevenson, *Home Book of Quotations*, 18.

[34] The Hunkpapas were Sitting Bull's tribe, and the Sihasapas were Blackfeet Sioux.

face of the earth by contact with incoming influence, before I can fairly begin to prepare them for a change. The worst of it is, I have not only the bad Indian element to contend with, but also bad whites, & false brethren, such as the Agent & his allies, & there is not a soul in sympathy with my efforts. If they don't oppose me through malice, they do it through a mistaken notion of my plan of action & the possibility of success, & even go so far as to misrepresent me to those who, they think, ought to compel me to direct my energies to some worthier & more helpful end.

Confound the miserable meddlers. If they don't want to aid me, why can't they let me alone. Good Lord, save me from my friends, & if you don't think these savage brutes worth saving, & won't help me save them, at least pull these just & wise men, these pious Catholics, off my back, & I'll show up the biggest fight with Satan & his allies ever recorded in sacred or profane history. But—great heavens, what a herculean task I have undertaken. How shall I ever succeed in turning through these worse than Augean stables a stream of God's grace large enough to sweep away this mass of filth & corruption? God's grace, like water, seeks its level,—but that level is the disposition to correspond to it, which must exist, or be made, in these brutal, corrupted hearts, before grace will flow into them. To that end, all my work is directed, and, were I let alone, I would, in time, succeed; but my opponents pour in filth upon me, almost as fast as I can remove it. I am wearied with labor, choked & suffocated with the stench, & half dead with sickness in these mephitic vapors. Still I'll work on. Tu autem Domine adjuva me. [But you, Lord, help me.]

By constant [contact?] with civilization, the Indian in his present state will be pretty sure to be uncivilized, & perhaps by contact with his uncivilized state I shall become more civilized, at least as far as disgust with the savage is concerned. This, like all other things here will probably go by contraries, according to the time honored custom of the "Heokas."[35]

[35] The visions of *heyokas* (free spirits within a tribe) led them to express themselves in a clownish world of "contraries," wearing strange clothing, living in ragged lodges, sleeping without robes and blankets in the winter and piling on these covers in the summer. Whatever was asked of them, they generally did the opposite.

March 31st [Holy Saturday]

Saddled up, & started with Mr. Wells for the Agency. Warm. Wind north-west. Roads not too bad for the horse, but very bad for either wagon or sleigh. Either bare ground, or deep snow, through which a loaded sleigh cuts to the ground. Started at 8, & reached the Agency at 4. There was no meeting of St. Mary's Society. Put away the horse & ate lunch at Mr. Bernard Pranges'. Emeran[36] in from Grand River for pay-day & reports. I must send out more provisions to Grand River school, & as usual must pay for part myself, through the delay in sending Emeran's back salary. I must, however, do what I can to keep peace in our own camp. Government payday delayed, consequent cardiac badness.

Today is the 5th anniversary of my ordination. He, he, he! Had I only known then what awaited me,—I didn't,—the fool's wit comes afterwards.

Soldiers from the fort came up to Father Bede's[37] this evening, & went to confession to me. They will go to communion tomorrow.

April 1st [Easter Sunday]

Easter Sunday. Rose at 6:30. Emeran went to confession. Said mass at 8. About 30 communions. Ate breakfast. High mass at 10:30. Preached after Vidi aquam ["I saw water," the "water rite" replacing "Asperges" in Easter season], on Easter & rising with Christ by repentance & confession (in Dakota). Read rules of St. Joseph's Society to some young men. They seem willing to follow them.

I have refused to hear confessions of Agency people, except at special request of Rev. Father Bede. I have various good reasons for so doing, not the least of which is a regard for my own safety from receiving "payment in abuse," & regard for my own dignity in repelling such a rabble of cowardly, cringing, treacherous lickspittles.

Meeting tonight of some young men who want to organize a St. Joseph's Society. Emeran went there, & read the rules again. I

[36] Emeran White Boy, often listed in agency reports as Emeran B. White, a full-blood Sioux who taught at the Grand River School.

[37] Bede Marty, OSB, (unrelated to Bishop Martin Marty) was a missionary at St. Benedict's Mission located near the Farm School, sixteen miles south of the agency in current-day Kenel, S.Dak.

FIGURE 5. Father Craft and Benedictine missionaries at St. Benedict's Mission, Standing Rock Reservation, Dakota Territory, ca. 1886–1888. *Left to right*: Father Martin Kenel, OSB; Father Craft; Father Bernard Strassmaier, OSB; Brother Meinrad Widmer, OSB; Brother Nicholas Enz, OSB; district farmer William Whitsell. Photographer unknown. *Courtesy of Conception Abbey Archives.*

can't get away from the Agency before tomorrow or next day, & yet it is far from pleasant here. I wonder how Father Bede manages to endure it. One constant conflict with corruption, lying, hypocrisy, etc., & eternal vigilance guarding against Catholic pharisees, going about seeking whom they may slander & destroy. This morning I took Holy Communion (Viaticum)[38] to Mrs. Jennie Primeau.[39] She seems about the same, but, I fear, cannot recover.

[38] The Eucharist given to a person in danger of death.

[39] Jennie Primeau, wife of Louis Primeau, is listed on agency reports as an assistant day school teacher through 1888.

FIGURE 6. Agency officials, Standing Rock Reservation, Fort Yates, N.Dak., 1889. *Left to right*: Interpreter Joe Primeau, Agency Farmer George Faribault, Physician E. S. Hart, Agent James McLaughlin, Secretary Bird M. Robinson, and Issue Clerk Jim Merrill. Photograph by D. F. Barry. *Courtesy of State Historical Society of North Dakota, B0114-2.*

Just heard that my little sister Jennie Bloody Knife died at St. Benedict's Mission School. Requiescat in pace, et oret pro me. [May she rest in peace, and may she pray for me.] "Say ye to your sister 'Thou hast obtained mercy.'"[40] For her there is nothing to regret. "After life's fitful fever, she sleeps well."[41] The pain & regret are mine. Jennie, Clara, Paul, Martin, Mary,—all have passed safely, but I, who helped them to reach heaven,—am still here, & for how long, & with what hope of meeting them in eternity? God alone knows. Can't you help me little brothers & sisters, & say to me as I did to you, "Thou hast obtained mercy?"

[40] Hosea 2:8

[41] Shakespeare, *Macbeth*, 3.2.23.

April 2 [Monday]

Said mass at 7. Mr. Wells & Mr. Hess received. Sent medicine to Išnala-wica's [Only Male's][42] child, & Ada M. Sweeny's grandmother, & got more for Zatela & Mary Agnes Black-horse, & Joseph Canwape. Mr. Coles[43] will try to bring my freight from Mandan. Went to Douglas'[44] & bought 200 lbs. flour, 20 lbs. pork, 4 lbs. baking powder, 15 lbs. coffee, & 20 lbs. sugar, for St. Francis de Sales School, & will get a box of crackers tomorrow. Talked with Merrill on Agency matters.

After supper went to a meeting of those who wish to start a St. Joseph's Society. Read rules, instructed them, & explained the rules. One tried to vent his annoyance at the strict rules by remarking that I once encouraged Indian customs. Shut him up, & explained matters quite sharply. The rest acted well. Will give crosses tomorrow. Must be kind but strict, & determined. The young men had their table set in real civilized style. Table-cover, china cups & saucers, & lots of good things to tickle the palate. The same rules will be observed as in Father Martin's[45] society.

Today I remembered at mass my little sister Jennie, who, though dead to earth, lives with the elect, & also here in the memory of those to whom her virtues, & especially her heroic patience, have endeared her. I know she will not forget her brother still "in tenebris et in umbra mortis" ["in darkness and in the shadow of death" (Luke 1:79)]. Something gives me sad foresentiment that "I shall see her, but not now; I shall behold her, but not near." Once, surely, in the valley of Josephat, when the last reveille wakes the "soldiers of the Great Spirit" for his last review. But why "not near," & what foundation is there for such gloomy forebodings? Can it be that God will take me at my word, and, as He does not mean to save my stubborn nation, that he will blot my name also out of the "book of life?"[46] As Moses said, so did I. Where he sent Israel, he himself could not

---

[42] Kingsbury, *History of Dakota Territory*, 1:950.

[43] Coles operated a general store on the reservation.

[44] H. F. Douglas operated a general store in Fort Yates, N.Dak.

[45] Martin Kenel, OSB, superintendent of the mission school at Fort Yates from 1884 to 1906.

[46] Rev. 20:12.

go. I have sent my best before me, & perhaps I must perish in the wilderness, for the same cause that kept Moses from his earthly reward. It really seems that I have

> "—forfeited to be their slave,
> All here & all beyond the grave."

As God wills it, so let it be. "Fiat mihi secundum verbum tuam." ["May it be done to me according to your word" (Luke 1:3).]

What I did I did for the honor of my colors, the standard of the cross, & if I perish in covering the retreat of my cowardly bands, it is, in some way, a satisfaction. I looked forward to eternal life with my little sister & her people, but "Dominus dedit, Dominus abstulit, sit nome Domine benedictum" ["The Lord has given, the Lord has taken away; may the name of the Lord be blessed" (Job 1:21)]. I will fight on still, "Ad maiorem Dei gloriam" ["For the greater glory of God" (the Jesuit motto)], & may He derive still greater glory from my sufferings here, & even my "pain of loss" hereafter. "Gwell angau na chywyllid!" [Welsh for "Rather death than shame!"] "En Avant Sainte Marie." [French for "Forward for St. Mary."]

My determination is finally taken, and, suffer as I may, I shall strike the enemies of God, our Lady, Holy Church, while one is left. If it is my last field, I will make it a bloody one, & make them remember,

> "In pride of place, here last the eagle flew,
> And tore with bloody talon the rent plain,
> Pierced by the shaft of banded nations through."

And, perhaps, if Dakota legends, & God's mercy fail not, the blood of the "Hovering Eagle," sprinkled here, where he died defending his nest, will bring down the rain of God's grace to take away the curse from this stiff necked & hard-hearted generation.

April 3d [Tuesday]

Groomed Pinch. Blessed & gave crosses to the 10 who form the nucleus of our new St. Joseph's Society. Gave Mr. Wm. Pamplin an order on Douglas' for a box of soda-crackers for Emeran, & also money enough to pay expenses on Emeran's trunk, about $6.50. Warm, snow melting fast. Many geese flying north. Perhaps this is the "anser" to our prayers for spring.

Mr. Pamplin will marry Mrs. Lanigan [*sic*], a full-blood.[47] Best thing he can do. "A broth of a boy was Johnny Lanigan," & his "widdy" seems to be a "raete & dacint craytur." "Long life to them," & may Mr. Pamplin never come to grief for disregarding the advice to "Beware of vidders." St. Paul says "The younger widows avoid," but as this one is "fair & forty," & therefore "no chicken," it's all right, no doubt. "Maidens, like moths, are ever caught by glare,"[48] & Pamplin does well not to tie up to a copper-colored maiden, who would be caught up by the glare of the first white-blanketed "ho-bu," whose skunk perfumed draperies, & "Itowapi kin le" [Image bearing] melodies, would be wafted towards her on Dakota's gentle zephyrs.

Besides, has Mr. Pamplin not been highly honored? Few men, living under our republican institutions, can attain to the high honor of being presented, with their brides, at court,—even a police court. His services to the Government have, evidently, been appreciated very highly, for has the Government not watched solicitously over each changing phase of his romantic courtship, until it was brought to a happy conclusion under its protecting aegis?

Wandering with his inamorata past the habitations of the dead, over the classic hills of Išna-paha [Lone hill], many gentle breezes from Mini-šo-še's silver-locked waves brought the roses to their cheeks, & gently waved their flowing šinas [blankets or shawls]; while beneath their feet the earliest blossoms of spring time, waking from their slumbers, tried to rise from their snowy couch, & gently sighed. "Dear friends, accept our sympathetic congratulations; we too are white-robed 'Ho-bu's."

---

[47] William Pamplin, carried on the agency payroll at $75 per month in 1892, was an "additional farmer" who settled a land claim near Selfridge, N.Dak., currently called Pamplin Hills. He reported to McLaughlin and was responsible for instructing Indians in their farming activities. Mrs. Lannegan may have been the widow of Barney Lannegan, a white man who worked on the construction of Fort Yates in 1874–75 (Hinton, *South of Cannonball*, 81; and *Annual Reports*, 1892, 832.)

[48] Lord Byron, *Childe Harold's Pilgrimage*, canto 1, st. 9.

The blue-robed guardian of Dakota's peace, followed afar, but ever vigilant, lest malignant spirits, wandering from their burial-place, on deeds of evil bent, should venture to distract a tryst so fair. Softly approaching, bowing low, while in his hand his gold-bound cap of office gracefully swept the snowy plateau in lowly salutation, with gently modulated voice he softly whispered. "Brave knight,—fair lady,—I come an humble ambassador from the palace of Justice to the court of Cupid. Bravest of the brave—fairest of the fair, graciously deign to accompany me to the royal residence, where honors meet will be duly rendered to you to whom such honors are most justly due." Gallantly he marshalled them; courteously, but pensively they followed. The knight escorted the lady to the palace of Justice, where rank on rank of blue-robed belted knights received them with martial honors & courteous salutation, & leaving the fair lady with her attendant damsels, he passed beneath the smiling moonbeams gentle rays to his lonely couch, to dream sweet dreams of the morrow & the morrow's joys.

Day dawned of Išna-paha's steep,
On Mini-šo-še broad & deep.
And pahin's [porcupine's] mountains lone,
The snowy plains, the palace keep.
The guarded cells where captives weep,
In yellow lustre shone.

The golden sunbeams had scarcely smiled their morning salutation to the fair river, & lonely hill in robes of white & silver draped, when the gallant Sir William presented himself at the palace of Justice, to kiss the snow-white hand of his lady, & to receive with her the high honors awaiting them. In the royal hall, surrounded by his blue-robed belted knights, his courtiers, & his venerable gray-haired counselors, the King of Justice, throned in state received them. What pen could record the splendor of that reception. What minstrel played or poet sang of honors high like those conferred upon them. Suffice it to say, that Sir William & his lady fair saluted amid applause of ladies & of knights as King & Queen of Love &

Beauty, were earnestly besought by the venerable gray-bearded Monarch, & his gray haired Chancellor, to grace the royal presence with their nuptials, & that they graciously consented. Modest & retiring as becomes a gallant knight, Sir William rode rapidly with his bride-elect to their residence, to avoid the proffered honors of a "shivaree"[49] or "skimmelton," & prepared to solemnize his nuptials with a splendor unequalled in magnificence & pomp.

Long may this worthy pair survive to bless our land with many worthy descendants, now that

"the rosebud the graces our highlands,
Is wreathed in a garland round William to twine."
& long may it be told in song & story, how—
The Black Robe heard their plighted troth,
And gave to them the nuptial oath.
How bluff King James the curtain drew,
While Caskes' hand the stocking threw.
And wished that every married pair,
Love like this Knight & lady fair.

The probability is that the gallant & amorous Sir William will, out of the goodness of his heart, wish happiness like his own to all misguided bachelors, & will contrive, too, that they come to it in the same way. That it is clearly a "put up job," there is none so blind who does not see. However, it serves him right, & may all those who, for the sake of corrupting the Indians, try to destroy the work of God's priests among them, come speedily & surely to the same trap, & be "double-dead immortal-cinched" in the same way.

Pamplin, fearing that the police & other Indians would expose his squaw-trading, took his stand with other cowards & enemies against me in the Sitting Bull affair, & now he is getting justly paid, by their exposing him. Had he then acted like a man, he would never have been compelled to marry such a worthless character, as there are others deeper in the affair than he, but now, since in consequence of his meanness "that has come to him which he feared,"

[49] A variant of the French *charivari*, a noisy serenade to newlyweds.

why, let him take it, & dandle on his knee, with other many-sired children.[50]

April 4th [Wednesday]

Warm. Wind south-east. Thunder & showers. The first lightning was seen last Monday evening. Told Pamplin that his affair was a put-up job to trap him & save someone else. Wanted me to help him. Of course I declined. Let him reap as he has sown. I can't fight the battle of those who serve under Satan's colors.

Saddled up & rode to Cannonball. Horse mean, but did not buck. Roads execrable. Big Head's bottom overflowed. Horse waded through knee-deep. Stopped, took lunch at Mrs. Van Solen's school. Case of small-pox reported near Big Head's.[51] Don't believe it. Probably a scrofulous eruption. Geese, ducks & crows flying north.

Stopped to see Ada's grandmother. Old lady better, liniment works well. Found a new mother, Ada's aunt. "Honor thy father & mother." Gave momma a cigarette. Smoked, praised little Ada. Shook hands all round, mounted, & rode to Mr. Wells' school. I'm tired out. The jolting of that rascally Pinch is tearing me to pieces. The Bishop is right. To what end is all this labor? Better spare myself now so as to work when I can work to some advantage. The bad element is getting weaker, & will soon be completely "cinched." They don't like me, simply because I am a priest, know too much about them, want them to do right, & work hard to save souls. I shall stay here & "down" them, & then I & my successors can succeed.

April 5th [Thursday]

Slept late. Tired, bruised & feverish. I never get saddle-sore, but such terrible jolting, on a hard-riding horse, over execrable roads, is a little too much for human endurance. Quite a number of scholars came. Announced communions for Sunday, instructed them, & read rules of St. Joseph's Society, advising them to join it. Gave

---

[50] Agent McLaughlin is the "King of Justice" and "gray-bearded monarch" in this lyrical account of a local shotgun wedding. His Indian Police are the "blue-robed belted knights."

[51] Na-su-lan-tan-ka (Big Head) was an Upper Yanktonai (Kingsbury, *History of Dakota Territory*, 1:950).

pictures & medals to those who went to their Easter Duties on Holy Thursday. Agnes "Comes-Last," my worthy cousin, tried to tear up a picture of the B.V.M. [Blessed Virgin Mary], belonging to Mary Agnes Black Horse, & when stopped by the others, threw it away with opprobrious epithets. I gave her a "blasting" such as she, probably, never got before, & won't care to get again. Had anything in the shape of a male Indian or white had done it, I would have left him but very little life, & very many broken bones. Miss Agnes prefers the white blanket of the "Ho-bu" to the white robe of innocence, & hence a picture of Mary Immaculate excites her deviltry, as a red rag excites a mad bull.

I took back the picture I had given to her nephew, Joseph Canwapi, as, being an Indian, he has not, probably, courage enough to protect it from insult. It is not well to "cast pearls before swine,"[52] & swine, lower, viler, filthier, more completely debased, & fonder of wallowing in filth, than these vile beings, I never yet saw or heard of. The demons cast out of more decent beings have entered as of old, into this herd of swine, & they are now running headlong over the precipice into the sea of eternal perdition which will soon swallow them up. My God! What can be made of materials so utterly & hopelessly rotten? It would be well if a Jew, or some other swine-hater could be made Agent here. Speaking of Jews, the history of these Indians, as one who knows them could write it, would be merely a reprint of the history of Jewish perverseness, as Holy Scripture gives it, merely changing Hebrew names to Indian, & somewhat intensifying the malice, brutality, & pig-headedness of the Jews to suit their worthy descendants, who have still further degenerated from most execrable ancestors. Moses got temporal punishment as a reward for his loyalty & affection for the Jews, but he would have been pretty sure to lose his soul into the bargain, had he done the same for these reprobates.

This evening Miss Agnes managed to get herself courted by two "Hobus" close to the school. They pulled her around, & threw her

[52] Matt. 7:6.

down, much to her delight & satisfaction. The devil is in her, as big as "woodchucks." She, & all those like her, have given up all that was good in Indian ways, & kept only the evil. I must refuse to recognize as relatives all who refuse to abandon Indian customs.

April 6th [Friday]

Warm. Wind south-west. Instructed scholars for their Easter communions. I much doubt whether many will come, as they understand thoroughly that they can't "Kiyugata" [serve] God & Satan at the same time.

Saddled up & rode to Parkins, but could not cross Cannonball. It broke today, & the stream is bank high with drift ice, & gorged by back water from the Missouri, as far as Parkins. The Missouri broken, & ice running as high up as the mouth of Cannonball.

"Strong-heart" came to say that his daughter, Mary Zuyawin [War Woman] is worse, & needs food, &, at the same time, "Two-bears'" mother came with a note from him expressing much sorrow for having deceived me about his marriage, & saying that he was sick & begging for food. I doubted both parties, because I had heard that Mary was much better, & that Two-bears was pretending sickness to escape arrest. Therefore, I refused to give "Two-bears" anything, & promised to go with Mr. Wells, in his wagon, after dinner, to see Mary; but before dinner time, I saddled Pinch & rode towards Parkins, &, when near Strong-heart's house, turned to the left, & dashed at a gallop through the camp to his house, so that they had no time to prepare for me. Just as I expected. No one at home, & the door tied up. In the next house I found Two-bears, perfectly well, with several others, & preparations for a feast of some kind, to which they were evidently waiting to add my supplies for the sick. Laughed at them, & after much good advice on fox-trapping, I rode off laughing & singing, rode round the house, & took another peep into "Strong-heart's." Still no one at home. Just then Strong-heart came up, the very picture of a detected liar, & badly disappointed glutton. Laughed at him, advised him, & rode off. What can be done for such a disgusting set of brutes? I must detect & expose some more frauds.

There will be a dance tomorrow. Zatela's daughters, Mary & Anna, have promised to let me know before Sunday whether they will abandon Indian ways. I will insist on an answer, just as I catch them on the way to a dance, whither they will go, of course. They know that I am much opposed to my sisters going to such places as common squaws, & being talked of like them, & they already complain of being slandered, & ask my protection. Pretty hard to protect them, when they "love the danger."[53] I have prepared to put them in good standing as decent white girls, if they obey me. They know it, but, I fear, will try to deceive me, & keep me in hot water defending their reputation, while they are soiling it by evil associations. I am trying to raise my relatives up, but I am determined they shall not pull me down. If they are sincere with me, as they know well—more than the rest—how to be, I will defend & elevate them; but if they deceive me, & try to get my aid, & at the same time get me laughed at, & even help laugh at me, for trying to save them against their wills, I must leave them to themselves. "Invitum qui servat, idem facit occidenti" ["Who saves a man against his will does the same as murder him"] sings Horace, & he sings in sooth.[54]

Gave a lecture to Ignatius for aiding his sister Agnes in her deviltry. The time has come when the Indians must choose between ruin & prosperity. The old ways have so far changed, that I cannot permit them to follow them any longer. The Indians here are not to be trusted,—even the best. It's all very true that rascals have caused this, but "what o' that?" They are base enough if they allow anyone to make them act as they have done towards me.

The Brulés—but why should I always remember them? I can't help it. See now

> "How selfish Sorrow ponders on the past,
> And clings to thoughts now better far removed!
> But Time shall tear thy shadow from me last."[55]

---

[53] Shakespeare, *Othello*, 1.3.167.

[54] Horace, *Ars Poetica*, 488–489.

[55] Byron, *Childe Harold's Progress*, canto ii, st. 96.

I can't forget them. They obeyed me, & stood by me like men. God, so far, has rewarded them. May He repay them tenfold as they merit.

April 7th [Saturday]

Warm. Wind south-west. Snow disappearing fast. An Indian told me that Zatela's family were on their way to a dance at Cottonwood's. Saddled, mounted, & rode towards Zatela's. They saw me coming, & turned their team to the left, to seem to be going another way. When I came up with them they said they were going to Bear-ghost's for a feast, but did not know what feast, & finally owned up that is was a "ghost-feast." (Wakicagapi) [Dance of the Ghosts]. Denied going to a dance, but at last Crow-ghost owned up. Asked for my answer. Anna & Mary wanted to put off. Wouldn't be put off. They asked if I wanted them to never go from home, & to die of ennui. Told them no, I only wanted them to be innocent, happy & prosperous. Finally consented to give up all Indian ways, but wanted me to clothe them. Told them that while always ready to share all I had with my sisters, as I had always done, I would not promise anything, as I did not want to have it said that I paid them to obey me for their own good. They said they would only look on at dances. I wouldn't hear of it, as just there lies the mischief.

Zatela's wife said that I was always saying that the girls were slandered, & made that an excuse to make them drop Indian ways,—that they always staid at home, & no one but I ever said so. I referred to Anna as having claimed my protection against slanderers & referred to my former advice at Parkins. Girls shut the old lady up. General silence. Got mad, hit Pinch, & started away with a growl of disgust, but turned back to give them a last chance, & asked them to answer me for the last time whether they would abandon all Indian ways, & neither dance, nor look on at dances. They did not answer, though Crow Ghost urged them to, & I rode away leaving them badly caught, & thoroughly ashamed. It was just as I expected. They are too weak to keep out of mischief alone,—too little confident in me to trust sincerely in my protection, & too malicious & fixed in "Indianism" to be sincere with the "wašicun" [white man]. What can I do? I am most anxious to aid them, for they are the best people on my missions, but they will be destroyed if they follow in the steps of the other Indians. They really like me, but not to the extent of doing all I tell them, though they realize & say that I say it for their good. I must persist in telling them the truth, though it may lose me their friendship, &, for their good, I must refuse to recognize them as relatives unless they will obey me, hoping that this course, aided by the little good sense which,—more than all other Indians here,—they certainly possess, may, in time, do away with their weakness, their want of perfect confidence, their malicious bitterness in clinging to evil, & their folly in treating as a "wašicun toka" [white man enemy] the best & sincerest friend & relative they ever had, or ever will have, just because he loves them well enough to tell them the truth, without regard to consequences.

Went with Mr. Wells to Parkins. Gorge broke this morning, & ice ran out, but the water is still high. Teams cannot cross yet. Foot passengers cross in small boat. Landing difficult on account of drift ice piled along the banks. We hear that the Agent ordered the police to isolate the supposed case of small-pox at Big-head's camp, but they are afraid of it & refuse. It is there yet. If I am called, or if the disease spreads, I will go down there, & make arrangements to remain out in the camps, as I could not go into the Agency or return here to Wells, for fear of carrying the disease to others. If I go there now to investigate, & it should turn out to be a real case, I will have to remain out, & as I have nowhere to stay among the Indians, I shall be in a predicament. Perhaps, however, I had better make arrangements to stay out, if I have to, & go down & find out, as the police won't do anything alone. I have no right to order them, & can't safely do it, while we have such a malicious Agent, & so I must do myself, or get the Indians to help me do whatever is to be done.

April 8th [First Sunday after Easter]

Dominca in Albis [Sunday in white],[56] 5th anniversary of my first mass. Full years truly, but full of what? God alone knows that. I

[56] Often called "Low Sunday," the Sunday after Easter in the liturgical calendar.

dare not judge as to the fullness of merits, for a convert, new to the faith, left alone to fight his own battles, & to guide himself by the principles of worldly rectitude & honor, with but few spiritual lights, cannot expect to merit much;—but I can safely say that those five years, except, of course, that spent at Rosebud, have been full to overflowing of infinite, unalloyed, hopeless misery.

Since I left Rosebud, I cannot recall one single day that a reasonable man, taking all things into consideration, would call happy. Yet none of this came from the trials I knew, & was told of, & counted on at ordination. All arose from that which I had no right to expect, & which God, certainly, did not *will* that I should meet, though He may have allowed it. And I have, by no means, seen the end of all this. It will go on just as long as I go on in the strict line of my duty, & that, Deo volente [God willing], will be while life lasts. Well, "what can't be cured must be endured,"[57] & though I must suffer, I will still fight.

1st mass at 7. 2nd mass (High) at 10. Only about 30 came to 2nd mass. Zatela had a big "wakicagapi" at "Bear-ghost's" & the smell of wasna [a mixture of marrow and cherries], beef, dog, & coffee, proved stronger than the allurements of grace, & led a big crowd by the nose. I talked about Holy Communion, & tried to feed their souls, but the hearts of my hearers had gone after their noses towards the "wakicagapi" & its steaming kettles, & as soon as mass was over they hastened whither their hearts & noses led them. Well, good appetite to them, & full stomachs,—at least they came to mass, while others were guzzling.

Little Ada Mary Sweeny wants to make her first communion, but she must be better prepared. Went to Big-head's camp & Mrs. Van Solen's school, after mass, to investigate small-pox reports. Nothing but a scrofulous eruption [i.e., having a diseased appearance].

On the way I saw a "Hobu" courting a girl. He was not acting quite right, & she tried to wriggle & twist away from him, making much more ado about it than they usually do. I galloped up, &

[57] Dickens, *Pickwick Papers*, chap. 48.

asked her if she was willing that he should court her; offering to let them alone or drive the "Hobu" off as she should decide. She did not answer, but tried harder than ever to escape, begging him to let her go. As it was evident that she was unwilling, &, from what I saw already, would probably be ill treated, I ordered the fellow to let her go. As he did not obey, I charged in between them, bestowing upon him a good sound kick as the horse dashed against him, & then, wheeling again on him, brought my quirt lash down across his shoulders. He broke & ran for the house, dodging right & left to escape Pinch's hoofs; but Pinch had entered thoroughly into the spirit of the affair, & no doubt, supposing that this big calf was a lost "maverick" strayed from some ranch, followed him close, doubling & tacking with him, as a good "cow-horse" only can do, until he ran him frightened & breathless into the shelter of his tipi. Hurling after him a volley of choice Dakota epithets, regarding the cowardice & meanness of persecuting a girl who didn't want to be courted, I rode away on my smallpox hunt. The girl probably made good time for home. I could see nothing of her after finishing up the dude.

I don't feel like taking the part of these ungrateful, treacherous squaws, but a woman in trouble, no matter who she may be, has a right to the aid of anyone who considers himself a gentleman. "Noblesse oblige" [French for "nobility compels responsibility"] is certainly true here.

Took supper at Mrs. Van Solen's. Gave pictures to her & the children. Smoked. Left in time to cross the worst streams & drifts before dark. Waived a brotherly salute to little sister Ada, who peeped out of a tipi on the right. Declined in choice & elegant Sioux an invitation from an old "cooler" to give away tobacco & halt for a palaver on the left. Got back to Mr. Wells in time to smoke, write, & <u>sleep</u>.

April 9th [Monday]

Wind N.W. Cooler but snow melting. Ada does not come as she promised for instruction. Very well, no communion for some time longer. I don't see how I can have any ready for confirmation, if they are not better disposed than now. I fear that, for the present, but little can be done in the camps, & only in the boarding schools & in St. Joseph's Societies. The worse the Indians become the stricter must be our rules for them. It's the only way. I have insisted that Agnes Comes-last must publicly acknowledge her offense, & her sorrow therefor, before I can allow her even to come to mass. As long as she is badly disposed, & under her father's influence, she will only come to make trouble, & I cannot permit it. Went with Mr. Wells to Parkins. Cannonball high, & ice still running. Crossed in the boat.

The Indians are the most abject cowards that men & angels out of sheer contempt ever permitted to live, as being not worth the trouble it would take to kill them, & sure to rot in their own corruption if left to themselves. Sinte-peta [Fire Tail], an Indian who is not ashamed to boast in dances of having crept up behind an unarmed white man, & murdered him in the most cowardly manner, today stood near Cannonball, waiting for some white man to cross his wife, who was waiting on the other side. The worthless poltroon, too cowardly to cross among floating ice, had sent his wife to Parkins to buy provisions. When the river runs out, three inches depth of water, may, possibly, not prevent his crossing with his wife, to "peddle" her to the whites, as usual. The other Indians were, for the most part, as cowardly.

The Missouri is broken as far as Fort Lincoln. Some of the Indians have commenced plowing, for spring wheat & oats,—if they can get any.

April 10th [Tuesday]

Woke up this morning, & the first object my eyes rested on, was old Frank Wakan-inyanka (or Ota-inyanka) [Holy Running], an inveterate cooler, unmitigated humbug, & consummate hypocrite. He will tiptoe piously into the house, making the sign of the cross, his lips pursed up like a dried up potato, & his ugly phiz devoutly elongated; & after making a genuflection before the stove, he will

FIGURE 7. Long Dog.
In the background are the Catholic church and
fenced-in priest's house at Fort Yates, Standing Rock Reservation.
Photograph by D. F. Barry. *Denver Public Library, Western History Collection, Call No. B-887.*

recite in the "holy tone" the Lords prayer, in Dakota, &, scarcely pausing to take breath he will launch into the most outrageous coffee-cooling for all sorts of things, from a pipefull of tobacco to some food or money. He can't be got to his duties, won't go to mass when there is an Indian feast within smelling-distance, & lives in the worst devil-worshiping outfit that ever brought God's anger upon a tribe of pagans.

His business here today, was to beg boards for a coffin for a two year old child just dead, so he said. Pretended not to understand when asked if it was baptized, but finally said it was. For various good reasons, I don't believe him. Either the child is not dead, & he wants the boards for other purposes, or else the child is not baptized. I never could baptize one in that outfit (Tokala's) [Kit Fox's], & if Father Bede has, he surely gave a baptismal card, & they can't have lost it in so short a time, as they carefully treasure up every bit of such paper for coffee-cooling purposes. Therefore, after Mr. Wells & I had soundly laid down to him our views on hypocrisy, we sent him to get the child's baptismal card, since when he has not appeared.

During breakfast Old "Long Dog" came in to shake hands. Refused to shake hands with him, & on his persisting in talking to me, ordered him out & slammed the door behind him. I cannot consistently recognize him after his outrageous conduct in supporting with loud yells of approbation Sitting Bull's filthy charges against me to Inspector Bannister last fall. He was most gorgeously arrayed in Indian costume, & paint, &, as usual, carried his three-knife war-club on his left arm. He is the same old "Long Dog" who, three years ago, when bleeding to death from nose, lungs, & stomach, & completely exsanguinated, recovered instantly, after I had anointed him, &, after taking a smoke from my pipe, walked off perfectly well. "When the devil was sick, the devil a monk would be, but,—when the devil got well, the devil a monk was he."[58] He is a thorough & paced rascal, &, though he probably has almost as much faith as Satan himself, he is a clear case of unmitigated "witkotko" [craziness].

Instructed little Ada & a few others for first communion. "Ada, sole daughter of my house & heart."[59] Sharp, intelligent, & plenty of faith, though only 10 years old. Better take them innocent, & full of faith, though young, than corrupted, & faithless, though older; for their riper intelligence is over-ripe & rotten; & little pleasure will our Lord take in entering into vice-rotten hearts & souls black with crimes "such as are not so much as named among the

[58] Bower, *Scotichronicon*, vol. 2, p. 292.

[59] Possibly a paraphrase of Milton, *Paradise Lost*, bk. 9, line 653.

Gentiles." What was good among the Indians is gone forever. The poor children, from earliest infancy, are reared in an atmosphere reeking with vice & the filthiest immorality. We should be ready, at the first dawn of reason & moral responsibility, to consecrate its first fruits to God,—if we do not Satan will take them for himself. The earlier they can understand & receive Holy Communion, the better. We have nothing, under present circumstances, to gain by delay, but much to lose. The children should be kept in boarding-schools, safe from the camps, without vacations, until civilized tastes are formed, & good habits firmly fixed, & time shall have changed the camp life, as it will soon. May Satan seize the Agent for his cowardly, selfish, malicious orders to the contrary.

Before school ended for the day, I asked Mr. Wells to instruct the children, after catechism, in making the sign of the cross, while I watched "from cover" & observed the effect of the instruction. The new scholars, who had never made the sign of the cross before,—the regular communicants,—& those recently baptized, all made it well,—the new scholars soon learning it: while all whom I had suspected of devil-worship, verified my suspicions by not making it, or,—when Mr. Wells watched them,—by half making it, although most of them could do it well two years ago. They did it when they discovered that I was watching them, as I had instructed them, & they knew I had not forgotten what they did long ago.

High-bear came to ask me to write a note for him. Read him passages from the Old Testament, describing Jewish perverseness, & its consequent punishment, & proved, much to his horror & astonishment, that it was identical with Indian perverseness, & would probably be punished in the same way. He might profit by it, if it were not quite certain that its effects will be washed from his mind by the first drink of coffee or dog-soup; for an Indian's thoughts are all centered in his stomach, & his ideas may be truly said to be well digested; those that are evil being assimilated, & those that might lead to good being cast off with other excrementitious matter, for which he has no earthly use.

Cottonwood (Waga) also came, to ask about issue, boss-farmer, etc. He smiled even unto his collar-button, assured us that he was a just man, & knew no evil, & was a great friend to the "wašicun,"—which must be true, as he kept the word "wašicun" under his tongue, & chewed & mouthed it, & dwelt upon it as long as possible, though, from the faces he made over it, it must have tasted very bitter. What a convincing proof of devoted attachment, when, for the sake of the "wašicun" he mouths so long & earnestly that "dear sacred name" in spite of its evident bitterness. Confound the dirty, cowardly hypocrite.

Mr. Wells skinned & prepared for mounting, a booted lynx, killed at Fort Rice bottom (poisoned). It must have died with a cramp in its stomach, or when trying to propitiate a much hated enemy who "had him down," for his grin strongly resembles the "fascinating smile" of Waga, when conversing with his "wašicun koda" [white man friend]. Sweet resemblance! Waga & a poisoned lynx! It's a fact, though.

Just before going to bed last night, I heard a drum at Waga's camp. A rapid beat, similar to the "wapiyapi" [curing ceremony] beat, but on a large drum, followed by a monotonous beat like the "Hanwacipi" [night dance] beat, but much more rapid, & more sharply struck. It's probably some new devil's affair, as it is in that quarter, & unlike anything I ever heard. Of course, they have no right to dance except on Saturday, but the police won't report it, & the Agent won't thank or protect them if they do.

April 11th [Wednesday]

Wind N.W. Cool, but snow melting, & nearly all gone. Ice running at Fort Yates. Many Indians plowing. Porcupine[60] can be crossed. Ice gone, & water about 3 feet deep. Found out today, through Tokala's wife, that the child for whom Frank Wakan-inyanka tried to get a coffin, was not baptized. Just as I supposed. It's almost impossible to pity these brutes. The children *may* be saved, but the older ones never can.

[60] A creek entering the Missouri River midway between Fort Yates and Cannonball.

Iyato came to show a coffee-cooling note, & ask me to intercede for him with the Agent. He is the one who, last year, started a small store between here & Big-head's, but, in spite of my advice, he gave credit to the Indians, & did not abandon their ways himself. Of course he failed. Half Indian & half white ways would seem to be the policy of the best of them. The "age quid agis" [do what you do] plan they won't understand,—& they can make up their minds that I won't aid them till they do understand it, for it's time lost.

Mary Agnes Black Horse, another little sister, & Mary Aniwin, both communicants, ask for the scapular. I will enroll them when I come again.

Blue-earth came to beg flour, lamp oil, coffee, sugar, tobacco, powder & shot. The worthless scamp,—after giving away all he had in dances & feasts.

Man from Fort Yates came with a team to meet Douglas at Parkins. He will stay all night. I must start tomorrow for the Agency, & take vestments, etc. on horseback to Mrs. Van Solen's, where I say mass next.

That drum I heard night before last was Ahewanka, using the "inakicipi" ["they purify themselves"; i.e., the sweat lodge ceremony] drum in some of his infernal incantations,—literally "raising the devil."

April 12th [Thursday]

Warm. Wind S.W. Sealed up the package containing my vestments, so that they cannot well be opened. Mr. Wells will leave them at Waslaya's near Mrs. Van Solen's school, on Saturday, so that I can take the hill road to the Agency. Saddled up, & started at 2 P.M. Roads pretty dry. Met a boy who told me that the dude maverick Hobu, that Pinch & I rounded up last Sunday, has a wife whom he wants to throw away,[61] in order to steal the girl I drove him from. I wish now I had let Pinch brand that maverick with the horseshoe brand as that pursuing four-footed cow-puncher so earnestly desired. I might, at least, have put the quirt brand on him,

[61] Divorce among the Sioux was a "comparatively simple method of disposing one woman for another" (Hassrick, *Sioux*, 122).

& will certainly do one or the other if I catch him following other people's cattle again.

Stopped at McFaddens. Douglas passed me near Beaver Holes[62] on his way to Fort Yates. Met Ed Coles at Beaver Holes on his way to Wells'. Reached the Agency at a quarter to 8 P.M. Jennie Primeau worse. Visited her. Little Mary Prange had a spasm, but is better. Bill Pamplin married his inamorata last Saturday. Exit the "widdy Lanigan"[*sic*].

The report of my rounding up the maverick Hobu has reached here, but the report of his deviltry would have slept forever by the way, had I not corralled him. Sometimes good deeds are more noised abroad than evil ones, though those who thus noise them love the evil better. Strange, isn't it? but thus the evil-doers attacking the champions of right, often cut off their own noses.

Satan is in charge of Indian Agencies; but it will go hard if Wakantanka-ta akinta [Soldiers of God], together with the Mission herder & his horse "Pinch," doesn't round up & horseshoe-brand him, with all his lost mavericks.

St. Joseph's Society is lively, will meet Friday night. Mrs. Ben Cadotte is sick. Bleeding from lungs. F. Bede [Marty] attends her. Holy Oils just came. Must fill my oil-stocks tomorrow.[63] Smoked, wrote this much, & will sleep the sleep of the just, tired, worried, busy, & thoroughly-disgusted-with-yellowness man. By the bye, I learn that no one took Emeran the supplies I left at Douglas'. He had to come for them. Waktešni, etc.

April 13th [Friday]

Wind S.W. Ice in the Missouri running fast. No mail can be crossed. I hear that Grand River is very high, & that Oak Creek [broke] last Sunday, & is now too deep to cross. Went to Douglas' to buy clothing. Miss Drexel again sent $25.00 for intentions.[64]

[62] Beaver Holes Creek, about five miles above Fort Yates.

[63] The oils of the catechumens, blessed by the bishop of the diocese, which are used in the sacraments of baptism and extreme unction (last rites).

[64] Intentions were generally a monetary stipend for a mass or prayer for a special purpose.

Bought a black coat $7.00, a pair of Irish corduroy pants (imported) $5.00, & from Coles, 2 pairs long stockings $1.25. Mr. McNeider & Capt. Ilsley of the 7th Cavalry got me a pair of cavalry boots. . . .

When a man is "clothed & in his right mind,"[65] he is supposed to be pretty well fixed. I am clothed, &—well, if not in my right mind, at least, I don't know it.

Blessed Joseph & Mary Prange, & gave Mrs. Prange the blessing after delivery. Begged some bread & sweetmeats for little sister Mary Agnes Black Horse, at Prange's. Groomed Pinch. Hear that Mrs. Cadotte is better. St. Joseph's Society met. Got there just as the Agent, whom they had invited there, had finished making them a speech. He told them they could meet in the council hall. After he left, they had the usual "civilized supper," Old Black Tomahawk[66] began with the rest, & continued eating for at least an hour after the others, & seemed still hungry. He carried away a big handful of the bread left over. Several promise to come to F. Bede tomorrow morning for instruction. Next meeting on Saturday, Apr. 21st. Meeting broke up at 10:30 P.M. Smoked, wrote, prayers, bedtime.

April 14th [Saturday]

High wind from the N.W. Today is the first killing of beef since last December, & the noble red is here in full force gorging himself sick on raw "tripe & guts." Mr. Wells came in with Mrs. W[ells] & Louisa. John Carignan[67] is in from Grand River. Wrote a letter for Pizi[68] to Giles Tapetola.[69] Six of Pizi's family died during the winter. Mrs. McLaughlin's[70] Rosary Society had their first meeting this evening. A little common sense, if they had any, would have led them to meet & dismiss before dark. Just remembered that

[65] Mark 5:15.

[66] Canhpi-sapa, a Minneconjoux.

[67] John M. Carignan, a teacher at Grand River Day School.

[68] Pizi is the Lakota name for John Grass, a chief of the Blackfeet Sioux.

[69] Giles Tapetola, a nephew of Chief Gall, had been sent by Bishop Marty to St. Meinrad's College in Indiana as a potential candidate for the priesthood. He returned to the reservation without completing the curriculum but served for many years as a teacher and catechist.

[70] Marie Louise McLaughlin, wife of Agent James McLaughlin and daughter of a full-blood Indian mother.

I forgot to give Maggie Good Day a ring to replace the one she gave me for a wedding a month or two ago. A small matter, perhaps, but very big to little people, & I should have had sense enough to remember it. A year ago I would not have run the risk of wounding the feelings of any Indian, least of all, one of the little ones; but now I scarcely can manage to do a priest's offices towards them, to say nothing of going outside the strict line of duty to think of them. Bought & gave to Maggie a ring costing over 100 times as much as the one I used for the wedding, & much more showy, which will perhaps convince her that I didn't forget it on purpose.

Interpreted for the Doctor. Would have gone to Wm. Halsey's[71] for St. Mary's Council, but no one seems to know whether there will be any. Perhaps it will be on Monday, as today they are gorged with offal, & unfit for anything but sleep.

Took a statue of the B.V.M. to B. Prange's for Mrs. Parkins, & will have it sent to her on Monday. Mr. Wells, finding no place near Mrs. Van Solen's school where he could safely leave my vestments, brought them here. Deuce take it! What a time I shall have getting them back.

The frogs are piping on all sides wherever there is mud or water, & have given us an occasional solo for the past week. Ice still running in the Missouri, but the mail can now be crossed. Took supper at Mr. Givens', after eating one at B. Prange's. Custom of the country; "Eat when you can, fast when you must," & that same "must" is likely to occur frequently. Hear that the 7th Cavalry leave here on the 15th of May. Sorry to part with them. Helped eat up F. Bede's lunch. Did it out of mischief, but I guess I needed it. I am certainly not getting stronger. One Bull at last made up his mind to have his child baptized, & brought it in. F. Bede baptized it. He wouldn't let me do it when I went to Grand River on purpose, but when I ceased to wish it, he asked for it, & when he found out that I didn't care to wear myself out seeking lost sheep that didn't want to be found, he packed up the lost sheep & brought it to me.

[71] William Halsey, a relative of Charles Halsey and grandson of Chief Kills Eagle, also served as an interpreter on the reservation (Hinton, *South of Cannonball*, 90).

Just so it is with all of them. Kindness has no effect; but neglect & contempt bring them to their senses. If they want "cold shoulder," & think they can live on it, they will be soon satisfied, for there is a large supply of it in this world. Charity & kindness are rare, & like pearls, should not be offered to such swine.

April 15th [Sunday]

Cloudy, threatens a big blow tonight or tomorrow. Wind S.E. Father Bede said 8 o'clock mass & went to F. Martin's. I sang the 10:30 mass, & preached in Indian on the sacraments,—channels of grace absolutely necessary to put our souls in a state for salvation.

Mr. Wells left for Cannonball, leaving me $75.00 to send to Joseph St. George. Got the address from Louisa at the school, dined, looked after my horse, & went to Pastor's house to instruct Indians,—who did not come.

Baptized a 1 month baby, gave a baptismal & also an Indian name, as it had none. Mahpiyata-iyoyanpawin, & may this little "light in the heavens" be a guide to its parents walking "in tenebris et in umbra mortis" ["in darkness and in the shadow of death" (Luke 1:79)]. The mother, Josephine Cinpi, was once a school girl. Vacations kept alive the camp-spirit in her, until, leaving school, she went back to the blanket, married in Indian style, & now cannot be distinguished from any other squaw. I remember her. A relic of the promising days of the missions, when much <u>might</u> have been done, had the laity not tied the hands of the clergy, & the Bishop found out in time the tricks of the laity. The Indians were bad enough then, but not as corrupt as now, & there was still hope, but now nothing can be done except with the young.

Just heard that McFadden soundly thrashed two married bucks for trying to steal his school-girls near the school. He says he will also have them sent to the guard-house. If the whites annoy him about it, I shall report them. He has done his duty & done it well. Mrs. Faribault came to excuse her little girl, on the plea of illness, for not coming regularly to F. Bede's instructions, as I had announced for him at mass. Good woman, & good child. Wish old Caske were like them. Robert Hehaka [Elk] came to record baptism of Mad bear's aunt, whom he baptized poir. in art. mort. [in danger of (at the point of) death]. Good boy. Sat up late with him, instructing, telling stories, smoking perfumed cigarettes, & otherwise encouraging him. Don't mind loss of sleep when it's likely to do any good to one who merits courtesy. Wrote a note for him, smoked, wrote this much, & now—to bed.

April 16th [Monday]

Got up late; someone beating reveille on the door. School-children in church, waiting 15 minutes for mass. He-he-he! However, they all need prayers. If they go home for vacation, they won't pray any, & will need all the grace they can get in that extra 15 minutes. Said mass & gave Holy Communion to the Sisters. Sad, Sad, Poor Sisters. Agent has too much to say in the school, & they are foolish enough to forget their true strength in God & their superiors, to trust such a wretch, who will slander them to his infidel employees at the earliest opportunity.

We are not of the world, & its votaries are not in sympathy with us. If we don't keep up our esprit de corps, & help & trust each other, small help will we get outside. The Church is Divine, but the ulcer that is sapping the vitality of its temporal part, is the want of charity, confidence, sympathy, Christian esprit de corps, & energy among those consecrated to God. Here am I, the least of all, a convert, & by no means holy, know at least that much, while the spoiled, petted, children of the Church, who have lived in the light of the Holy Spirit from their cradles, can't be made to see it. It proves, it is true, that I am enough outside of God's Church, to take an outside glance at its workings, & therefore, so much the worse for me, but that I can't help. It also proves how much more easily than I, the more favored ones should see the weak point in their line, but they won't try to see it, &, therefore, so much the worse for them. It would be well for all of us if the convert had more of their innate, though not practical, sanctity, & if they had more of his practical, though worldly, ways of looking at things.

Peter Skunk is in charge of Coles' stable, & Pinch got no grain this morning, until the erudite quadruped looked at me with such a yellow, hungry look of disgust, that I suspected something wrong, found it out, & fed him myself. Must feed him myself. Skunk can't be trusted. Visited Cadotte's & Wm. Halsey's. As I led out Pinch to start, Andrew Fox, a son-in-law of Sitting Bull,—a Hampton [Virginia Indian boarding school] graduate returned to the blanket, began to sneer & laugh at me. Gave him a "blasting" & threatened him with a thrashing, & he immediately became quiet. While I was saddling, he came up to talk. Silenced him, & ordered him off, informing him that he would be at once knocked down if he came nearer than a certain post in the fence. After remaining quiet awhile, he crossed the limit, & I at once pitched him headlong into the middle of the road. He sneaked away, & I sent after him the information that all dogs who followed Sitting Bull would be served in the same way. I will take no more abuse from these brutes, & will meet sharply & sternly the slightest aggression.

Mrs. Cadotte is better. Halsey's family all well. Hard rain from N.W. just as I reached Cadotte's. It moderated while I was at Halsey's, but began again just as I left to return here. Rain-coat comes in very handy; put it on, but owing to the wind, & the plunging of Pinch, who didn't like the wind, rain & a few hail-stones striking his face, I could not keep my knees covered. However, I didn't get very wet. Fed & watered Pinch. Met young Bull-head (Lieut. of Police)[72] in Coles' store. He is much changed. He don't like the idea of casting off all Indian ways at once. Young men of St. Joseph's Society came to see Father Bede about their meetings. Now that they have agreed to cast off all Indian ways, their actions manifest sincerity. How different from the treacherous conduct of the "old-timers."

About noon, F. Bede returned from F. Martin's [Kenel's]. I shall have to be there next Sunday to help F. Martin in starting St.

[72] Henry Bullhead, lieutenant of McLaughlin's Indian Police, would later shoot Sitting Bull during the latter's arrest in 1890 and was himself killed by Catch-the-Bear in the same fracas.

Joseph's Society. At 9 P.M. the rain has ceased, & there is not a cloud in the sky. If tomorrow is clear, will go to Cannonball. . . .

April 17th [Tuesday]

High wind from the N.W. Wrote to Miss L. B. Drexel,[73] to my mother, & to James Bear-robe at Hampton. Scholars persecuted at Hampton. Punished if they go to mass, & urged to become Protestants. Advised James to go to mass, & to complain to the priest near him, & to F. Stephan, whose address I gave him, if punished for it, & to return home if Hampton is made too unpleasant. Told him to tell the other Catholic scholars what I say, & to show to his teachers my letter, which contains abundant reproaches for their proselytizing, & their broken promises to us of religious toleration for the scholars.

Young Bull-head promised to bring his child for baptism next issue, as today is too windy to keep his team standing out. Tried to start for Cannonball, but the wind was too high for me to travel against it fast enough to reach Wells' before dark without hurting the horse. Will start tomorrow, early.

Barney Prange went to St. Benedict's with the Agent, & returned this evening. Father Martin will now know how to look out for the Agent's tricks, as I sent him by F. Bede a letter from F. Stephan, exposing his attempts to attribute to his (the Agent's) intercession favors obtained from the Indian Department by F. Stephan & the Bishop for parties here.

I suspect that someone steals my horse from the stable to ride at night, & therefore groomed him carefully, so that he would show saddle marks if rode, & went tonight to watch the stable, but I found him safe.

Cetan-wicaša tells me that when Emeran came here last, he left Anowankte to watch the school. Anowankte's wife cooked up for an iwakicipi beans obtained from my school supplies. I don't think Emeran would give them away, & she must have stolen them. Per-

[73] Louise Drexel was the sister of Katharine Drexel, a wealthy heiress who was a major benefactor of the BCIM.

haps she has a key to fit the door. I sent her word that I had heard about the beans, & that if Emeran had not given them to her she must pay for them. They stole our pork in that camp, & now the beans, but they will not set well on their stomachs when I come to investigate it.

Shell's wife, who lives with an Indian, after leaving Shell, wants to join the Rosary Society, & marry the Indian, & the Indian wants to join St. Joseph's Society. F. Bede told the woman it was impossible unless they separated. I must hunt up the Indian & tell him the same.

11:00 P.M. bedtime, tired, sleepy. My eyes are very weak. Office don't improve them, but I can't carry a larger book. I dare not try to finish it when I feel that it is hurting my eyes, & finish with the rosary. Heaven only knows what will become of a missionary in a place like this, with the malicious surroundings & the probability that the Bishop may be deceived by their false statements. I have determined to remain here, or in the vicinity, to fight Satan & his allies, &, if they succeed in setting the Bishop against me, I may need all my sight & strength to make my living. Truly a priest is an unfortunate being. There is much he <u>might</u> do, even though it seems too much to expect of him, if he could trust his superiors; but, under the circumstances, there is much that he <u>cannot</u> do, even though it might seem to others that in not doing it he is willfully negligent of his duty. However, God understands it, & will, no doubt, requite according to their works those who torture his priests, & annul their work, & their usefulness. Had I only known all this in 1883, but I didn't, &—regrets are too late.

April 18th [Wednesday]

Wind N.W. Some snow in the air, but cleared up at 10 A.M. Cold. Went to Mr. Wells, by hill road. Before starting wrote to F. Stephan,[74] stating that the Agent had written or would write to Department, to get Joe in as clerk. Gave account of Kemp's case, &

[74] In the letter (Craft to Father Stephan, 18 April 1888, BCIM Records), Craft warns against McLaughlin's attempt to have Joe Primeau appointed chief clerk.

the consequences of Joe's getting the place, & left it to him to act as he pleases. Stated that McLaughlin's strength was our weakness.

Bought 500 cigarettes at Douglas'. Stopped at school to see Louisa, & at McFadden's. Left Agency at 9:30 A.M. & reached Wells at 2. P.M. Gave scapular to Ada Mary Sweeny, Mary Auiwin, & Mary Agnes Black-Horse. Bob Brown, Iato, & Crazy-man came. Instructed Mr. Wells' 3 boys for confession. Today I got a letter from Maggie Goodwood, Hampton, Va. She says she goes to mass on Sunday. Can't understand how she can do so, while the others are not allowed to go. Must enquire. Received from Yankton the prayers to be said before & after mass, & the Bishop's circular regarding cathedvaticum [a fee assessed on each parish for support of diocesan operations] & prayers.

April 19th [Thursday]

Warm. Wind N.W. Wrote letters for Mr. & Mrs. Wells, one of them to Maj. Cramsie[75] at Devil's Lake. Mr. Givens, the District Farmer, got back from Parkins. Talked about Agency crookedness at Fort Berthold [Indian Reservation]. Givens started on his rounds among the camps. Mr. Wells promised to persuade Ada Mary Sweeny to go to school at St. Benedict's Mission. Howard Coles came with Aleck Faribault,[76] on his way East for some weeks. Sketched out a caricature of the woodchuck, the eagle, & the fox, & parodied Childe Harold, on the back of a package for Lulu St. George.

Saddled up, & went to Mrs. Van Solen's. Saw Red-swift, a boss farmer, & boss liar. He sympathized with the Hobu maverick I rounded up. Gave him "fits" & my opinion of Indian brutality in the strongest terms. The scoundrel has a daughter in the sister's school; intelligent, speaks English well, & might become a good woman, but will inevitably go to the dogs here & to the devil hereafter, if she is not kept out of her father's control.

If, like Korah & Co.,[77] & Sodom & Gomorrah, these dogs could

[75] Maj. John W. Cramsie, U.S. Indian Agent at Devil's Lake Reservation.

[76] Alexander L. Faribault, assistant teacher at Grand River Day School (*Annual Reports*, 1892, p. 856).

[77] Num. 16, 17:5, and 26:8–11.

be swallowed up by the earth, or consumed by fire from heaven, their children might save their souls, but otherwise I see no hope. I am anxiously awaiting the land survey & allotment,[78] hoping that it will be a step towards civilization.

By the bye, the girl I drove the Hobu maverick from, turns out to be Hanpa-napin's daughter, baptized, & once quite devoted to the Church, but now as wild a skipper as any in camp. The Hobu I thrashed claims, they say, that she was willing to be courted, & that he was not treating her ill, but that she pretended to be unwilling, & tried to get away, & got him in trouble, because she feared I would recognize her. I did not recognize her, & know, from what I saw, that he was taking a mean advantage, & treating her immodestly; but the rest of his statement may be true, judging from what I know of these squaws. Therefore, I am glad I treated him as I did, & only wish I had given her also a severe reprimand. He claims he is not married. In fact, few of them are, except as the brutes are.—Ate supper, smoked, talked of various things. Gave Mrs Van Solen a medal for Lita, Leo Ota apapi's wife, wrote this much, & now,—to bed.

April 20th [Friday]

Fed Pinch. Prepared for mass. Went on the roof to fix the bell, slipped, & nearly fell off. Climbed up on the other side where cleats were nailed on, & fixed the bolts. Forgot to put the rope over the wheel. No matter. The bolts are worn out & wouldn't hold.

Said requiem mass for Eddie DeGrey, Mrs. Van Solen's son. Scholars sang Indian & English hymns during mass. After breakfast, Mr. Parkins, Ed Donohue, & Mr. Angevine drove up. Mrs. Van Solen, Lucille, & little Caske went to the Agency. Saddled up Pinch & rode in with them. Sent off a $3.25 P.O. Order for Mr. Wells. Bought a hat & black ribbon for my cross at Douglas'. Took gloves to Lulu St. George at the school. Helped F. Bede

[78] The Dawes Act, or General Allotment Act of 1887, provided for general distribution of up to 160 acres of land to heads of Indian families. Undistributed land would then be made available for settlement under the Homestead Laws (*Annual Reports*, 1887, pp. iv–x and 274).

instruct young men of St. Joseph's Society. They wanted us to fix up the marriage of a young man who had taken the discarded wife of Shell,—a white man married by F. Jerome.[79] Explained to them the indissolubility of matrimony. The fellow is in a bad fix. He has children by the woman. Serves him right, for his former opposition to the Black Robe's ways.

Tired & sleepy. I want to write to the Bishop, but must do it in the morning. "In pace in idipsum dormiam et requiescam." ["Totally at peace I will sleep and rest" (Psalm 4:9).]

April 21st [Saturday]

Rose at 6 A.M. Clear & warm. Wind S.W. Said mass at 7 A.M. Wrote to Bishop, saying I had not written before so as not to trouble him to answer while he was unwell. Explained the necessity of having no vacation for boarding schools, & recommended that it be stopped. Mentioned Emeran's 5 month's back pay. Asked of Indian Catechisms, & "Ladders of Heaven."[80] Saddled up & left for St. Benedict's Mission at 2 P.M. Forgot to mail letter to Bishop, & went back after going 1/2 a mile.

Stopped at Cadotte's & Halsey's. Wrote to the Doctor for Mrs. Cadotte. Several Indians signed to me to stop & talk. As they probably only wanted tobacco, & as it is my policy just now to treat them coolly, to bring them to their senses, I paid no attention to them, & rode on.

Reached here (St. Benedict's) about 6:30 P.M.. Gave perfumed cigarettes to my little brothers George Canteiapešni & Jacob Halsey. Indian relationship is "fearfully & wonderfully made."[81] I miss little sister Jennie. Gone to heaven during my absence. "Now staid to welcome here her wanderer home."

Those who hate Indians, or Pharisaically sympathize with them at arm's length, could never understand how I could sincerely love

[79] Father Jerome Hunt, OSB, a founder of the Agricultural Boarding School near Fort Yates; in 1888 he directed the Boys Industrial Boarding School at Devil's Lake Agency.

[80] Possibly a reference to a visual teaching aid similar to the "Two Roads Map," which depicted the good and bad roads to eternal life.

[81] Ps. 139:14.

them, & claim kindred with them. And yet God, who searches all hearts, & from whom no thought of motive can be hid, knows well that I was sincere & earnest in my affection for them, & am so still, in spite of their follies & malice. The death of one of my Indian relatives is soon forgotten by those who should cherish them most; while I who loved them most living, & yet was most hated by them for my efforts to save them, I, who, of all others, could not even have what consolation could be derived from seeing them in their last moments, I whom they were taught to hate & slander while living, & whom their last glance refused to recognize,—I am the only one to cherish their memory, &, through the Holy Sacrifice, refresh & release them from Purgatory, in return for the exquisite tortures they made me suffer while on earth. Well, so be it. "Noblesse oblige." I shall act well my part towards them, though they forget their duty to me. I am now, through policy & necessity, compelled to treat them coldly & distantly; but my apparent dislike for them is all on the surface. As the Good Shepherd looks anxiously for the return of the lost sheep, so I look anxiously for the moment when they will see things in their true light, & give me a chance to treat them as I did once. God grant that it may be soon. As for those who have caused this, may God avenge me upon them, & deal with them according to their work.

The Agent & his white allies are chiefly to blame. They look upon me as the chief cause of their failure to corrupt the Indians, & abuse priests as before, & are doing their best to get rid of me. Thus far I have out-generaled them, but still the fight goes on. A fine position, truly. Wolves & sheep alike hate the shepherd. It is very hard to bear, but it cannot last forever, & I am determined to stay with them "exceedingly late." Other priests have left, without trying to save the sheep or punish the wolves, because they were unwilling to risk losing caste, position, &, possibly, their souls in the attempt. The enemies of the Church know this, & try to drive me off also. But, for once, they have mistaken their man. I can't suffer keener mental torture than now; & I am prepared to risk all & lose all, & I <u>will</u> succeed.

April 22d [Sunday]

Cloudy, damp, wind East, threatening rain, but cleared up at noon. Said mass at 6:30 A.M. Feast of the patronage of St. Joseph. Preached before High Mass on St. Joseph, the Holy Family, Marriage, Sacraments, St. Joseph's Society, Indian ways, etc. After sermon F. Bernard[82] married 5 Indian couples, (all married before in the Indian way). They & others went to communion during mass, & took breakfast at the school.

After dinner the men met in F. Martin's room. We read rules of Society, & founded St. Joseph's Society, with 13 members, all of whom begin as practical Catholics, having abandoned all Indian ways. It was a sore blow for the old chiefs, who were sad & silent, the only growl coming from Bear-face.

After Benediction the women met, & we read them the same rules, adapted to them, & founded the woman's branch of St. Joseph's Society. Paul Ptehincala was made by F. Martin the president of the men's society, & Mary, his wife, president of the women's society, beginning with 8 members & about 7 postulants, some of whom are to be instructed for all the sacraments, & some for confession & communion only. All hearts good, & the work now well established on a firm foundation. This society is one & the same with that at the Agency, & under the same rules. I am sure that my little sister, Jennie Oyanke-lutawin, is at the bottom of all our success. God has, no doubt, taken the "Angel of the Mission," because we had need of such an intercessor. Wm.& Charles Halsey were here, & Wm. Halsey promised to do his best as president of St. Mary's Society (for neophytes), to prepare & send to St. Joseph's Society all the members possible.

After supper took care of Pinch. An Indian came to ask for baptism. Told him to come with his wife for instruction, cut his hair, & give up Indian ways. Smoked, talked, got tired, & prepared for bed.

---

[82] Bernard Strassmaier, OSB, a Bavarian priest who arrived at Standing Rock in 1886, where he labored faithfully until his death in 1940 (Duratscheck, *Crusading Along Sioux Trails,* 107).

April 23d [Monday]

Said mass at 7 A.M. (requiem for Jennie). I ought to remember little sister, but I doubt much that she needs our prayers. Brother Nicholas [Enz] went to the Fort at 6 A.M. & returned in the evening. Examined a sick boy. Bones of the feet carious. Froze his feet in the camps a year ago. They became ulcerated, but he wore his moccasins until the matter glued them to his feet, & formed a crust, under which the ulcers were eating into the bones. We had to soak the feet in warm water, & then cut the moccasins off in strips. Now the bones are carious, & it seems that our only hope is in amputation.

These Indians are rotten. Their changed life, & remaining too long under the miseries of their state of transition from barbarism to civilization, has produced scrofula, & syphilis has done the rest. Translated prayers to be said before mass from English into Sioux. Took off Pinch's shoes. They have been on all winter. F. Bernard instructed women to receive the sacraments before entering the Society. One came to say that her husband would listen to us, but his father & mother (Red-horse & wife Blackfeet) are holding him back in Indian ways. Smoked, tired & sleepy,—bedtime.

April 24th [Tuesday]

Very high wind from S.W. Blew the earth & seed from the fields & gardens. Thermometer went up to 85° above 0. Fahr. Said mass at 7 A.M. Finished the translation of prayers to be said before mass. F. Bernard instructed women for the Society. F. Martin talked with F. X. Taku hokipešni, the school policeman, giving him his choice of being helped to build his house, or getting wheat to sow his field, & also gave Isidore Miniowicakte, the secretary of the Society, blank book, paper, pens, pencils, ink, etc. Two school-boys, playing, started a fight in earnest, & school policeman stopped them. Advised F. X. Taku hokipešni, just as I did the Society at the Agency, about the Indian superstition regarding the conduct of husband & wife from the beginning of pregnancy to the weaning of the child. An evident trick of the devil to perpetuate polygamy & immorality.[83]

[83] Sioux belief, as with many other cultures, discouraged intercourse during this period.

Two old coffee-coolers came to "cool." One of them, Little Bear, an arrant scoundrel, came to get a coffin for his mother-in-law, who is not yet dead, & who refuses to receive the last sacraments, pretending deafness when the priest questioned her. Little Bear's wife also treated F. Bernard with the greatest contempt at his last visit. The rascal blamed his mother-in-law, but tried to shield his wife, pretending it was someone else. Informed him that those who wished to die impenitent could not be buried here, as we thought too much of little Jennie, & other good children buried here, to place a reprobate among them.

Red-bear & his wife came to "cool" for tripe & guts. He has a boy at school, so F. Martin gave him a paper entitling him to tripe & guts at the next beef killing. He has a girl who ought to go to school, but refuses to send her. His wife gave as an excuse first, that she herself did not get anything to eat here, & afterwards said that she was keeping the girl to have a feast & throw away a horse, etc. next summer, at her "Išnati-olowan," a feast given for each girl at the first appearance of the menses,—a kind of "bringing out" in Indian Society, & advertising for marriage sale, or stealing. It is worse now than ever, & lets loose the camp bucks to court the girl, & gives her to understand that she is a squaw, & is expected to act like one. It should be stopped. We gave Red-bear our opinion of it in strong terms. He admitted everything, but evidently with a very bad grace.

Little George Canteiapešni, Jennie's brother, is very delicate, has sore eyes, & swollen glands in neck, & seems likely to run down. It seems as if Jennie is after him. So much the better for him. I wish she would come after me; but there's no such good fortune in store for me I fear.

Fed & groomed & watered Pinch. Tired, sleepy, smoked, bedtime.

April 25th [Wednesday]

High wind from S.W. still continues, but is shifting round to W. & N.W. Said mass at 7 A.M. Remembered the Bishop's mother, whose death in Switzerland is announced by the St. Paul "Pioneer

Press." Copied out my translations of yesterday, for my own use. The first was for F. Martin. F. Bernard instructed Indians for the Societies. Some, of their own accord suggest abstaining [from meat] on Friday, though, on account of their poverty, & other causes, the Church does not insist in their case. Still, it shows their sincerity.

Red Horse came to "cool." Gave him a sharp reprimand for interfering with his son & daughter-in-law, & trying to keep them from marrying properly, & to hold them in Indian ways. He admitted dissuading them from marrying, & gave, as a reason, that his daughter-in-law was too bad for his son to marry properly. Of course she is sometimes cross—like everyone else—& has sometimes gone with her brothers to Protestant meetings, but is now sincere, & tries to do well since F. Bernard instructed her. We know well that the hare-brained old scoundrel thinks of nothing but dances & other Indian puerilities, & that this is his only reason for holding them back; but it shows how cunning he & all the others are, in seeking to gain their point by alleging,—not their real reasons—but something which, they rightly judge, will accord with our views, & which might lead us to doubt a well disposed person, &, perhaps, by an injudicious reprimand, to "froisser" [French for "to crease or rumple"; "to hurt one's feelings"] a character scarcely warmed up to make a right step, & crush down one scarcely able, though willing, to rise from the mire of savage vices & ignorance. This is the very plan they have always laid to cause the removal of priests, as soon as they had become too zealous & successful. They gave to the Bishop, not their real reasons,—which would, of course, have led him to support, instead of blaming, the priest,—but other false reasons, apt to influence one already prejudiced in their favor, & against the ones they sought to ruin. They, & bad Catholics, who act on the same plan, will, undoubtedly unite their forces, & bring every pressure to bear on the Bishop against me, whom they regard as the chief stumbling-block in their evil ways. Their cunning is truly Satanic, & their cleverly laid plans, may, I fear, influence the Bishop to say or do something that he could not in a long lifetime undo. May God expose their villany, & enlighten the

Bishop, & avert any such fatal misunderstanding between me & him; for if a trouble should arise from this cause, I have finally determined to fight it out to the bitter end.

I have studied carefully the evils that have, hitherto, annulled the efforts of all former missionaries here, & I have planted myself squarely in their course, & mean to check them now & here, & drive them back, even though they close in on front & flank, while those who ought to aid me, attack me in the rear. The crisis of the Missions has come. I brought it on with a full & clear knowledge of the consequences to myself, & I mean to abide by those consequences. I am not going to be driven away, as others were, by the fears of temporal & spiritual dangers, but will remain here, or in the vicinity, & will see that the Church triumphs. I have much to lose, I well know, but I am prepared to lose, & all of the "yellow-government-mule stickability" that is in me, shall appear A.M.D.G.

Francis Taku hokipešni told us what all the Indians know about Red Horse's daughter-in-law, & verified our former views. There was nothing bad about her, but what we already knew, & even <u>that</u> has now ceased.

Old Belly-fat came in on a "cool." A good old "gent-chief." Ever ready to speak in favor of the Black-robe, & regular in attendance at mass; but, pleading old age, & old traditions, could never be got to approach the sacraments. He meant no harm, however, & always urged the young Indians to obey us. He now promises to complete what may be wanting in former instructions, & go to his duties. He is almost the only one who, even while unwilling to do all he should, still, listened respectfully to advice, & never abused us, or gave us occasion to regard him as an enemy.

Bear-face came in, furious against Hampton School,[84] for refusing to pay his sick daughter's fare home. He says he sold a horse for $30.00 & sent her the money himself. Serves him right. I tried to persuade all those Catholic girls to go to Avoca[85] last fall, but

[84] The Indian boarding school in Hampton, Va.

[85] The Sisters of the Holy Child Jesus (SHCJ) operated a school for girls at Avoca, Minn.

they preferred Hampton, though they knew of its corruption & deviltry. But perhaps that was just the attraction. Went to see little George Canteiapešni. Not in immediate danger, but Jennie evidently wants him. Gave him a cigarette. Mr. Whitesell[86] returned from Oak Creek. Brother Meinrad[87] gave seed wheat to Francis Taku hokipešni. Wrote prayers before & after meals in Sioux for F. Bernard. Heavy thunder showers from N.W. in the evening. A boat with lumber for new school building is expected here every day. The first boat came from Bismarck to Fort Yates on the 23rd. Shaved, smoked, wrote, prayers, bedtime.

April 26th [Thursday]

High wind from N.W. Clear. F. Martin went to the Agency. Saddled Pinch & started at 11 A.M. Stopped at Halsey's & Cadotte's, & reached Agency at 3 P.M. Hear that P.[rotestant] Episcopal young men's society is breaking up. They want to join us, but must make a long probation, as they have been, like all Indian Protestants, great scamps & arrant hypocrites, & can't be trusted. St. Mary's Society has been much benefitted by the formation of St. Joseph's. It's time for them to wake up, & keep their long forgotten promises to abandon all Indian ways, & they just begin to see that they had better do it. I shall have more work & fighting, but more of the only peace worth having,—the "peace of victory."

Mrs. Cadotte & Adele are better. Jennie Primeau is worse. My flour, pork, beans, & groceries landed by boat at Douglas'. Received letters from Miles Gibbons, & from John Owl-ring, Rosebud. Young Spotted-tail is sick. My sister Grace Waštewin died 3 months ago, R.I.P. et oret pro me [May she rest in peace and pray for me]. Poor little sister. Very much like Jennie Oyankelutawin. Quiet, modest, devout, & sincere. One of my first Rosebud converts, &, I think, my first penitent. I took her away from the Episcopalians. A convert, like myself, but worthier of heaven, may God

86 William Whitsell, a district farmer assigned to Standing Rock.

87 Brother Meinrad Widmer, OSB, industrial teacher at the Agricultural Boarding School near Fort Yates.

FIGURE 8. Belly Fat. Photograph by D. F. Barry. *Denver Public Library, Western History Collection, Call No. B-23.*

have mercy on her, & may she pity me. All the rest of my relatives at Rosebud are well.

The postulants of St. Joseph's Society came for instruction. Instructed them on the Sacraments, prayers for the dead, patron saints, communion of saints, etc.

I learn that Mrs. McLaughlin not only holds her women's meetings at night, but has had the cheek to enroll three school girls, take them from the school to the meetings under some other pretext, & keep them out of the school all night. Advised F. Bede to set his foot squarely down on such things at once. Two of the girls are candidates for the novitiate. Confound her impudence, whether it arise from ignorance or malice.

Mrs. Prange still quite sick. Asked Fathers Martin & Bede to remember my sister Grace at mass. I must get the particulars of her death. She was the best of Spotted-Tail's daughters, & my best sister at Rosebud.

Soldiers of 7th Cavalry, Rice & Young came up as usual in the evening. Got from Mr. Charles Primeau[88] the address of T. Bruguier [*sic*],[89] Sioux City, Iowa, to whom I shall write to find Mad Bear's nephews, the sons of Francois Laframboise. "Wamahèl" (Louis Sitting Bull) is in the guard-house for various "sculduggeries." He is regarded by poor Lo as a big "wakan" [holy man]. Such as their gods are so are they. They are pantheistic only in deifying the worst side of nature,—& all vices. Juvenal's[90] deity cultivators, & fine deities they are causing to sprout up here. "O sanctas gentes, quibus haec nascuntur in hortis numina." ["O holy tribes to (for) whom these deities are born (spring up) in (your) gardens."]

Late, tired, sleepy, smoked, wrote this much, bedtime.

April 27th [Friday]

Raw, sharp East wind. Threatening rain or snow. Mr. Wells came to pick out Nellie's grave, & to arrange for putting up a stone.

Mrs. Van Solen came to bring girls & boys for first communion, & boys to join St. Joseph's Society. Emeran came in from Grand River. As his back pay ($125.00) has not yet come, I took his two store accounts. (Coles' $64.00, Woolfolks[91] $61.00) on my own account. Letting him to pay the balance of the $75.00 of his account at Woolfolks.

F. Martin went back to the Mission. Wrote out 5 marriage certificates to be recorded in Agent's office, for 5 couples married last Sunday at the Mission, & wrote application for 6 licenses for the 6 couples to be married here on Tuesday next. I instructed, with F. Bede & Emeran, 20 of St. Joseph's Society for the sacraments. Mrs. McLaughlin came with Mrs. Van Solen's girls to see F. Bede. The young men of St. Joseph's objected to receiving 5 boys from Mrs. Van Solen's school. Explained to them why they should be received,

---

[88] Charles Primeau appears as an interpreter and witness for the November 30, 1882, Standing Rock agreement with the Sioux (*Annual Reports*, 1862, 379).

[89] Theophile Brughier, an early pioneer in DT (Kingsbury, *History of Dakota Territory*, 1:135).

[90] A Roman poet.

[91] Woolfolk was a fur and buffalo robe trader who settled in Bismarck, N.Dak. (Kingsbury, *History of Dakota Territory*, 1228).

but while I was consulting with F. Bede about it, the meeting broke up, & the young men began to break away. Called them back, but 4 of the boys did not come. Some of the turbulent spirits tried to win F. Bede over to their views, & Mrs. McLaughlin took their part. I let F. Bede settle it, & we tried to console the boys by promising to start a separate society for them at Mrs. Van Solen's school.

I explained to all that the first & most essential condition for keeping the society in decent order, was obedience to the priest. F. Bede weakened, & let them have their way, fearing that they might break up. Had he stood firm all would have gone well. I am thoroughly disgusted & shall let F. Bede run things in his own way. I don't care to lead rebels. They now want wedding rings for the 6 couples to be married on Tuesday. Tired, sleepy, disgusted, & don't care to think about it. We should be firm with these brutes, but rather than risk a dispute with my brother priests, I shall drop entirely out of the affair, & let them find out things for themselves, as they won't listen to me. Smoked, wrote, bedtime.

April 28th [Saturday]

Wind N.W. Cold, raw. Cloudy. Sharp snow storm, but cleared up at noon. Said mass at 7 A.M. A steamboat fast on a bar about 10 miles above. Went to Douglas'. Arranged to have my freight sent to Grand River by Išnala-wica, a policeman, & to pay him $2.25 for freighting about 500 lbs. Bought a sack of oats for Emeran's pony, for which he will pay. Completed arrangements for taking $125.00 of Emeran's store bills on my account, so as to pay up his 5 months back pay. If the Bishop sends it, so much the better, & if not so much the worse for me.

Met Josephine Crow-feather & Lucy, going from the school to visit their parents in the camp near the Agency. There is a big dance today, but I forgot it until they passed. Enquired of the Indians, & found that the dance would be near where Crow-feather was camped. Was afraid that Josephine, my sister, would be annoyed by some of the Hobus near the dance, & would have called her back, or gone out there to take care of her; but being sure that she would not thank me for my interference, I told F. Bede & sent word to the Sisters that there was a dance in camp, & told Emeran, who was going that way, to the St. Mary's council, to see where Josephine was, & to inform those who would circulate it, that it would be best for any Hobu who thought of annoying Josephine, to get a coffin first, & settle his affairs, as she has a brother who will inflict summary punishment upon anyone annoying her. Coles told me that he saw the two girls looking on at the dance, & Father Bede prepared to send or go for them, but they came back before dark. The Sisters did not know of the dance when they let them go.

Waited some time for 3 couples to come for instruction, but two only came. Instructed them for their 1st communion tomorrow. Mr. Halsey came to arrange for communion tomorrow.

Wm. Herr, Rissa, & Young, soldiers from the Fort came up, & another soldier went to confession. My sister Emma Halsey came to teach me the melody of St. Joseph's hymn in Dakota. She was quite timid, but I managed to get the tune. Tired, sleepy, smoked, prayers, bedtime.

I sent today for a Remington revolver & "drop shoulder holster" to Montgomery Ward & Co. Night rides are getting unsafe. I have but little of the spirit of the martyr, & knowing the motives of the rascals here, feel sure that death would not be martyrdom. Therefore I wish the best next to martyrdom, viz. a soldier's death, & I will take care that the soldier dies hard, &—not alone.

April 29th [Sunday]

Clear, but raw & chilly. Said mass at 8. Before mass heard confessions & gave communion to Wm. Halsey, a soldier of the 7th Cavalry, & Anselmine Wapelinawin, & 1st communion to Peter Hchaka-onzinca & his wife, & Leo Hehaka-gi [Brown Elk] & his wife, who could not wait for Tuesday. Leo Ota apapi & wife did not come. He don't want to cut his hair. Rather queer. He has given up all other Indian customs, & is a very good fellow.

Preached at High mass on the gospel of the day. Church crowded with Indians. Many could not get in. F. Bede blessed medals for women's society. In the evening instructed & heard confessions, at the school, of the 5 boys & four girls from Mrs. Van Solen's, all but one of whom make their 1st communion tomorrow. F. Bede baptized 2 children. 1 for young Bull Head, Lieut. of Police, & one for Yuzuzupi. Visited Jennie Primeau & got medicine for Anselmine. Jennie Primeau is much worse, & will probably die. Sat up to write letters, but was too tired to do much. Went to bed at 11:30 P.M. Today 1st horseback procession of St. Mary's Society to church.

April 30th [Monday]

Still raw & cold. Wind S.W. Some rain in the evening. Said mass at 7 A.M., & gave communion to Mrs. Van Solen's boys & girls. Bought wedding rings. F. Bede & I instructed members of Societies, & heard about 65 confessions,—all Indians & mixed-bloods. Mrs. McLaughlin is doing her best.

Sent to Agent for marriage licenses, but, so far, did not get them. Emeran left for Grand River. Mr. St. George, who came with Mrs. Wells, went to confession in French, as also Mr. Ben Cadotte. Young John Grass started to go to St. Benedict's School. Mr. St. George gave me some maple sugar, which I handed over to my little sister Josephine Crow-feather. "Sweets to the sweet."[92] Gave her a medal of B.V.M. Grand preparations for 1st of May. Our Lady is now rousing up faith, & leveling heresy. A grand start, & we must take advantage of it, & work to hold it.

Dr. Caskie[93] is just finding out the treachery of the whites on the Agency. It's about time. In spite of his professional skill, & his Christian character, his ignorance of, & dislike for, "snakes," blackguardism, & "five-ace-tricks," is not conducive to popularity. Tired, & must be up early to say first mass at 6 A.M. Cigarette, prayers, bedtime.

May 1st [Tuesday]

. . . F. Bede sang high mass at 7 A.M., & before mass married 5 Indian couples. One forgot his ring. I ran to the house to get one,

[92] Shakespeare, *Hamlet*, 5.1.265.

[93] Ambler Caski, a physician at Fort Yates.

& ran back to the church, and, in consequence, was hardly able to interpret for the marriages, owing to spasmodic heart's action. During mass 22 made first communion, & among them John & Sibly McLaughlin,[94] & Lulu St. George, & 25 others also went to communion. The couples married today all received. After mass we gave the scapular to the communicants who had not received it before. Before mass I gave an instruction in Dakota to prepare them for marriage, communion, & receiving the scapular.

After mass, I got Dr. Caskie to examine my heart's action. He can detect no enlargement, nor valvular trouble, but finds great rapidity, & functional derangement. Exposure, hardship, & continual anxiety & trouble for the past few years, keeping me under a severe mental strain, & deranging nervous functions,—all combined have caused it. He gave me digitalis, & also pepsin, to correct the stomach, also much out of order, & a belladonna plaster to put over the heart.

Mr. Prange employed a woman from Winona[95] to work. Nothing going on in these new frontier towns: Even the <u>saloons</u> closed. Made out & sent to Agent 5 marriage certificates. May devotions at 7 P.M. Soldier & Protestant girl married at 9 P.M. The man wouldn't go to confession. He'll catch it in good style. One who marries a Protestant is sure to have a hell upon earth.

I just learned that Louis Manina died at Clontarf [Minnesota]. He was the best scholar at Mr. Wells' School, & a very good Catholic. I won't forget him, while I am able to offer the Holy Sacrifice for him. The dead seem closer to me than the living,—nearer to me now, I fear, than they will be hereafter. At least they know <u>now</u>, & will do for me in heaven what I did for them on earth. Lowell is right, & one who has borne the torture, that has been my daily portion, from the estrangement of those nearest & dearest, & trusts that now, enlightened by God, they will see & amend their mistake, can well feel the truth of his beautiful lines—

---

[94] John (Jack) and Rupert Sibley McLaughlin, 13- and 11-year-old sons of Agent McLaughlin.

[95] A town across the Missouri River from Fort Yates; consistent with the "wild west" aura of some communities of the era, it was also called "Devils' Colony" (Hinton, *South of Cannonball*, 55).

"Tis the void chair our surest guest receives,
Tis lips long cold that give the warmest kiss,
Tis the lost voice comes oftenest to our ears,
We count our rosary by the beads we miss."[96]

How often would the "Hovering Eagle" have covered & protected his little ones here, but they would not; but now, from the "spirit-land" they know him, & fly to him, & he gathers them again under his wings. Here in spite of their perverseness I cherished them & fought for them: & can they refuse now to use for me their power with God? Surely not. There is no ingratitude in heaven. Through me they have obtained eternal life; & may I obtain it through them.

May 2d [Wednesday]

. . . Dr. Caskie started for Mandan on his way East & South to be married. Wrote to Bertha Tapatiwin, my sister, at Avoca, in answer to one just received from her. Received letters also from my mother, from Miles Gibbons, from J. H. Strait, Fort Totten, & from J. B. Catanduta, Hampton. The last complains that he is punished if he goes to mass, & is almost forced to join the Protestants. I must send such letters to F. Stephan.

I learn from F. Bede that there is some chance that Josephine Crow-feather, Annie Pleets, Emma Archambeau & others, who were to go to the convent as postulants, may not go. I examined them, and, if there is such a thing as a vocation, they certainly have it. It might be possible that they would lose it, but they can not have lost it in so short a time. Why should they be kept here in this hotbed of vice, to risk losing it. Why expose these poor Indians, to whom God offers His mercy, to such temptations as would destroy even the strongest. It really seems to me that those who have it in charge fear to act lest they may get themselves into trouble. The girls should be taken to the convent at once. One excuse is, just now, that no one can take them. I will offer to do it, or to replace for the time any priest who will go. If they won't act then, when I take all the risk which they fear, then may God take

[96] James Russell Lowell, "Agassiz," lines 7–13. First published 1866 in *Heartsease and Rue.*

vengeance upon those who seek the ruin of the souls whom He has chosen. This same Catholic Church has a human side, & it is here something less than human. We read much of holy people who did their duty to God & their neighbor without fear of Satan or Satan's allies; but there's precious little of their spirit in this part of the world. Well, I shall offer my services, at the risk of having a grand first class racket, & of finding, besides, all my good friends join Satan against me. Tomorrow I shall propose my plan, which I now commend to the Sacred Hearts of Jesus & Mary, & to Holy St. Joseph, patron of novices & those seeking God's service. Little love would I have for my relatives if I should neglect that part of their interests for which alone I became their relative; & small loyalty would I show to God if I allowed Satan to seize His chosen souls without a sharp fight, which I shall at once begin.

May 3d [Thursday]

Said mass at 6:30 A.M. Offered to take girls to the convent. Sister Gertrude[97] says that all but Emma Archambeau are firm, that Crow-feather offers no opposition, & that Emma Archambeau is too weak & morally cowardly to resist her mother's importunities, & would even abuse us for our charity. All this is very true. She deserves nothing, but still I offered to take the blame for the whole affair, if at any time it should be thought prudent to send her to the convent. I fear that before Mother Gertrude[98] gets her, some of the scoundrels on the Agency, who seek the destruction of the poor girls, may work with the Agent, or in some way alarm the Sisters, or, through relatives, dissuade the girls, to prevent them from going. Should such an attempt be made I will do my utmost to prevent its success, & to take summary vengeance upon the rascals. It is evident that the Sisters do not desire my assistance, & if they can get along in the affair without it, I shall be much pleased, but as two of the girls are my sisters, I shall be ready to help if necessary.

[97] Sister Gertrude McDermott, OSB, superintendent and teacher at the Industrial Boarding School.

[98] Mother Gertrude Leupi, OSB, superior of the Benedictine convent at Yankton, DT.

Josephine Crow-feather will visit Mandan with the Sisters tomorrow. Gave Sister Gertrude $1.00 for her, to enable her to enjoy her visit better. Wrote to F. Stephan, enclosing Douglas' bill for provisions for St. F. de Sales School. Douglas made out my bill also at my request. Bought 5 large packages of cigarettes at Coles. There is a plan on foot to put O'Brien in place of either Wells or Carignan as teacher. My informant told me, that I might warn Wells. Left a note for Wells with F. Bede, in case I should pass him on the road, & not see him. Advised F. Bede to keep McLaughlin's boys in St. Joseph's Society. I like the poor little ones, & they should be saved if possible, no matter what their father's faults may be.

I started for Cannonball at 4:30 P.M. to have Wells' team ready for the Sisters tomorrow. I'll take any trouble or suffer anything, if it will contribute in the least towards securing my sisters' vocations, & for Josephine, especially. She was the only one who did not fear to show a sister's sympathy & affection for me, when I was so foully slandered last summer, & I have not forgotten it.

Reached Mrs. Van Solen's at 7:30 P.M. Ate supper, started again, & reached Wells' at 10:30 P.M. Put up the horse. Warned Wells about school matters. Arranged for team for the Sisters & Josephine. Smoked, prayers, bedtime.

May 4th [Friday]

Clear, like yesterday, but cool. Sister Mary Adele[99] & sister going East, & Josephine Crow-feather, reached here at 11 A.M. Showed Josephine the school & classes, & gave her another dollar which I borrowed from Mrs. Wells. Lent her my oilcloth "slicker" in case of rain. They ate dinner with us, & started at 12 M. ["meridies," Latin for "noon"] Levi Dezera was to drive the team, but fearing that he would be sick on the way, I got Mr. St. George to go, & it was lucky I did, for Levi was quite sick after they had gone.

Announced mass for Sunday to the scholars. Mrs. Van Solen left my vestments here. Went with Mr. Givens to Parkins & interpreted

[99] Sister Adele Eugster, OSB, matron at the Industrial Boarding School.

on the way, & sent a telegram to Sister Mary Adele to let her know that she could get a team here to take her through to the Agency tomorrow night, if she wished.

High Bear wants me to report Frank Gates[100] for "squaw business." Referred him to the Agent & Faribault.[101] I imagine that the plan to give O'Brien a teacher's position may mean that Jack Carignan is disgusted with the Indians on Grand River, & wants to resign unless he can exchange schools with Wells. If he resigns, then O'Brien, the only available one, will take his place, or else Wells will take it & O'Brien will take Cannonball. Most probably Wells will exchange with Carignan. Such an arrangement would be satisfactory to both, & it may be that this is the real state of the case. I have just heard something that makes it seem probable, but we can't tell yet.

Young Bull-head's prophesy is coming true. The brutes on Grand River will be punished for their rascally treatment of Louis Primeau[102] & myself, & will get as teacher one who will stand no nonsense,—unless he is totally blind to his own interests & safety.

May 5th [Saturday]

Clear. Cool. Wind S.E. Looks as if it might rain if it tried hard. Washed saddle blanket. Mr. Wells went duck-shooting with Miss St. George. Interpreted for boss-farmer.

I have heard something that causes me considerable anxiety. It seems that the Agent [McLaughlin] has been threatening to annoy & "investigate" "the Catholics," stating that he is not afraid of them,—that they cannot remove him from office, etc., & his threats seem to be directed against all the priests, but especially against me. I can't see how he can hurt me, as I have done nothing to give him any hold on me, but perhaps he may intend to get the Indians to

---

[100] Frank Gates (Blackfeet Sioux name Saswe), an assistant farmer on Standing Rock Reservation.

[101] George Faribault, responsible for Indian farming operations on Standing Rock Agency.

[102] Louis Primeau was a day-school teacher on Standing Rock (*Annual Reports*, 1886, 1888), an interpreter with Buffalo Bill's Wild West Shows (Hinton, *South of Cannonball*, 90), and a trusted interpreter for Agent McLaughlin (McLaughlin, *My Friend the Indian*).

renew Sitting Bull's filthy charges, which he, probably, instigated before. My informant was not sure whether I would be attacked through Inspectors, or Commissioners, or by reports & charges sent to Washington. The Agent seems to be under the impression,—at least, he is said to express himself so,—that I & other priests are trying to have him removed, as he richly deserves, & now wishes to begin an attack on us to save himself. It may be that tale-bearers have so informed him, for a liar's track no one can follow; but I imagine that, finding us determined not to submit to his abuse, & be ruined & removed at his pleasure, & attributing his failures to destroy us, to my determined, and, hitherto successful, defense of myself & other priests, he wants to make an effort to get rid of me, & won't scruple to use any vile & unworthy means to gain his end.

Certainly we have made no attempt to have him removed, though he certainly deserves it, & all our reports to the Bishop & Catholic Indian Bureau have been in regard to his attempts to injure & remove us, & his neglect to protect us from the attacks of bad Indians, & they have been made merely for our own protection. His policy is "rule or ruin." I therefore went to Parkins, & wrote a letter to F. Stephan,[103] stating what I had heard, & promising to telegraph if any action in the case should be needed, & what I heard should prove true.

I sent the letter to Gayton (Kennedy's) Post Office, over the river, by Peter Scheuer, whom I met at Parkins. I got from Mr. Parkins a list of the lawyers in Bismarck. I thought of sending one of them a retaining fee, & stating what I know & suspect, so as to be ready to call on him in case the Agent should annoy me; but, so far, I am completely in the dark as to what he is about. I have no desire to get into trouble nor trouble anyone else, but if the Agent attacks me again I mean to defend myself in a way that he will remember.

Mr. Wells & Miss St. George returned from duck-shooting. Sister Mary Adele & Josephine [Crow-feather] returned with Mr. St.

[103] Craft writes of McLaughlin's past and potential treachery to "make trouble for the Catholics" as well as the agent's failure to come to his defense in the charges brought by Sitting Bull (Craft to Father Stephan, 5 May 1888, BCIM Records).

George from Mandan [North Dakota]. They passed on the road, Rosa Bear-face[104] & Josephine McCarty, returning from Hampton School.

Josephine [Crow-feather] is tired riding, & has a headache. Gave her hartshorn [a preparation of ammonia used as smelling salts], & tied up her head with a hot cloth. Sent Lulu St. George to put her to bed. Josephine wanted to go to communion tomorrow, but in order to reach the Agency in time for high-mass, they will have to leave here long before mass. Must write to the Bishop, & send the letter by Sister Mary Adele & Josephine to F. Bede to be mailed.

May 6th [Sunday]

Clear. Sister Mary Adele & Josephine went with Mr. Givens to the Agency, starting at 6:40 A.M. They took to F. Bede my letter which I wrote this morning to the Bishop, containing the same warning about the Agent that I sent to F. Stephan, & also expressing the hope I felt that I could rely on him in any emergency.

Josephine's headache had disappeared by this morning. Wished her God-speed in her efforts to become a Sister, & promised to pray for her today at mass. Said mass at 10:30 A.M. Indian prayers (imperata) ["directed" prayers] before mass. Mass said to obtain God's help against the Agent's persecutions, & also for the vocation of my sister Josephine to the convent.

Only about a dozen Indians at mass. Big dance last night, & all are asleep today. After mass two Hobus appeared on the hill, waiting to "catch" a girl going from mass. I rang the bell for the policeman, who did not come. I then saddled Pinch & rode after them, but they left when they saw me coming, & disappeared in Waga's camp.

Sent my vestments by Mrs. Van Solen to her school. Mrs. Parkins takes her down. To avoid any possible misunderstanding with the Agent, & to get what information I could about his proposed attack, I let Mr. Wells go this morning to the Agency &

[104] Teacher at Number 3 Day School, ten miles west of the Agency.

told him to say to the Agent that if he feared that I or other priests were trying to get him removed, he was much deceived, & might be at rest about it; but if he should attack me or any other priest, for this or any other cause, we would make a defense that he might well fear. I had not attacked him but he had thrown me on my defense. I never would aid him in Washington again, & did not care to meet him except for business purposes, on account of his meanness in the Sitting Bull affair.

I am only a missionary priest engaged in converting & civilizing the Indians, & wish to be let alone; but if he will persist in attacking me, I shall wait for him to begin, & then begin a defense which he will have cause to fear. If Mr. Wells can open his eyes, & stop his deviltry, well & good,—if not I suppose I must fight. It seems as if there is no rest for me, & all my trouble comes from false brethren whom the Church has aided until they are strong enough now to strike it in return for its aid. It is well that there is one Catholic (Mr. Wells) who has faith & courage enough to stand by his priests, & demand an account from the Agent, & let him know that he cannot attack us with impunity.

May 7th [Monday]

Clear & warm. Took the school in Mr. Wells absence, & examined the scholars in their prayers, etc., & taught them hymns. Baptized the 3 week old child of Joseph Wakute-waken, Paul Wicahpi-iyega. Gave my little sister Ada Mary Sweeny a medal of B.V.M.

Mr. Wells returned from the Agency. The sum of the Agent's reply to Mr. Wells' demand for an explanation, was—eliminated from lamentations about the trouble I give him, & his good intentions towards me, etc.—simply this. He admitted using the language reported to me, when angry, & after listening to lies told him by someone, who, he now believes, intended to make trouble for him, as well as for us. He said he never meant to do what he said, & regretted having said it. He probably may not attempt anything now, as he knows I am on my guard, but I must look out for him. To avoid possible complications, & save the Bishop & F.

Stephan anxiety & trouble, I went to Parkins & wrote to them stating facts as Mr. Wells learned them; & stating that he probably would do nothing now I was on my guard, but that I should watch him, & would inform them if anything should occur worth noticing; & that I wrote now to save them trouble & anxiety.

Rode back from Parkins with Mr. & Mrs. Wells, & Joseph & Lulu on horseback. Mr. Givens returned from the Agency.

I know perfectly well what I have to expect here. A priest, at all times, & in all places, must advise his people & instruct them, & do what lies in his power, by entreaty, command, remonstrance, & reprimand, to check their vices & lead them to keep God's commandments. It is especially necessary here, where Satan & his works have such a strong hold upon the Indians, & he will often be compelled to protect those who wish to do right, & are too weak to protect themselves against the attacks, moral & physical, of God's enemies. The bad element among the Indians is bitterly opposed to such things, & those who wish to do right, are too weak & cowardly to say a word in their own defense, or in defense of their priest, when he is attacked & slandered by Satan's allies for his efforts to save souls.

The attacks made upon priests cause much uneasiness to the Agent, as they draw attention to his neglect of duty in checking evil practices; & he is therefore anxious to get rid of the priest whose efforts to save souls, make a noise that endangers his quiet possession of his position; to hold which he is willing to silence his conscience, & allow evil to continue, as long as it is secret, & does not annoy him. He is therefore very likely to sustain all charges made against the priest, in order to make it appear that the priest is attacked by his own fault, & <u>not</u> for doing what God & his conscience command him, & what the Agent should do in accordance with his instructions, & he might even instigate such charges, if he thought the blame could be laid on the priests & not on him, in order to get rid of one whom he considers a troublesome cranky zealot.

Nearly all the whites on the Agency stand ready to instigate such charges, & to sustain them, in order to get rid of the priest who keeps out of their grasp the women they wish to corrupt, & whose unceasing exhortations to virtue, are an endless reproach to their vices, by letting the Indians know that the sins they wish to keep them in, are not the rule among civilized people, as they would like them to believe, but are condemned by God & man. Therefore, the bad element among the Indians, the Agent, & nearly all the whites on the Agency, will lay snares for the priest, & make charges against him, & misrepresent him to the Bishop, & to Government officials, & to all who may be able to annoy him, or cause his removal.

Now the question is, how far can they succeed? If the Bishop & the Inspectors, & other Government officials, knew the real state of the case, they could not succeed at all, but, would, on the contrary, be punished. But do they know the real state of the case? I do not think so. The real state of the Indians is not understood outside of their immediate vicinity. The Bishop, even if he should happen to have confidence in his priests, would be likely to be slow in sustaining them, when a prompt response to their call for aid would be most necessary; & he might even listen to vile accusations, without rebuking the accusers, or make such replies as to convey the impression that the charges had, in his estimation, some weight,—even though this should not be his intention. There is little hope that he would be as zealous & active in defending the honor of his priest, as that priest had been in defending the honor of his God, & the souls of his spiritual children. Government Inspectors & other officials, are very likely to be prejudiced against priests, & the least word from the Agent would turn them against him. In all cases, I might rest assured, that an attack from the enemies of God would find me left alone to meet it, & would be sure to injure me.

Where is my redress? In the law of the land, & in my own hands. For the first, I would need money, the cooperation, or, at least, <u>not</u> the opposition of the Bishop, & time to prepare & act,—none of which I am likely to get; & it would end in the loss of my position as missionary, the suspension of my priestly faculties, and, in the finale, the loss of my soul. For the second, to take the law in my own hands, by chastising the rascals as they deserve, would certainly terminate in the same way. I cannot let them attack me without resistance. If I resist I am lost. If I try to avoid the attack, I must either submit to them,—which I could not think of,—& which would make God condemn me, or I must leave, & go among the whites, which, again, I could not do, as I was ordained for the Indians, & would not have consented to assume the burden of the priesthood for any other people.

There is no chance of martyrdom among these vile cowards,—too utterly base & degraded to muster up courage enough to kill an unarmed priest. There is nothing to expect but slanderous attacks, a smirched reputation, the scorn of enemies & nominal friends, & the exasperating pity of those who ought to have been friends,—Then a determined effort to obtain redress: appeals to law, & a long legal fight, finally successful, but leaving me out of my position, & away from my field of usefulness; at variance with the Church, that should have aided me, & seeking the end in some foreign military service, closing my house's history, as it has always seemed destined to close,—where it began, in blood,—in battle,—in much worldly honor,—& eternal misery.

For all this I am prepared, & fully expect it. I can see no honorable escape. I have done my duty as my conscience & the Church's teachings have laid it before me. This is my recompense. If there is such a thing as predestination, in spite of our will & deed, here I have it. God can avert all this, & severely chastise the enemies of His Church, & in Him alone is there any hope, for if I am attacked I shall fight, & the end is clear. But I will do what I can to make my defense a stubborn & desperate one.

May 8th [Tuesday]

Clear & warm. Helped Mr. Wells cut out his cattle for branding. Pinch did not sustain his reputation as a good cow-horse. He was very wild, & hard to rein. Once, to stop his plunging, & fearing the weak bridle rein would give way, I had to cut him across the nose with the quirt-lash. Happened to hurt his eye, but not seriously.

Took the school for Mr. Wells while he branded the cattle. Gave instruction on commandments of God & the Church, explaining how most of the Indian customs, as they are now corrupted, conflicted with them. Taught the scholars hymns in Dakota. At first bashful, as usual, but afterwards sang well. Charlie & Johnnie McLaughlin[105] came up with Ben Gillen, who came to build Mr. Givens' house. Both boys belong to St. Joseph's Society. They are both naturally good & intelligent, & it seems a pity to keep them in such a place as an Agency. Mr. Wells gave Red Tomahawk[106] his dinner, as he is one of the very few who deserve it. Little sister Ada came to school today wearing her cross, medal, etc. to show how little she cares for the talk of the bad element. I hope to get her in a school soon. She is too good to grow up in the camps. Charlie & Johnnie helped rope calves. In the evening heard the first confessions of James, Frank, & Joseph Wells.

May 9th [Wednesday]

Went before breakfast to help Mr. Wells find his horse Daisy, who ran away last night trailing a 70 feet lariat, which, Mr. Wells fondly imagined, would not be stolen, because it was soaked in red paint, & could easily be identified. I maintained that, paint or no paint, the lariat would be taken. After sending Antony & Andrew Ireland[107] to look for the horse, we found it with the field-glass, only a mile away. Of course, the lariat was gone,—neatly untied from the short halter-rope. The halter & short rope were not taken, & therefore the thief must have some remains of conscience,—a rare thing in this neighborhood. He must be one of our best Indians, & by searching among them, we may find the lariat.

Johnnie & Charlie left for the Agency, about 8 or 9 o'clock, A.M. Saddled up; packed up corn for Pinch; took mail for Mrs. Wells,

---

[105] Sons of Agent McLaughlin, aged 15 and 13, respectively.

[106] Ta-can-hpi-lu-ta, a Two Kettle Sioux serving on McLaughlin's Indian Police, was also involved in the attempted arrest of Sitting Bull in December 1890. In 1893, Marcellus Red Tomahawk was captain of the Standing Rock Indian Police (*Annual Reports,* 1893, 559).

[107] Anthony Ireland was a district farmer on Standing Rock Reservation in 1893 (*Annual Reports,* 1892, 833).

& went to Mrs. Van Solen's. As I started Daisy got away again. I looked for her, but in the wrong direction, & sighted her with the glass, just as the boys caught her.

Stopped to see Ada's grandmother. Promised to get liniment for her, & gave her an order on Parkins for provisions. They are certainly starving. In all except beef, one person's rations for two weeks cost the U.S. Government about twenty-five cents. I offered to give Ada's grandmother an order on Parkins entitling her to the same amount of flour, bacon, coffee & sugar she gets at issue, on the Saturdays between issues. Thus giving her double rations, if she would let me put Ada in one of the boarding schools. She was willing, but Ada cried & refused. She says she is afraid the sisters will whip her. She will probably reconsider it, just as she did baptism.

It's very strange how these people refuse to listen to their best friends, but will readily listen to all others. Ada told Mr. Wells she was anxious to go to boarding school, but now that I want it, she won't hear of it. Just as, in India, the priest devoted to the pariah caste has to share the contempt & abuse heaped upon that caste by all others, just so I am called a "crank," & abused by the whites, for devoting myself to the Indians. But the pariahs appreciate the sacrifices made for them by their priest, & he has, at least, their affection & confidence, while these Indian pariahs here, treat me worse than the whites do, & refuse me the slightest mark of affection or confidence, & confide willingly in others, while I am almost the only one they hate. Well, they will see their mistake—too late.

Reached Mrs. Van Solen's in time for supper. Unsaddled & picketed Pinch. Tokala-luta [Red Fox] came in, & wanted to be very pleasant. The scoundrel went last week to the Agent, & wanted him to put me in the guard-house, because I reprimanded him as he deserved for encouraging vice. I treated him with contempt, & took no notice of him. He left immediately.

Just heard from Mrs. Van Solen the stories told about other priests who have been here. Every one, without exception, has been charged with drunkenness,—after he left, & was not here to answer them. Catholics are the worst enemies of God & His priests. I knew, personally, many of the priests they slandered, & know positively that their stories are false. If we should have a few of such lying wretches dragged into court to answer for their villainy, the rest would govern their lying tongues.

May 10th [Thursday]

Said mass at 9 A.M. Gave instruction on the Ascension; on imitation of the life of Jesus[108] at Nazareth: & rising with Him, by rising from sin by penance, & ascending with Him by being above worldly thoughts & desires, & keeping our thoughts & desires with Him in heaven. After mass I picked up some new Dakota expressions, so as to facilitate & make clearer the instructions & advice to be given in the confessional.

Took the names of some boys to prepare to begin St. Aloysius Society. Taught the children St. Joseph's hymn, & copied it out for them in Dakota. Left Mrs. Van Solen's at 2:30 P.M. & reached the Agency a little before 6 P.M. Frequent showers & high wind from N.W. Met Charles Halsey near Porcupine Creek. He wants to fix up his marriage, but has not yet heard from Santee Agency. It may be that the woman, to whom S. D. Hinman[109] married him there, was not baptized. He is anxious for Sam to go East to school.

Received from the Depart. a copy of the Indian Reports of 1887, & a copy of the correspondence in the affair of prohibiting Indian teaching in schools. Went to May devotions. One of my saddle cinches is wearing out, & none to be had on the Agency.

May 11th [Friday]

Wrote letters this morning to Bertha Tapatiwin, Mr. T. Bruguire to find Mad Bear's relatives, to F. Stephan[110] enclosing one for Ind. Commissioner Atkins,[111] acknowledging receipt of his book on

[108] A spiritual devotion with Christ as a model, from the 1417 book credited to Thomas a Kempis.

[109] Rev. Samuel Dutton Hinman, Episcopal missionary and official interpreter.

[110] Craft to Father Stephan, 11 May 1888, BCIM Records.

[111] J. D. C. Atkins, U.S. Commissioner of Indian Affairs.

FIGURE 9. Flying By.
Photograph by D. F. Barry.
Denver Public Library, Western History Collection, Call No. B-497.

Indian teaching affair, sympathizing with him, & approving his course, & sent receipt to Sec. of Interior for copy of Ind. Reports. Flying-by[112] brought in a letter from Emeran. Gave Coles Emeran's list to get soap & medicine at Mandan. Bought at Coles a box of 500 cigarettes, $3.25. Meeting of St. Mary's Society at Halsey's. Sent them some cigarettes, but can't go on account of my defective saddle cinch, as I don't want to injure the horse's back by using another saddle.

Visited Jennie Primeau. She is getting worse. Went to May devotions in the Church. Mrs. Van Solen & Lucille came to the Agency. Mr. Young, Herr, & Rissa came up. Robert Hehaka & an Indian of Mad-bear's band came up to F. Bede. Instructed them on the "Ladder of Heaven."

[112] George Flying By, first lieutenant of McLaughlin's Indian Police in 1892 (*Annual Reports,* 1892, 833).

May 12th [Saturday]

Said mass at 7 A.M. Anniversary of the death of Paul Teziopila at Yankton in 1884. Ordered a riding bridle & a saddle cinch at Coles'. Met Riggs,[113] Protestant minister, at Coles'. Zatela took pains to treat me with especial politeness & reverence for Rigg's edification. Jack Carignan & his mother in from Grand River. Warned Jack against Bill Pamplin, a tale-bearer, liar, & mischief-maker. Black-bull & High-bear came to me for help & advice in the land-in-severalty & Dawes bill affair.[114] Explained the benefits of the land survey. Referred them to the Agent, from whom, they say, they got their information, for any further explanation they need. Told them I had nothing to do with their business with the Government, & would attend to my work as a missionary only, as they had slandered, or allowed me to be slandered to Inspectors, etc., & they should be ashamed to ask me for help under the circumstances.

Wrote to Maggie Goodwood at Hampton, & John Owl-ring at Rosebud. Instructed Frosted about the care of families, protection of sisters & other relatives, & other civilized ways. Meeting of St Joseph's Society. Did not go, as I have two high masses tomorrow & need rest. Meeting of Women's Society at Wm. Halsey's. Mrs. McLaughlin got Emma Halsey & Emma Archambeau, very much against the wish of F. Bede & Sister Gertrude, to go to the meeting to help them, saying that there would be white ladies there, & the girls would surely be back before dark. F. Bede lent them his horse & buggy to ensure their quick return, but it was 9 P.M. before they got back. Went with F. Bede, stumbling through roads & holes in the dark, to Wm. Cadotte's to look for them, as we thought we heard them go there. They had not been there, & we found that they reached the school while we were looking for them at Cadotte's. We learned that there were no whites at the meeting.

---

[113] Thomas L. Riggs, Congregational missionary, son of Rev. Thomas L. Riggs and grandson of Rev. Stephen Return Riggs. The Riggs family served the Sioux for almost fifty years (Hinton, *South of Cannonball*, 109).

[114] The Dawes Commission would soon be arriving at Standing Rock, authorized by Congress to purchase eleven million acres of Indian land.

F. Bede & I thought over a plan to form a Society of St. Agnes, at the school, for the girls. It will be started tomorrow, & will, no doubt, be of great service in putting into the girls' minds civilized & Christian notions, & giving them something better to look forward to than camp vices. A soldier of the 7th Cavalry came to confession.

May 13th [Sunday]

F. Bede went to Winona. I sang 2 high masses,—one at 9 A.M. for the Indians; preached in Sioux on the Ascension, & explained Indian exemption from fast & abstinence;—the other at 10:45 for the whites. Church full. Boat came, but did not bring Emeran's organ & freight. Went to Douglas' & told them to look after our freight when it comes, & pay all charges. Tried to find a cinch & bridle, as my bridle reins are getting cracked & dangerous, but could not find any suitable. This morning at 5:30, a soldier of the 7th Cavalry went to communion. . . .

May 14th [Monday]

Said mass at 7 A.M. Mrs. Duprée & Mrs. Marciana Cadotte went to confession & communion. Sent by Flying-by things ordered by Emeran. Flying-by also took out a bell & books & other things for the school. Hunted for Dr. Diebel to get medicines for Cannonball & Grand River [schools], but could not find him. Sent F. Martin's mail & package by F. [Frank] Taku hokipeši. Bought new bridle reins at Coles, & blue & red ribbon, the colors of our societies, for my horse's bridle.

Yesterday, F. Bede started a St. Agnes Sodality at the school here, for the girls. Josephine, my sister, showed her charity, politeness, & common sense. In the election of officers, there was something like a "draw." F. Bede could have decided in favor of Josie, & proposed it. No one objected; but Josie, fearing that it might not be quite satisfactory to all, declined. She is a lady, & deserves the vocation which God seems to have given her. May she persevere to the end. Her father is willing to let her be a Sister, & seems quite proud of it.

Mr. McNeider gave me an old cinch, which will save my neck, until the new one, ordered from Mandan, through Coles, comes. . . .

May 15th [Tuesday]

Said mass at 6:30 A.M. Mr. Riese of 7th Cav. received. Gave my sister Josie Crow-feather a blue ribbon for her medal. Got her to aid me in verifying some new Dakota expressions. Wrote to John H. Strait & William Tiwanzilan, my cousins at Devils Lake, & sent crucifixes to John. Saddled up, & rode to St. Benedict's Mission, after giving F. Bede some Dakota sentences arranged to facilitate asking questions in confession.

Stopped on the way at Wm. Halsey's. He tells me that at the council the chiefs held on Sunday, to select the speakers to talk with the [Dawes Bill] Commissioners, the Indians said they did not want Sitting Bull & Antelope & such people to speak, as they always talked foolishly, & got them into trouble. Mad-bear was proposed as the chief speaker. It is the first time they have acted sensibly. Now it remains to be seen whether they will continue to be sensible.

I found the Mission very busy building, & moving buildings. F. Bernard has not yet returned from his mission among the whites across the river. I hear that Bishop Marty is proposed as one of the Commissioners to treat for the purchase of Indian land. Apart from the natural dislike we have to see our Bishop on a footing of equality with the Protestant "Bishop" Whipple,[115] who is also proposed, it seems hardly prudent for him to take part in it, as he will be placed in the dilemma of offending the Government, anxious for the purchase, or of alienating the Indians, bitterly opposed to it. I shall write to him, & tell him how the case stands, & leave him to judge what to do.

May 16th [Wednesday]

Said mass at 7 A.M. Took care of Pinch. Corrected Indian prayers, & wrote out expressions for the confessional, for F. Martin. Gave

[115] Henry B. Whipple, Episcopal missionary bishop at Lower Brulé Indian Reservation.

cigarettes to my brothers Robert Gaudreau, & little George Cantesàpešni, who now seems better, & to a sick boy in the infirmary. Practiced on the organ in church. Wm. Whitesell, the District farmer, went to Oak Creek, to look after the farm work of the Indians. Brother Nicholas returned from the Agency. Wind S.E. & promises rain, but, like all other promises in Dakota, it will probably disappoint us.

Young John Grass was hovering around since yesterday. He was not received into the school as he expected, & now expresses a great desire to receive the sacraments. F. Martin told him to come on Sunday. He is probably trying to get one of the school girls. He acted so once before, when he wanted to marry Maggie Goodwood, & when he failed, he went back to the Protestants. If he went to confession with such intentions, he would probably conceal his stealing & throwing away "Bad-hair's" daughter, on Grand River, last year. He will bear watching, & plenty of it. His father is the cause of all his perverseness. This evening attended May devotions in the church.

May 17th [Thursday]

Said mass at 6:30 A.M. Practiced on the organ in the church. Carpenters finished the boat, & finished moving building. In the afternoon we launched the boat, & I went with two boys to meet F. Bernard over the river. Having no oars, we used paddles. Found that F. Bernard went to the Agency via Winona. Some time after we got back, F. Bernard came in F. Bede's buggy, with Charlie Peerman. In the evening after May Devotions, I instructed Henry Agard [*sic*][116] & his wife for confession & communion. Wind S.W. & an occasional slight sprinkle of rain. Air cold & damp. The spring is very backward. No leaves on the trees yet, though there is grass enough for pasture.

May 18th [Friday]

Said mass at 7 A.M. Got pictures from F. Bernard. Wind S. W.,

[116] Henry Agaard was an interpreter on Standing Rock Reservation (Hinton, *South of Cannonball*, 140).

but clear & warm. Saddled up & rode to the Agency. Charlie Peerman brought back F. Bede's horse & buggy. On the way blessed Henry Agard's house & fields. Jennie Primeau gave birth yesterday to a 6½ months child (boy) which died soon after baptism. She is very weak, & seemed to be dying, but rallied again. F. Bede gave her all the Sacraments yesterday.

In the evening, some soldiers of the 7th Cav. came to take leave. They start tomorrow for the Indian Territory. One had been, with my advice & aid, trying to break himself of the morphine habit. He asked advice of Dr. Diebel, the contract doctor at the Fort, & the scoundrel told of it, & had him arrested, confined, & court-martialed, but he was acquitted. Diebel is a rascal, & has now forfeited the confidence of everyone. A doctor who betrays professional secrets, is unfit to live.

May 19th [Saturday]

Said mass at 7 A.M., & blessed the water. Gave some pictures to my sister Josephine Crow-feather. Talking with her about Purgatory, & stories regarding the return of souls to ask for suffrages, I made an agreement with her, that the one of us who should die first must endeavor, through Jesus, Mary & Joseph, to get permission to return, or to send word to the other, to state just what suffrages would be necessary to release the soul at once from Purgatory, & that the other must at once use every means in their power to obtain those suffrages. I promised to take Josephine's sufferings in Purgatory on myself if necessary to release her.

I wrote to the Bishop to post him about the dispositions of the Indians, in case he should be on the Commission to treat for land, & also to suggest that Mother Gertrude should come at once for the girls who are to go to the convent, before their parents or evil disposed persons can take the usual occasion, at the close of the school, to get them away.

Jennie Primeau is sinking, & will soon die. Went with F. Bede to see the 7th Cavalry leave. Our best soldiers are all going, & but few real practical Catholics remain. The Protestant "Bishop"

Haire[117] [*sic*] is at the Fort, & Dunbar, the chaplain came to get Victor Ahewanka to visit him, but Victor refused.

May 20th [Sunday]

Just before mass (7:30 A.M.), Susan Primeau came up to tell us that Jennie was dying, & wanted to see a priest. F. Bede & I at once went down. We found her holding the blessed candle, & just about gone. They said she died just as we came in, judging from the last breath they could notice. I gave her the last absolution, sub conditione [conditionally], & held my indulgenced crucifix to her lips. I am quite certain that she was still alive. She was well prepared, & merely sent for us, as we had directed, to be with her when she died. As soon as we were sure she was dead, I went up to church & said the first mass (8 A.M.) for her, announced her death, & asked all to pray for her during mass. I wrote to Maggie Goodwood at Hampton to inform her & Jennie's relatives there of her death.

F. Bede sang high mass at 10:30 A.M. & gave Indian instruction after mass, & took up the collection for the Cathedraticum. I measured Jennie for the coffin. Sister Gertrude, & another Sister laid her out. Funeral tomorrow, with requiem high mass, at 7:30 A.M.

In the afternoon the sodality girls from the school came to visit F. Bede. They are much changed for the better. Lizzie Fox, formerly stubborn, brazen, & mean in every way, is now docile, & modest, & among the best of the girls. For all this, many thanks to our Dear Mother Mary, who has done it all. I told them stories of saints & guardian angels, & other things which I thought might be interesting, amusing, & instructive. Josie Crow-feather was much interested in a German grammar. Young man promised to come for baptism, but failed to put in an appearance. Mr. Herr of the Infantry gave me some cigarettes.

May 21st [Monday]

At. 8 A.M. Jennie's funeral. Officiated, & sang a requiem high mass, but did not preach, though F. Bede invited me to. There were

[117] Episcopal Bishop William H. Hare.

many whites & few Indians present, & sermons to the whites here do but little good. I belong to the Indians, & do not care to waste the time & breath that belongs to them, in tickling the ears of those who listen only to criticize, & not to learn.

Bought a hair cinch at Coles' for 50 cts, & put it on my saddle. Saddled up, & started after dinner for Mrs. Van Solen's. Learned at Angevine's store (Woolfolk's) that Sitting Bull told them that the Bishop promised to pay his store bills. He said I had acted as interpreter for the Bishop, & he had the "cheek" to refer them to me. I exposed the lie at Angevines's, & also told Coles', saying that a liar & slanderer of priests had nothing to expect from priests or Bishop, & warned them not to trust Sitting Bull on our account. I asked when he contracted the debt at Angevine's, & reminded them that, about a year ago, when Bull pleaded poverty, I had gave security for him to the amount of $5.00, & if that still remained unpaid, I would pay it, if they could not collect it from Bull,—merely to keep my word, but told them not to charge it to me before trying to collect it from Bull. I warned F. Bede against the old rascal, but F. Bede knows him, & will not do anything for him.

The horse traveled well today, with a very easy, though rapid, trot. Never went so well before. Stopped at McFadden's school, near where I met Sister Gertrude & Mrs. Faribault. Left McFadden's at 4:30 P.M. & reached Mrs. Van Solen's at 7:40 P.M. Wind shifted from E. to N.W. A few drops of rain fell.

Met Leo Ota apapi. He was hunting muskrats with an old flintlock shot-gun. He had caught a turtle, & shot a muskrat, & was watching for another. Gave him some cigarettes, & smoked with him, & instructed him about confession & communion. Met my little cousin Susan, with her little relative, a lame boy, quite bright & intelligent. Gave him a cigarette. After supper at Mrs. Van Solen's, we sang Indian hymns with the children. I told stories about Purgatory, Angels, etc. Willie Cadotte[118] picketed my horse. Smoked, wrote this much. Bed time.

---

[118] William Cadotte was an "additional farmer" on Standing Rock Reservation (*Annual Reports*, 1892, 832).

Tuesday, May 22d

Said mass at 9 A.M. Explained about the children's societies we intended to form. After mass formed the Society of St. Aloysius for the boys, & the Society of the Holy Angels for the girls, & appointed Presidents, Vice Presidents, Secretaries, Treasurers, & visitors of the sick. Wrote rules for the two societies, & ordered the prayer to the Guardian Angel for both. Went to Mr. Wells, & stopped to see Ho-tanka [Big Voice] & Ada's grandmother, & arranged for Ada to go to St. Benedict's Mission School.[119] Reached Mr. Wells' about 6 P.M.

Wednesday, May 23d

Learned from Ada that Ho-tanka intends to take her to the Agency school. It won't do. It's too near by, & as the Agent may want the children to go home for vacation, I don't want her there. I found that Ada wanted to go with Ho-tanka and, as she is probably acting under his direction, I rode over to see him & her grandmother about it. Explained that I wanted her at the Mission, to keep her at school, & out of the camps, & would give no provisions unless I had my way. Promised to make up the loss if she should be taken off their ticket. They consented, & promised to send her with her aunt tomorrow early. I will borrow Mr. Wells' horse & buggy, as Pinch is too wild & tricky to drive single. Went with Mr. Wells to fence in a spring, to keep his cattle from spoiling the Indian's water, & then we went to Parkins. Bought 3 packages of cigarettes, & arranged about rations for Ada's grandmother.

Examined Louisa St. George, case of spinal curvature, & consequent deformity of chest & shoulders, & also tendency to irritation of synovial membranes about knee & hip joints. She is 13 years of age, delicate, lax fibre. The spine straightens when stooping, or drawing herself erect. Will mention it to Dr. Caskie. In the

[119] Craft later mentions that Ada was an orphan, so it is unclear precisely what Ho-tanka's relationship to Ada was. Indian relationships were broadly applied; thus, Ho-tanka may have been Ada's guardian—he may have adopted his deceased brother's or sister's children. Craft, too, often claimed the same sort of relationships, though he would identify orphans to get them into boarding schools.

meantime recommended friction of the whole body, & especially along the spine, one hour horseback exercise morning & evening, sitting erect in the saddle, & tonic treatment, & out door exercise. The phosphate of iron would, I think, be beneficial.

The Red Fish outfit are trying to marry Mary Skecawin to a man about 40 years of age, who took & threw away Deer-neck's daughter. He offers a horse for her. They came to see me before I reached here, saying that they wanted her to be properly married. It's the "devil dreaming" outfit. They want the horse, & only talk about marriage, to use me as a shield to ward off the consequences of giving a school girl to one who, by Agency rules, has no right to marry her. I have not seen any of them, as they have kept away since I have been here. I sent for Mary to know whether she had consented, & told them she must speak to the Agent,—or rather sent them word to do so. They won't trap me; & I shall inform [George?] Faribault about it. Spring backward; no leaves yet; grass short. A few plum blossoms.

Thursday, May 24th

After waiting until 10 A.M. for Ada & her aunt, I saddled up Pinch & started for the Agency. Stopped at Ada's & asked why they did not come. Ada was off somewhere, & they said that she was not willing to go to school. The real truth probably is that some camp Indians have dissuaded them from sending her. Informed them that I would do nothing for them, & would not again ask her to go to school.

Stopped at Mrs. Van Solen's. St. Aloysius' & the Holy Angel's Societies are doing well. The old Indians think the rules too strict, but the children are pleased with them, & are doing well. Reached the Agency at 7 P.M. Coles' gave me my cinch.

The Agent has been notified by the Indian Department that we can have 160 acres of land, not claimed or occupied, for mission purposes. F. Bede was notified by the Vicar General, & told to inform F. Martin. The land should be taken near St. Benedict's Mission, & that is probably the Bishop's intention. The Agent is quite dissatisfied because he was not consulted.

Friday, May 25th

Said mass at 7 A.M. Bought riding gloves, stockings, & 2 boxes No. 44 Winchester cartridges, to use at Grand River,—by deputy, of course. The antelope & deer are coming close. Emeran wanted me to give some to an Indian, & sent a note to that effect, with a list of things to be bought for the school. He evidently forgets that we can't give ammunition to Indians, so, of course, I couldn't run the risk.

Instructed some Indians at F. Bede's for the sacraments. One woman cross, & evidently unwilling. Told her to come when her temper was better. Baptized a child of Chief Mad Bear. Went to see Victor Frosted's wife. Severe pain in stomach. She vomited bile, & was relieved at once.

Mrs. McLaughlin came to see her & brought with her Miss Collins,[120] a Presbyterian "woman missionary" who pretends to know about medicine, but their services were not needed. Fine Catholics, to be sure. Mrs. McLaughlin is trying to get two school girls off to her woman's society meeting. F. Bede & I & the Sisters won't consent. She will probably have Miss Collins at the meeting, "to make a few remarks." If she does, she will hear of it in good style. We must not let wolves into the fold. The spirit of Alexander the coppersmith is again abroad. May God help us to exorcise such heretical ghosts. Bad Catholics, whose want of self respect, & want of realization of the dignity & superiority of their church over all this, leads them to be flattered by the notice of Protestants, are too apt to betray the Church to Satan & his allies. We must watch them, & oppose their bad influence at any cost.

Saturday, May 26th

Said mass at 7 A.M. Hunted a long time for Mary Agnes Black Horse, who said she wanted to go to the Sister's school, but I could not find her. Looked after my horse, in Coles' stable, to be sure he gets proper care, & gave him hay, which the man in charge had

[120] Mary C. Collins, Congregational missionary on Grand River, ten miles south of Sitting Bull's camp (Hinton, *South of Cannonball,* 171).

forgotten. Jack Carignan is in from Grand River. Dr. & Mrs. Caskie reached here in the afternoon. The womans society met in the council hall. I saw a crowd of disreputable-looking bucks looking in the windows, & ridiculing the meeting. Told young Bull Head, Lieut. of Police, to scatter them. He ordered them off, but, after he left, they did not go. I ordered them off promptly & sharply, & they left at once, & did not return.

Went with P. Hogan, a soldier, to see a dying woman at Leon Primeau's house. No one there, & house locked. Found a woman a quarter of a mile distant, in another house, who turned out to be the one I went to see, but she was not sick, & only remembered that she had a pain in her back some time ago. . . .

Sunday, May 27th [Sunday]

Sang high mass for the Indians at 9 A.M. Preached on the gospel of Trinity Sunday, & mentioned the Indian trick of going to dances, & into occasions of sin when they think the priest will not see them, though they promised to stop such things when they joined the Societies. Church quite full. Met Iron Eyes going with "Two-packs" to an Indian council. Gave him advice about bad companions, & reminded him of today's sermon. Explained to Mad-bear the meaning of Land in Severalty, survey, etc. Called on Dr. & Mrs. Caskie, & welcomed them to Dakota in the name of the Indians. Went to the meeting of St. Mary's Society in Bull Head's house. About 30 or 40 present. All spoke well, & St. Joseph's boys gave them good advice. . . .

Monday, May 28th

. . . Prepared to start for St. Benedict's Mission, but a rain & wind storm from N.W. came up. Took a picture of St. Joseph to Dr. Caskie at Coles' house. Went to the Post Office & found a letter from the Bishop. He can't prevent the school vacations. We must do it ourselves. F. Bede wrote to the Bishop & Abbot that he doubted his fitness for his place here. It's all nonsense. He must stay. I wrote at once to the Bishop to encourage him, & make him stay, & will write tomorrow to the Abbot to that effect. We can't afford to lose him. It would cause a terrible break-down in our work. The Agent went to Goose's camp,[121] & Cannonball to visit the camps. The Bishop says that Giles Tapetola is sick, & is coming here on a visit. I answered that we will try to make his visit pleasant, & he can help with the societies.

Tuesday, May 29th

Said mass at 7 A.M. Would have gone to St. Benedict's Mission, but rain storm from N.W. prevented. Sent off letters to the Bishop & Abbot Frowin.[122] Brother Nicholas & 2 boys came from the Mission. A soldier was buried at the Fort. Name Myers; probably a Catholic, but not certain. Buried by the Protestant Chaplain.

Wednesday, May 30th

Said requiem mass at 7 A.M. Put new cinch on the saddle, & saddled up Pinch to go to St. Benedict's Mission. Sisters received a letter from the Bishop, saying that Mother Gertrude will be here about the middle of June. Went to the school to ask F. Bede about news from the Bishop. Talked with Sister Gertrude about the best means to keep the children in school during vacation. She spoke of their unwillingness to remain, on account of the severity of Sisters Maura[123] & Anselmine. I know it to be true.

Started for the Mission at 1 P.M. & stopped on the way at Douglas' store, & wrote to the Bishop, suggesting that he tell Mother Gertrude to ask about & correct the harsh treatment of the children, so that F. Bede's Sodality may have its effect in keeping them at school. Stopped at Henry Agard's to see the children. Reached the Mission at 5:30 P.M. Spoke to F. Martin about the location of the 160 acres for mission purposes, & suggested that it be taken at St. Benedict's Mission. May devotions & Benediction in the evening.

[121] Near present-day Selfridge, N.Dak. (Hinton, *South of Cannonball*, 59).

[122] In the letter, Craft updates Abbot Frowin Conrad on the state of the mission and praises the efforts of Fathers Bede and Martin (Craft to Conrad, 29 May 1888, BCIM Records).

[123] Sister Maura Weyer.

Thursday, May 31st

Feast of Corpus Christi [Body of Christ]. Sang High mass, & gave benediction at 9 A.M. Preached in Sioux on the feast. Went with F. Bernard to High Eagles. Wahacankayapi's, Mato-cuniyaka's [Bear's Rib], Crow-feather's, & Hehaka-he-maza's [Iron Elk] to see a boy 4 years old, with a broken arm. Told them to take him to the Doctor, & borrowed Crow-feather's harness for them. Sister Mary Adele & Placidus [*sic*][124] came in the evening.

Friday, June 1st

Said mass at 7 A.M. Saddled Pinch, & started for Flying-by's camp, Grand River. Stopped for rest & lunch at Oak Creek, & met Išnala-wica coming from the Agency. He told me that Emeran had gone to the Agency sick, & that the school was locked. I therefore cut across the country to Antelope's camp, & went to Carignan's school, at St. Mary's Mission. The camps seem deserted. Many Indians absent on an antelope hunt; & the only sign of life was a dance at Tahca-ska's [White Deer's], in the Long-feather camp, in defiance of the Agent's order. Reached Carignan's at dark.

Saturday, June 2d

Left Carignan's at 10 A.M. Heard the confession of Gicciya's wife, & started for Little Oak Creek to see Frances Wircan, who is sick, but hearing on the way that she was not at home, I turned back, & found her near Circling-bear's house. Inflammation of hip joint, but improving. She had nothing to eat, & I gave her a note to Jack Carignan to get something. Succeeded in persuading a man & his wife that their Wanbli-cinca-aglahpaya [Hovering Eagle] was dead, & that I was quite another person.

Met Gall,[125] & told him that Giles Tapetola was coming back. Big dance near Long-feather's. Came by the "Antelope Road" to the Mission. (St. Benedict's) Met Bill Pamplin on the way, above

[124] Probably Sister Placida Schaefer.

[125] Agent McLaughlin established Gall as a Hunkpapa chief and John Grass as chief of the Blackfeet Sioux as rivals to Sitting Bull (Vestal, *Sitting Bull, Champion of the Sioux*, 249).

Antelope's. Stopped at Oak Creek, & again within 5 miles of the Mission to eat lunch & rest the horse. Reached the Mission at 9 P.M. Pinch got in fresh & wild as ever, after making 110 miles in 2 days. (today, nearly 60).

Sunday, June 3d

Said mass at 6:30 A.M. High mass at 9:30 A.M. Preached on the gospel of the day, in Sioux. After mass procession of the B.[lessed] Sacrament. Meeting of St. Joseph's Society after dinner, & St. Mary's (women's) Society after afternoon service. Rain began from S.E. about noon. I interpreted for F. Martin at both meetings. Word came that a nephew of Mato-watakpe [Attacking Bear] was dying. Rode hard to get there in time. A miserable hoax. Bilious vomiting,—had fainted once, but now all right. He didn't want baptism. "Natapeha cincapi [Toad children], etc."

Monday, June 4th

Said mass at 7 A.M. Heavy thunder showers from S.E., shifting to S. & S.W. Abundance of rain now. In this country, we get all things—good or evil—in real bonanza style, rather too much than too little.

Francis Aglila, who had sneaked off from school Saturday night, returned, after being called by police, about 11 P.M. yesterday. F. Martin demanded his reasons for leaving, but could get no answer. A half-witted fellow came to say that Black-bear's wife had just been struck by lightning, & was still alive, & wanted to see a priest. He told his story straight, & had evidently been sent by some one. Doubted the story, but went on foot with Waterbury, Baker, & Bob Gaudreau, the carpenters, to investigate. All humbug. No one sick; but saw them preparing for a "Heoka dance," which came off, much to Sport's disgust.

Helped F. Bernard instruct Sport for the sacraments. He will soon be received into the Church, with his wife. Interpreted for F. Martin, who gave some advice to the girls, & afterwards to the boys. Devotions to the Sacred Heart in the evening.

I learn from F. Martin that the Agent is getting alarmed about Sitting Bull's actions in organizing the Indians to oppose the sale of land, when the Commissioners come. Had the Bishop & Bureau taken my advice, & the Agent acted with them, to remove him, all would now be quiet. The cowardly policy now pursued will cause great trouble. I feel much worried about the prospects ahead. All the Bishop's promises have failed. He does not move against Bull, nor even refer to the matter. He says he can do nothing to keep the children in the boarding schools out of the camps, & even sanctions a short vacation. He says nothing about his promise to pay Emeran's 5 months back salary, & I shall, probably, have to pay it, as it is now charged to my account at Coles' & Woolfolk's stores. Should I be attacked again by the Bull party, for my efforts to convert & civilize the Indians, I shall get no help, but must fight alone. My only recourse is the law; & if I commence proceedings to defend myself against the common enemy, I shall probably be opposed in some way by the Bishop, & cannot even have the same standing before the courts that any private citizen would have. I shall, of course, go on, but I shall have to pay dear for it. Truly a priest is between many fires. It is really hard to keep our "esprit de corps," & keep from a very bitter feeling towards our officers, who turn their heaviest artillery on our rear, while the enemy charges us in front & flank.

Satan & his allies know their enemy, & attack him persistently. I feel much honored by their enmity, but my party also turns against me, & I have to take the attack on all sides of my square. I am crushed, wounded, & exhausted; my ammunition is about gone, & the fight now goes on "with sword sway, & with lance's thrust," at close quarters. All that keeps me up is the unbending, stubborn determination inherited from a fighting race; but I have much of that, & the fight will be bitter, stubborn, & desperate. I may, possibly, be cut to pieces, but the enemy will have small cause to rejoice. "Gwell angau na chywyllyd." [Welsh for "Rather death than shame."]

Tuesday, June 5th

Said mass at 7 A.M. This morning it is clear; no rain; wind N.W.

Everything growing well. Gave Black-lightning some advice about his boy Waanakikšin [Subjecting one's self to danger for others], & told him to watch him, & keep him from insulting school girls. He probably spoke to him about it.

After devotions in the chapel, in the evening, a young man came to speak to me, on the porch. He said he had heard something that he did not like. I asked what it was, & he said that he heard that someone had told me that he had caught school girls. So far, I had not recognized the fellow. It was getting dark, and, besides, I do not know Waanakikšin by sight. I supposed it might be one of the Society boys. What he said about "catching school girls" made me suspect it might be Waanakikšin. I asked his name, & when he told me he was Wannakikšin, I ordered him to leave at once, as I did not wish to talk to him. He still persisted in talking, & I pitched him off the porch, & repeated the warning I had given his father, viz., that if he ever insulted a girl whom I claimed as a relative (meaning especially my sister Josephine) I would send a pair of bullets through his brain. He began to talk louder & ask who told me, & wanted to call on the school-girls for evidence. This was carrying insolence too far; so I caught him by the neck & shoulders, & pitched him headlong from the house. He stopped at the corner of the boy's building, & I ran at him, to give him a sound thrashing, for hesitating to leave, but he ran like a deer. F. Martin came up in time to see the race, and, as he goes to the Agency early in the morning, he requested me to tell the policeman to keep the rascal from entering the school enclosure, even to go to mass. Brother Meinrad says that he often saw him watching the girls from the window of the boy's quarters. Nothing could equal the scoundrel's impudence,—to come here to justify himself, when his rascality is common camp talk. I will not permit him to speak to me, and, on the next occasion, should he attempt it, I will punish him severely.

Wm. Waterbury went to the Agency, will return tomorrow. Arranged with Frs. Martin & Bernard to compile & translate a prayerbook & catechism in the Titonwan[126] dialect, & have it printed at Conception [Abbey in Missouri]. We need one in this dialect, even if F. Jerome should publish one, as his will be in Isanti.[127]

Wednesday, June 6th

Said mass at 6:30 A.M. Exposition of B.[lessed] S.[acrament] & Benediction after mass. F. Martin went to the Agency. Wrote the index & order of arrangement of the new Indian prayer-book & catechism, to be compiled chiefly from the Mission Book of the C.S.S.R.[128] & from Deharbe's[129] little catechism.

Went with Sport, after dinner, to look over the Blackfoot camp. Found my little sister, Frances Wapešawin, dying in the camp. She belongs to the Agency boarding school. I heard her confession, & sent her cousin to the Sister Superior & F. Bernard to get provisions for her. She will go to the Agency tomorrow to die near the church. I told the school policeman what F. Martin said about Waanakikšin. He came to the school, & found the rascal near the stable, watching the girls, & at once drove him off. His mother came afterwards, & wanted to scold the policeman, but he drove her off. I regret now that I did not beat the fellow. Wapešawin's cousin came for food for her. I gave the note I wrote for her to the Sister Superior, who gave her food. Bill Pamplin got in here from Grand River, & will stay tonight.

Thursday, June 7th

. . . F. Bernard finished instructing Wm. Whitsell (Sport) & heard his confession, & profession of faith, & baptized him, & absolved him. I stood as sponsor.

The school policeman told me that the treasurer of the Protestant Episcopal young men's society, has decamped with the funds,

---

126 The Titonwan dialect of the Teton Sioux.

127 Isanati is the dialect of the Santee Sioux.

128 CSsR stands for Congregatio Sanctissimi Redemptoris, or Congregation of the Most Holy Redeemer.

129 Joseph Deharbe, Society of Jesus (SJ), author in 1848 of a catechism popular in Europe and among German parishes in the United States.

& taken someone else's horse with him. Two-packs, one of the same party, & a polygamist, has been caught with another squaw, & will be tried for it next issue. . . .

Friday, June 8th

Saddled & fed Pinch. Said mass at 7 A.M. Started for the Agency. Wind N.W. & rain beginning. Found 4 Mile Creek very high. At Wm. Halsey's crossing I tested the depth with Mad Bear's tipi pole, but finding it too deep & the mud bad, I went to the lower crossing, & crossed with Catka & another Indian. Took dinner at Wm. Halsey's.

Shell King & his son Edwin were killed by lightning in their tent last night. A child in Shell King's arms was not hurt. Mr. Prange made coffins for them, & I helped the Indians put Edwin near the church, & Shell King in the corner of the cemetery. They will be buried tomorrow. Shell King was not baptized, & will be buried without any ceremonies by St. Mary's Society, to which he belonged.

Frances Wapešawin was brought to the school dead. She died before they could get her over 4 mile creek. She was still warm, and, I think, alive when brought in, & I gave her the last absolution sub conditione [conditionally]. The girls carried her in. I measured her for a coffin, & told Mr. Prange to make it. Met Mr. Wells & Louisa St. George.

Three mounted Indians of Sitting Bull's outfit stared insolently at me on the way in from Halsey's. I rode round them, & asked what they meant. They were frightened, & "took water," & I warned them to be more careful, wheeled my horse round them, & left them.

. . . Emeran received my revolver & 100 cartridges. Louis Primeau wants 5 masses said for Jennie. Heavy rain in the evening.

Saturday, June 9th

Said requiem mass at 7 A.M. for my sister Frances Wapišawin & Edwin Wawiyohikiya [To make sad]. At 8 A.M. I attended the requiem high mass for Frances, with the Sodality in the Sister's chapel. Instructed those who are to be married & receive communion tomorrow, & heard their confessions. Helped Joe Helmig[130] dig the grave for Frances, & attended her funeral as mourner. Father Bede officiated, & afterwards buried Edwin. The boys of St. Mary's Society attended the funeral. When F. Bede left the cemetery, I went with St. Mary's Society & buried Shell King. As he died unbaptized, we buried him without ceremonies in a corner of the cemetery. I said a prayer for him; we lowered the coffin, & then we said one Our Father & Hail Mary, & then I made a few remarks on the necessity of preparation for death, & the danger of delay.

Rain in the morning from N.W. but cleared up by noon. Bought 500 cigarettes at Coles', & also candy for my sister Josephine.

Sunday, June 10th

Sang High Mass at 9 A.M. Sport confessed before mass, & Emeran received. Preached in Indian. Before mass I married Sport, F. Fast-horse, & G. Hinska-maza. During mass they received, & after mass I gave them the scapular. Made out marriage records & certificates. Wrote a verse to the Sacred Heart for the hymn "Nearer My God to Thee" (in Sioux).

Josie Crow-feather & Maggie Good Day went with F. Bede's carriage to visit Maggie's father. I watched them with the glass through the camp, to be sure they were safe. They returned bringing Maggie's little sister to school. At dark, F. Bede & I went to visit Ursula Winyanwašteka, who is dying. She refused to return to the school, or to confess, wishing to put it off.

A man we saw would be baptized if we gave him clothes. He may wait until he learns that God's grace makes better clothes for the soul, than the white man's cast off duds do for the body. We returned about 11 P.M. I baptized 2 children during the day.

Monday, June 11th

Said mass at 7 A.M. Got provisions for Emeran at Douglas'. Ordered a hat & riding gloves. Sent word to Mr. [George?] Far-

130 Joseph Helmig, an industrial teacher at the Industrial Boarding School.

ibault to go to the school to control Black Bear & an old woman who were annoying the Sisters & trying to take away Cunegunda. The child herself acted well, & scolded & sent them away. Interpreted for the doctor. Visited my little sister Josephine at the school, & gave her some pictures to remind her to pray for me. At her request I wrote my name on some of them. Found that a photographer is established at Fort Yates, & will go with Josephine to have our photos taken. . . .

Tuesday, June 12th

Said mass at 7 A.M. Went with my sister, Josephine Crowfeather, to the fort, & had our photos taken. I borrowed $5.00 from F. Bede, & the same amount from Douglas to pay him back. Promised Sister Gertrude [McDermott] to pay Josephine's dowry, if Mother Gertrude [Leupi] would not take her without it, & also to pay for whatever clothing she needs at Douglas', & also gave orders at Douglas' to that effect, when I went there with Josephine today. . . .

Fearing that, at the last moment, Satan might try to prevent the girls from going to the convent, I made a vow, that in case M.[other] Gertrude should at once take Josephine & Annie [Pleets] to the convent, as novices, I would, for one year from the date of their starting, (if they persevere for that time) fast & abstain, (as in Lent) every Friday & Saturday, in honor of the S.[acred] Hearts of Jesus & Mary, & entirely abstain from smoking, in honor of St. Joseph. Also, if Emma [Halsey] & Helen also go, I would devote the cost of that tobacco to having masses said according to the intentions of St. Joseph. Also, that if Josephine & Annie persevere, I would, as long as they both live, & persevere in their vocation, add in every mass a memento for the souls in Purgatory, according to the intentions of St. Joseph, & should Annie die, I would continue it for Josephine. It is chiefly for Josephine's sake I do this. When all others left me to fight alone against slander & calumny, she was the only one to give me a sister's sympathy & affection; and, when I forget it, may my right hand be forgotten.

Wednesday, June 13th

Said mass at 8 A.M. Took to the Sisters the music of the Sioux creed. Went to see a sick boy in Charging Thunder's camp. Another "bogus" sick call. Met F. Bede on the way, coming from the Mission. Gave Josephine the "proofs" of our photos. Severe hail storm in the afternoon, from N.W., followed a very hot & sultry morning. It turned on Išna-paha [Lone hill], & did not reach the Agency.

It seems that Mother Gertrude is sick, & can't come, & sends another sister. I am terribly worried, fearing that something may prevent the girls from going to the novitiate. I again remembered my vow of yesterday, & added another, to perform the same acts, for the same intentions, & under the same conditions, in case they leave here by the 1st of July. All this business could be easily settled, if the Holy Catholic Church were only as energetic in saving souls as Satan & his allies are in destroying them. God alone is my hope now in this matter; though I shall spare no effort to carry it out. J. M. J. miserenomini. [Jesus, Mary, Joseph have mercy on us.]

Thursday, June 14th

Said mass at 7 A.M. Called on Sister Gertrude, & arranged to aid in getting the girls safely off to Yankton. Arranged with McNeider to get a team if necessary. Gave the photographer a list of prominent Indians. Wrote to my Mother & F. Stephan. Hail storm from N.W., but turned on Išna-paha, & only gave us a slight shower. . . .

Friday, June 15th

Said mass at 7 A.M. Wrote the Bishop about Bull's movements, Sport's conversion, Societies, Sisters expected, postulants, Josie, & Annie, especially, & about their fear that Maura or Anselmine would have charge of them at Yankton, but that they were satisfied on hearing they would be near him, & that postulants are taken care of by their superiors, like tender plants in a garden of their own,—just as I told Josie & Annie today. . . .

Saturday, June 16th

Said mass at 7 A.M. Arranged with Mr. Wells & McNeider for teams to take postulants & Sisters to Mandan. Met Giles Tapetola, who came last night, with the Agent. Meeting of St. Joseph's Society. Went with Giles, & made them a speech. Weather still very hot. Thermometer 110° in the shade.

Sunday, June 17th

Said mass at 8 A.M. F. Bede sang high mass at 10:30 A.M. Bought a linen duster at Coles'. Went to Douglas' to get one, but they had none. Steamboat "Missouri" came from Bismarck. Arranged with Sister Gertrude to get F. Martin's consent for the postulants to leave. I sent him a note for the Sister to take tomorrow, begging him to hasten it, & offering to take them myself, as I have the teams ready. F. Bede seems inclined to oppose my getting the teams, for fear the Agency people might blame him because I interfere, so he says. He would see my sister remain here in danger, & try to stand in the way of my saving her, all because of his selfish, unreasoning panic.

These people talk smoothly, when I don't need their aid, & are ready to desert, & even attack me at the moment of my greatest trouble. They would oppose their brother priest to gratify the allies of Satan, if it would save them the least feeling of anxiety. It was the same in the Sitting Bull affair. And yet these are holy religious.

I am in such mental torture that I can hardly decide what to do, but I must keep cool, for Josephine's sake. When she is safely in the convent, I shall leave them room enough to break their necks, which they would have done long ago, had I not risked everything to prevent it. Their cold, unfeeling, cowardly, selfish, malicious disregard of the misery they cause me, & their Satanic conduct in endangering my sister, by delays, will not be forgotten. I keep quiet now, because it would endanger her more to quarrel with them, and, for her sake, I will endure in silence, until I get her safely away. But should they in any way prevent her from going, I am prepared to punish them.

There is nothing I can do to allay their miserable, suspicious fears. I cannot cut my heart open to let them read in it that I have every desire to help, & none to hurt them, & they have not sense enough to see it in all my actions towards them. May God enlighten them, for I cannot. When Josephine is safe, I shall take care how I trust them, & shall leave them alone, to find out what their folly costs.

Monday, June 18th

Said mass at 7 A.M. Sisters Gertrude & Bernadine[131] went to the Mission. Baptized & gave communion to John Ikanwicaki. Išnalawica brought in Hupahuozanzanwin, the sick girl they wanted to die, from Grand River. Sister Gertrude returned from the Mission. F. Bede says he will not object to our plans for Josie & Annie. He seems satisfied as to my motives. Thank God.

Tuesday, June 19th

Said mass at 7 A.M. Major McLaughlin went to the Mission & returned. F. Martin writes that Josie & Annie will go without delay. All is arranged to start Thursday morning, at 5 A.M. I will go with them to Mandan, & if Sister Maura is cross to my sisters on the way, I must go with them to Zell.[132] Arranged to borrow $30.00 from Douglas, & $25.00 from Coles, for the trip. The Agency teams will take up the trunks. My fasting, etc. will begin the day they leave here. Thank God I can suffer a little to save sister Josie, & may He grant her & Annie perseverance.

Wednesday, June 20th

Said mass at 7 A.M. Requiem. Anniversary of death of Mrs. Annie Kennedy (Galpin). Borrowed $30.00 of Douglas, & $25.00 of Coles. Photographer finished & brought up 6 pictures. Gave 2 to Josephine, 1 to Annie, 1 to Mr. Prange, & 1 to Sr. Gertrude, & kept 1 for Mr. Wells. Watered & fed Pinch. Went to John Pleets[133]

---

[131] Sister Bernardine Wachter.

[132] The novitiate of the Benedictine convent was located at Zell, DT (in what would later become S.Dak.).

[133] John Pleets held the position of stableman in 1893 (*Annual Reports*, 1893, 559).

to see a sick child, but it had gone home. Met Josephine & Annie there. I took the photos to them there, so as to be sure no one would annoy them. Fortunately, Scott brought the photos to F. Bede's, just as I had come from Pleets, after meeting Josephine & Annie, & I took them down to them at once. Walked up with them on their way back to school. . . .

En Route to Mandan, DT, 1888

Thursday, June 21st

Went to Douglas' & got team & driver. Left Fort Yates with Sisters Bernardine & Maura, Josephine Crow-feather, & Annie Pleets at 5:30 A.M. Wind N.W. Rain, cold. What the Indians call a "dog's day." Got to Wells' at 8:30 A.M. Got a lunch. Left Wells at 11 A.M. After passing Fort Lincoln the pole broke, on one side, from the front hounds [framing], while going down hill. Turned into the bank, & let the Sisters get out, while I held the horses' heads. Mended the break with a halter. Reached Mandan at 6 P.M. My sister Josephine showed me the way. Put up at Peoples' Hotel. Bought 2 black veils for Josie & Annie. Today I begin to pay my vow, regarding fast, abstinence, & abstaining from tobacco.

Friday, June 22d

Rose at 4:30 A.M. Begin my fast according to vow made for Josie's & Annie's vocations. Arranged about the Sisters' & Josie's & Annie's trunks. Helped get their tickets. Train late, & they did not get off until 12:30 P.M. In the meantime, I got their lunch at the station; bought peaches & eggs for them; took them to see the bear; seated them safely in the car. Kissed them good-bye, left; came back, & staid with them till the cars started. Gave them the parting blessing (at the hotel, & also on the cars) shook hands again, and, after thanks, blessings, recommendations to each others' prayers, etc., I jumped off the cars, just in time for a parting salute to my sisters as their window passed me,—So,—they have gone,—to peace. through light, & through light to eternal peace & happiness.

Josephine, my pet sister,—the only one who stood by me in need,—the only one who really loved her brother, & merited his love & respect,—has been placed, as far as possible, beyond the reach of Satan & his Agency allies,—& I am at last, contented, & believe that peace exists. As she guided me on the way here, so may her prayers guide me on the way she follows, to peace, light, & eternal rest with her in heaven. But for her, I should have hated the whole Indian race. She has hitherto been my guardian angel. May she still guard & guide me by her prayers. Annie, too, will, I am sure remember me, & obtain God's grace for me. So we all can obtain eternal rest & light, they through peace, & I through unceasing conflict,—what matters it? "Say to your sister, 'Thou hast obtained mercy.'" God grant them final perseverance, & to me, through their prayers, the same, & eternal happiness with them in heaven.

Paid blacksmith for mending wagon. Bought some things for F. Bede, Sister Gertrude, etc. Called on F. Perrault [*sic*],[134] & staid to supper. Went to the church & thanked God for our success in getting Josie & Annie so far in safety, & begged Him to grant them final perseverance, & eternal life. Rain, cold, & raw.

Saturday, June 23d

Left Mandan at 8 A.M. After passing Lincoln Sergeant Petit overtook me. Came with him as far as Parkins. He went there, & I turned off to the upper crossing & went to Wells. Just had time to shave, when Sergeant Petit came up. I rode in his buggy to the Agency. Rain, cold, & raw.

At Standing Rock Reservation, DT, 1888

Sunday, June 24th

Said mass at 9 A.M. Preached on the Epistle of the day, & mentioned their trying to cheat us, by slyly following Indian ways. Mrs. McLaughlin came up to talk about Societies, etc. Went to St. Joseph's council. Took dinner with Mr. Gilbert. Paid Douglas' (per

[134] Father Joseph G. Perreault of Mandan, DT.

McKenzie) the $30.00 I borrowed last Wednesday. Also gave Ed Coles $7.20 on the $25.00 I borrowed on Wednesday last. Tore my cassock on the gate, & took it to Sr. Gertrude for repairs. Gave Douglas & Coles lists of goods I want tomorrow. This morning Leo Hehaka-gi [Brown Elk] & wife received, & in the evening Mr. Cadotte, Sr. went to confession. Clear, but threatening rain.

Monday, June 25th

Rain. Said mass at 7 A.M. Sent supplies to Emeran. Dyed a cincture. Clear in the afternoon, & would have gone to the Mission but could not start in time. Met Spotted Elk from Rosebud, & told him of the rascality of these Indians. He is not the best of the Brulés, & goes with a bad element here. However, now that sister Josie is safe in the convent, I care but little for any of them.

On Saturday last the Indians chose Mad-bear, Big-head, Gall, & Grass, & an half-breed, to be their speakers before the Commissioners. Antelope wanted [Sitting] Bull chosen, but he couldn't get it. Bull, Antelope, & Circling-bear kick, but the nation seems to have cast them off in good style. They begin to open their eyes.

Tuesday, June 26th

Wind S.E. Hard rain. Can't go to the Mission today. Brother Nicholas is here also stormbound. The boat "Missouri" came yesterday. Met Grey Eagle[135] in Coles' store, & repelled his attempt at friendly advances by treating him coldly, & pretending not to know him, & threatening to knock him down if he persisted in speaking. He can't follow Bull & the "Black-robe" at the same time. Old Bull had a long talk with the Agent last night, & again this morning, complaining of the conduct of the Indians in throwing him away. He will have another council next issue day, & try to get some on his side. He claims to have letters from Rosebud & Pine Ridge.

Wednesday, June 27th

Clearing off. Wind S.W. Said mass at 7 A.M. Went with Giles as far as Išta-maza's [Iron-eyes], & then went on to the Mission.

---

[135] Grey Eagle served as a judge on Standing Rock Reservation in 1893 (*Annual Reports*, 1893, 559).

FIGURE 10. Grey Eagle. Photograph by D. F. Barry. *Denver Public Library, Western History Collection, Call No. B-489.*

Took package for Charlie Peerman, but did not meet him. Gave Josie's kiss & message & photo to Claudia & Matilda. Arranged with F. Martin to try to keep all the girls at school.

Thursday, June 28th

Returned from Mission to Agency. Returned Charlie Peerman's package to Sister Adele. Sent note to F. Martin so as to have unity of action between both schools in holding the children. Sent him also notes of Indian creed, & blue ribbon for Claudia & Matilta. Giles went to Mr. Wells via Mrs. Van Solen's. I left the Agency about 4 P.M. & reached Mrs. Van Solen's at 8:30 P.M. She had gone to Parkins, so I went on to Wells'; after shaking hands with boys & girls.

Friday, June 29th

Very hot. Ho-tanka tried to cheat Givens, who advised him to send Ada to school, as she is an orphan. She tried to pass her aunt off as her real mother. I exposed the fraud, & reproached him with opposing our efforts to help Ada, out of his selfish opposition to the Agent. He began to quarrel. I frightened him into silence by promising him a thrashing. He began again & I repeated my threat, & ordered him off, & pushed him away. He threatened to kill me, & I seized him & pitched him down the hill. As he found I was in earnest, he left.

Very heavy shower at night. The hail made a terrible noise west of here, but we got none. . . .

Saturday, June 30th

Very hot, worse than yesterday. Went down to Mrs. Van Solen's & got my wine & vestments. Alice & Jane, & Leo Ota apapi & Zita [Smoke] were there. Big dance at Big-head's camp, & also at Cottonwood's, the latter lasting very late. Zatela's girls persist in attending the dances. My advise is worse than lost, & I shall cease to trouble them with it. . . .

Sunday, July 1st

Said mass at 10 A.M. Very few came,—about 15. Too sleepy after the dance,—which lasted till nearly morning. Sent messages regarding Indian customs, etc. to those who did not come, through those who did. Rode to Parkins. Met Leo Harmon & Mrs. Galpin[136] & Bob & Sam Gaudreau. Heavy rain in the evening. Had to stay all night. . . .

Monday, July 2d

Clear, but occasional short showers during the morning. Returned from Parkins, after giving much good brotherly counsel to Mary Ehakewin, regarding dances, etc. Ta-šunke-wakan's wife promises to send Mary Agnes Black-Horse to school at the Agency. When the promise is kept, I may believe it.

---

[136] Mrs. Galpin was a full-blooded Sioux, whose first husband was Henoré Picotte, an Indian trader from St. Louis, Mo. Their daughters were Louise and Lulu. Louise became Mrs. Van Solen, and Lulu became Mrs. Capt. Harmon (Holley, *Once Their Home*, 288).

Tuesday, July 3d

Went to High-bear's. Levi Dezera & Black-bull returned from the Agency. Went to Parkins, & brought up flour, etc. for Wells. Cannonball very high on account of the rains, & we had to use a boat. Showering in the afternoon.

Wednesday, July 4th

Gave a scapular to James Wells.[137] Left Wells at 12:30 P.M. & came by the telegraph road to the Agency, reaching here about 6 P.M. Porcupine high, but crossed safely.

Found that the affair with Ho-tanka had been much exaggerated, & that Wells & Givens had explained it properly. Wells seems very reticent, & is, I think, insincere. He is keeping out of the affair,—& he may keep out. I don't need such false friends.

Thursday, July 5th

Scott sent up more photos. Received letters for Bishop, F. Willard[138] (enclosing $5.00). . . .

Friday, July 6th

. . . Telegraphed to Sr. Bernardine when the trunks were reported received at Mandan, & sent word by Ed Coles to have them traced.

Saturday, July 7th

. . . Received telegram through Coles that trunks were sent forward, & would be traced. Sister Gertrude just heard that trunks have been received at Maria Zell.[139]

No beef issue today. Cattle here, but no Dept. permission yet to issue, as the contracts have not yet been signed.

The Indians brought up that Ho-tanka case against me in the Police court. If [George] Faribault & the Agent were good Catholics, they would teach these wretches a severe lesson. As it is, they do nothing, & allow the bad element here to make a priest's work as unpleasant as possible.

---

[137] James, Frank, and Joseph Wells were the sons of Aaron and Josephine Wells.

[138] Father George L. Willard of the BCIM.

[139] The Benedictine convent at Zell, DT.

Sunday, July 8th

Sang high-mass for the Indians at 9 A.M. About 30 or 40 went to communion. 4 were first communicants. I strongly doubt the sincerity of many of them. . . . St. Mary's men's society came, but not mounted.

Monday, July 9th

. . . I learned that my sister Emma Halsey wants to go to the novitiate, but her father cannot get her the necessary outfit, without selling cattle. I arranged with Sister Gertrude to get the things as cheap as possible, & have them charged to me.

The Indians, headed by John Grass, met in the Police court, & got up a petition to the Bishop to have me removed. The Ho-tanka case, & a reprimand I gave a policeman for slandering me, is taken as the motive, but the real motive is their desire to get rid of me, on account of my knowledge of language, customs, etc., which makes it impossible for the hypocrites to deceive us. Mad-bear & Waga were there, and, though they claim they did not give their names, still they said but little against it. Treachery, always, where it is least expected.

High-bear told me about it. I asked [George] Faribault, & learned from him that, when the case was brought up on Saturday, (or rather Friday, as he says) in the Police court, he only heard my accusers, & told them that "they should not retaliate, but bear it quietly; that I was a priest, & a white man & could not be brought before an Indian court; that I was under the Bishop, & he alone could do anything in the case."

He is against me, & blames me for all the attacks the Indians make against me. He won't listen to reason, & is, evidently, as badly disposed against us, as he was before his pretended conversion, only he is more sly. I laid the case before the Agent, who pretends to know little about it, but says he will stop it. I told him I did not ask him to keep the petition from reaching the Bishop, but only in case it went through his hands, as I heard it would, to send a true statement of the case, to explain whatever lies the Indians might tell. Emeran & Giles will give them a blasting in their next council.

When I attempted to tell F. Bede what I had discovered, he seemed to be seized with a panic, fearing to get into trouble, & refused to listen, or believe anything against Faribault, & even when I tried to tell him something about the Women's Society, which he ought to know (in reference to communion) he would not hear a word, even to know what I was going to say. Such false brethren are our worst enemies. He will yet have trouble with the same people as other priests have had, & will have to ask aid from others, & perhaps from me, though I do not ask it from him. I hope he will find enough of Priestly & manly spirit left in the Church to aid him, instead of deserting & abusing him in his necessity.

I hear that the members of Mrs. McLaughlin's Women's Society, President & all (Mrs. Clifford) went to the dance on Saturday, but won't "give each other away." Three, also, received communion yesterday, after a good breakfast. Mrs. Louis Agard, & old Mrs. Kezi forgot, & broke their fast, but put off their communion until this morning.

Tuesday, July 10th

. . . Indians got a beef issue today. In the evening they had a council in the Hunhpati[140] camp. Giles & Emeran went, & gave them a blasting, for their attack on priests. Black-bull spoke in my favor, but Antoine Clement, the only fool among the mixed-bloods, interrupted him, & broke up the council,—not on account of enmity to me, but because he is more "Indian" than the Indians, & wants to have nothing but "old time talk." I staid at F. Bede's, & wrote letters to Josephine & Annie. F. Martin came at 11 P.M.

Wednesday, July 11th

. . . Bought 4 arrows at Coles, & gave one to each of the 4 bands of the Sioux, as a reproach for their cowardly lying, advising them to use them, instead of their lying tongues against me. Continued letter to Josephine & Annie & Sister Bernardine. . . .

[140] Hunkpatis, also called Lower Yanktonais, are a band of Yanktonais Sioux.

Thursday, July 12th

. . . Finished & mailed letters to Josephine, Annie, Sister Bernardine, the Bishop, & F. Stephan,[141] enclosing in the last, bills for goods for St. F. de Sales' School. F. Martin went home. Gave him my & Josie's photo; & two crosses for Claudia & Matilda. Letter writing is bad for my eyes. The truth is, hardship & worry have broken me down.

Friday, July 13th

. . . Wrote to my sister Bertha, & to F. Willard. Mr. Wells came in to see the doctor about an injury to his eye. Went with him & Dr. Caskie to Military hospital. . . .

Saturday, July 14th

. . . Harmon's herder broke his leg by the fall of a horse. Helped take him to Military hospital. Philip Wells[142] & the son of Col. [Hugh D.] Gallagher, Agent at Pine Ridge, reached here from Pine Ridge, on their way to Devil's Lake, & left in the afternoon for Cannonball. A. C. Wells will go with them to Devil's Lake.

Scott gave me more photos, & one of Crow-feather. . . .

Sunday, July 15th

. . . Went to the School & saw Bernard Akanakitan, sick. Went for doctor, but he passed me on another road, & went to the school. After dinner the Sodality girls came to see F. Bede. Told them stories of saints, & holy deaths, & tried to amuse & instruct them.

In the afternoon Charlie Marshall broke & rode a bucking mare from Harmon's Montana herd. Young men of Society came to F. Bede's, & told of [George] Faribault's attacks on them for doing right, & his assisting rascals & opposing us. May God treat him as he deserves, & stop his opposition to us.

[141] Craft's letter explains that school attendance in the prior quarter was adversely affected because the Indians were off on antelope hunts and had taken their children with them (Craft to Father Stephan, 12 July 1888, BCIM Records).

[142] Philip Faribault Wells, called "Fox" by the Indians, was an interpreter for the Dawes Commission and was later wounded during the Battle of Wounded Knee.

Monday, July 16th

. . . Very hot. For some days past the mosquitos have been almost unbearable. "Smudges" are smoking on all sides. Wrote letters to John Owl-ring, & Rev. F. Willard, to see if I could get some money to buy an outfit for postulants of Sisters of OSB in case there should be any more, & my purse should be too low.

B. Nicholas came up, & Giles went with him to the Mission en route for Oak Creek & Grand River. Received a letter from F. Stephan.[143] I am somewhat "out" as to the Dawes bill. I thought it for the benefit of the Indians, but it seems safest to have nothing to do with it.

Tuesday, July 17th

Went to St. Benedict's Mission. Warned the priests to remain neutral on the Dawes bill question. Met old Belly-fat & reproached him for his treachery in signing that petition against me. Talked with Charlie Papan. Returned to Agency at about 11 P.M. . . .

Wednesday, July 18th

. . . F. Bede wanted to go to St. Benedict's Mission, after I got back from a visit (with his buggy) to Leon Primeau's wife's sister, who is dying in the Hunhpati camp. She was not very well, & gave it up. Very hot. Many mosquitos.

Thursday, July 19th

. . . F. Bede went to St. Benedict's Mission. The woman I went to see yesterday, died last night, & Black Tomahawk buried her here, but did not inform us until it was over. He got the grave out of line.

Giles & Emeran returned from Grand River. I gave all the last sacraments to Bernard Akanakitan, at the school. In the evening the girls came up to visit. Gave them candy. Answered Stephan's letter.

---

[143] Father Stephan's letter identifies the members of the Dawes Commission, advises Craft that it "means danger ahead for our missions and schools," and warns him to avoid any contact with the commission (Stephan to Craft, 10 July 1888, in the author's possession).

Friday, July 20th

. . . Received letter from Bishop enclosing $180.00 to pay Emeran's back salary of $125.00, & the remaining $55.00 for me, paying up to the end of May, & $10.00 on June. He wants me to go to Fort Berthold to prepare to found a mission for the Indians there,—but not to remain there. I won't quit here until the enemy is crushed. Answered, stating amount needed for the trip, & telling him that the Indians here would probably complain against me, & asking him to give them a sharp reprimand. I told him I mentioned it, fearing that to relieve me, & give peace to the Mission, he might remove me to quiet the noise, but that such a move would give full liberty to the current of vice, that, naturally, makes a great noise around any obstacle in its way

The Commissioners arrived tonight,—that is, Pratt & Cleveland.[144]

Saturday, July 21st

. . . Giles & Emeran went to the council after the beef-killing. They say the Indians are uncertain what to say, but all will oppose the bill. Sport tells me that they will make charges against me & the boss-farmers, & Agent, & all. [George] Faribault is at the bottom of it all.

A boat came from Bismarck. Bernard Akanakitan died at 11 A.M. I was with him & prepared him. F. Bede buried him in the afternoon. I blessed the grave of the woman buried on Thursday. . . .

Sunday, July 22d

F. Bede went to Winona. I said masses at 9 & 10:45 A.M. Preached on gospel of mass, about Christ weeping over Jerusalem, & gave a sound blasting to the Indians for doing against me what the Pharisees, etc. did against Christ. After mass Young Men's council in Agency warehouse. I did not go. Let the cowards pluck up enough courage to speak for their priests. Had they done so earlier, I might

---

[144] Captain Richard H. Pratt was superintendent of the Indian school at Carlisle, Pa, and Rev. William J. Cleveland was an Episcopal missionary at Rosebud Reservation.

have thought more of them,—but now it is almost too late. I can never do for them what I once did.

After last mass, I took dinner at the school. Met there Emma Archambeau, to whom I gave advice to obey God & not men,— & Mrs. McLaughlin arrayed in the latest style of cane & cavalry gauntlets. . . .

F. Bede returned from Winona. The young men promise to send a letter to the Bishop, exposing the villainy of John Grass, Faribault, & Co.

Monday, July 23d

. . . Commissioners held a council with Indians at about 10 A.M. The Agent acted as the fourth Commissioner. The only thing done today was to explain to the Indians how they should carry on the council, & confine themselves to the bill, & not mention other business. The Indians were allowed to choose two interpreters, & chose Louis Primeau & Eugene Bruguier. The preliminaries being now arranged, they will meet again tomorrow.

Wm. Halsey learned from young Bull Head that the policeman Yellow-wolf is collecting names against me, by stating he was ordered to do it by the Agent & [George] Faribault. Mr. Halsey told the Agent, who was angry, denied it, & promised to "go for" Faribault. I gave photo & oil of anise to Crow-feather. Tonight the Indians are holding a council in camp, & resolve, so far, not to consent to the bill. Rode Pinch for exercise.

Tuesday, July 24th

. . . Council at 9 A.M. Today nothing was done but to "call the roll" to see if all were present, & then copies of the bill, with maps of the proposed reservations, were distributed. Brother Nicholas [Enz] came yesterday, with larger school-boys, to be present at council. He cut my hair. The Indians in council last night were very decided in refusing their consent to the bill. The Indians are to be required to sign either "yes" or "no." Gall suspects this method, and, to tell the truth, it <u>has</u> a queer look. The Indians will suspect something wrong. It seems to me a serious blunder. I hear of a council at Halsey's tonight. Who, & for what, I don't know.

Wednesday, July 25th

. . . Council called at 9 A.M. Judge Wright[145] spoke, scolding the Indians for not taking the maps, & put up a large map, from which he explained how the new reservations were to be formed. They still refused to take the maps.

Pratt spoke against the Indians allowing Barry[146] to take a photo of the council, but Barry put his camera on Coles' stable, & got it anyway. At 5 P.M. I went to Wells. Got caught in the big storm, & got into an empty Indian house near Waga's camp. After the wind & rain ceased, I went on, & reached Wells' at 10:30 P.M. Met Charlie McLaughlin & a boy from the Fort, taking freight for Coles from Mandan to Yates. Charlie will take Giles' trunk to Yates.

Thursday, July 26th

Helped Wells draw up papers in Indian depredations claim. Flying Hawk came up in the afternoon, & reported that Cleveland only, spoke in the council at the Agency this morning, explaining the bill. The Indians will answer tomorrow. Ta-šunke-wakan came to ask for medicine for his little girl. Case of sore eyes.

Friday, July 27th

Wrote a letter for Mr. Wells to his lawyers in Washington in claim business. Came back to Agency. Rode in with young Greenplum & Red-ear (from Clontarf—runaway) whom I met on the way. Reached here at 2 P.M. Mr. Halsey informs me that John Grass spoke for all the Indians in the council, & told the Commissioners that the Indians had unanimously decided <u>not</u> to sign <u>either</u> paper, & that they would expect the Commissioners to help them get from Government all due them by past treaties, & that the Commissioners might now go away, as this resolution was final, though the Indians were willing to respect the Commissioners by

[145] Judge John V. Wright of Tennessee, the third member of the Dawes Commission.

[146] D. F. Barry, photographer for the *Bismarck (N.Dak.) Tribune*.

remaining as long here as they wished, but would not change their resolution. Mr. Barry, photographer, & Mr. Quinn, reporter went to Bismarck. Quinn will give the Commission, & especially Pratt, a terrible raking over for their conduct towards him.

I called at the school, & agreed with Sister Gertrude to watch the Commission when they visit the school, to keep them from sowing the seeds of evil; & to be ready to report them at Washington in case of necessity. Refused to attend Mrs. Galpin at Faribault's. F. Bede displeased. He seems to side with the enemy.

Saturday, July 28th

. . . Commission visited the school. Pratt spoke of teaching the children individuality, & recommended separate rooms for them. The sisters have invited the Commission to visit the school tomorrow afternoon, & they also intend to accept the Commissioners' invitation to take the school-girls to the council, on Monday. The poor Sisters are completely deceived by these Protestant rascals. I have no authority, & can do nothing.

Bought a vest, & pair of shoes at Douglas'. Received a letter from F. Stephan, asking me to meet him at Chicago on telegraphic notice, & to confer with the Agent about boys for his Indiana school. Spoke to Agent. He promises to help & thinks we can get at least 10. Get the permit, & he will aid us, he says.

Sunday, July 29th

Said first mass at 8 A.M. F. Bede sang high mass at 10:30 A.M. John, Charles, Sibly, & Melda McLaughlin received at 1st mass. The Indians had a council in the Hunhpati camp after mass, & renewed their decision not to sign. The Indians of John Grass' protestant outfit, held service with Cleveland in the lower camp.[147]

Monday, July 30th

. . . Indians held council with Commissioners at 10 A.M. Wright, Gov. Church, J. Grass, Agent, Pratt, Cleveland, & Mad Bear

[147] John Grass was a convert of the Episcopal Church.

spoke. Cleveland read letter of Bishop Marty to Chairman of Committee in 1882, & tried to persuade the Indians that Bishop Marty would be glad if they should sign. The Indians seem to weaken & may sign. Sitting Bull was at the council, but said nothing.

Went to Douglas' & bought satchel & purse for my sister Emma Halsey, & gave her 2 dollars to use on the way to Zell. She gave me a lock of her hair to remind me to pray for her.

Pacified Ta-sunke-wakan, who wanted to take Mary Agnes Black-horse home. Gave her candy, & left her happy & contented. Saw Bismarck paper. Quinn lashes Pratt, and, worst of all, tells the <u>truth</u> about him.

Tuesday, July 31st

. . . Went to Mission, & met F. Bede at Cadottes'. Took down F. Martin's mail, & letters from F. Bede & Sr. Gertrude. Claudia Crow-feather not yet returned to school. To save sending the policeman for her, & to keep her from danger, I went for her, & coaxed her back, & paid Pte-pa to bring her in his wagon to F. Martin's school. I promised to intercede for her with F. Martin & Sr. Rhabana,[148] so they would not punish her. I did so, & they promised, but I have reason to suspect that Sr. Rhabana has, at least, scolded her. It is a pity that a little Christian courtesy can't be found among Christians. There seems to be little else than jealousy,—both of the prosperity of others, & ones own prerogatives. In the great Catholic Church, & in what should be its holiest part,—the religious orders,—where unity & charity, & Christian courtesy & honor should abound,—there, especially, we look in vain for it. I brought back a scholar, saved them trouble & annoyance, & gave them a chance to get out of a difficulty in which their own statement proves them to have acted rashly & harshly,—by pardoning my sister on my intercession, as a special favor to me, & to be asked but once; & they act with dignified reserve, stinted acquiescence, jealous suspicion, & a general manner that seems to say: "Yes, but we don't like it; we have our own system; we don't thank you for your interference; we

[148] Rhabana Stoup, a teacher at the Agricultural Boarding School.

can get along well without you." And yet, had I not brought back Claudia myself,—the fact that she was alone, among distant relatives, near a notorious rascal, & in positive danger, would not have moved them to use even the doubtful means of sending an unreliable policeman, until they got ready. F. Martin, too, shows a disposition to take the part of that scoundrel [George] Faribault. God will not let this pass unnoticed. I have suffered & sacrificed much, to keep peace, but I fear it will not long be possible.

In the evening I instructed Atkuku-ota-win, my sister, baptized 4 years ago by Protestants, & will see her again in the morning.

Wednesday, August 1st

Raining. Fed & saddled Pinch, and, when the storm ceased, I rode to see Atkuku-ota-win. Heard her confession, baptized her conditionally, & gave her the scapular. She seems to be dying. Gave her a dollar to buy food. Went back to Mission, got lunch, packed up letters & chalice & patens, for F. Bede, got some onions for Mary Atkuku-ota-win, took them to her on the way, & rode in to the Agency.

Yesterday & today's councils, same as usual. The Indians won't sign either way.

Got shirt & gloves for Sport from his wife, & left them with Agent. Talked with him about Commissioners. I declare in favor of bill, when speaking to whites, & remain silent with Indians. . . .

Thursday, Aug. 2d

. . . Council still goes on, & Indians still determined. Got proofs of Emma's & Miss Mary's photos, & took them back for them to Scott. Gave Emma my & Josie's photo. Someone cut the telegraph wire 2 or 3 miles beyond Cannonball. Commissioners & Agent visited St. Benedict's Mission, to inspect.

Friday, Aug. 3d

. . . Council again, & Indians still determined not to sign. After dinner I rode to the Mission to see what the Commissioners had been about. Stopped at Halsey's. Enquired for my sister, Mary

Atkuku-ota-win, but she had gone to the Agency. Sport & Barney came home.

Saturday, Aug. 4th

Left the Mission at 6:45 & reached Wm. Halsey's at 9:15 A.M. Emma home for a visit, but returns today. Heavy shower. Just reached Coles' stable in time, by riding hard. Met Cleveland & Pratt in Agent's office. Took care not to speak of their business. Agent informs me that they may ask our help. Told him that we could not, prudently, aid them, and, though we wished to aid the Government, when we safely could, we must keep away from the whole affair. I agreed with F. Bede what we should say & do, if asked to help, & also wrote to F. Martin to warn him.

In the afternoon the Agent came with letter from Capt. Pratt,[149] Chairman of the Committee, to me & F. Bede, asking us to go to the council on Monday, & speak in favor of the bill, & aid it. He asked a reply in writing. After talking with F. Bede, & agreeing upon our answer, I went to the Agent, & spoke for both. (The Agent sent F. Martin's letter by a policeman.)

I said to the Agent that no written answer, or other formality was needed, as we were free to do as we pleased,—that it was most proper for us to answer, verbally, through the Government Agent, as through him alone, we could recognize messengers from Government; & that our answer was this. 1st. As priests & missionaries, our general orders are to never meddle in secular or Government business not connected with our work, unless in some special case where it is sure that we can do great good to our people & the Government. 2nd. In this particular case it is certain that we could do no good, & would injure both the Government & ourselves. The Indians are excited, & any interference from us would increase the excitement, & lessen the chances of the Government

[149] Pratt's not-so-subtle letter states, "The failure of the Indians to accept the offer now made will necessarily leave their future condition and the further action which may be taken in regard to the reservation problematical and uncertain" and that "every true friend of theirs should at once use all honorable and fair means to induce the acceptance of the [government's] offer" (Capt. Richard H. Pratt to Craft, 4 August 1888, in the author's possession).

succeeding with them; & we would also, by exasperating the Indians against us, seriously injure our mission work; & while waiting long, in vain, for the bad feeling against us to subside, many would, in the meantime, die without the sacraments. Therefore we must, though anxious to aid, decline to interfere.

I further reminded the Agent of what he & Herbert Welsh[150] knew, viz. that I had written to Bishop & Bureau to keep Catholic papers from attacking the bill, & that my sentiments in favor of the bill are well known. I would gladly aid it now, as I did then; but there is question now of dealing,—not with intelligent whites,—but with corrupt savages, infuriated & unreasoning; & I have no right to endanger the work of our missions by interfering. The Agent thought we took the only prudent course in the matters.

In the evening I called on Sister Gertrude & Emma Halsey to ask for Emma's photo. Mr. Scott brought up 3 photos for me & owes me 3. I paid him in full $2.00.

Sunday, Aug. 5th

Sang high mass at 9 A.M. Preached in Dakota on St. Paul's II Epistle to Timothy, on persevering to the end, in spite of opposition. In the evening, about 9:30, F. Martin came. After consultation, he authorized me to give verbally through the Agent his refusal to attend councils, or interfere in any way in the Commission's business, & to give the same reasons as I & F. Bede had already given. The letter he received from Pratt is the same as mine & F. Bede's. F. Martin also told me to explain to Agent why he could not stay to see him & Pratt. No one at school, etc. & also, in addition to his former reasons, to add that he now brought the school so far, & with so much trouble, he would not like to break down now; & he had reason to fear serious injury to his school-work, if he should in any way interfere in the Commission's business.

Monday, Aug. 6th

. . . I went to the Agent, & said as F. Martin had requested. He replied that he had already told Pratt what F. Bede & I had said,

[150] Herbert Welsh, secretary of the Indian Rights Association.

but he cut him short, & said he required an answer in writing. He (Major) asked if we could not in some way write, or do something to satisfy them. I asked "how?" He said he didn't know, & could see no safer way for us to act than the way we were now doing. I told him that Pratt had now from us all he would ever get. We had answered him through the same Agent through whom he addressed us, & he (Pratt) throws our answer back in our faces. He has no right to seek our aid,—much less to demand a written answer, or other formality. If he misrepresents us, the Law, & public opinion will protect us, as both are on our side. The Agent understands, & approves our position, & will speak again to Pratt.

I wrote to F. Martin the result of my talk with the Agent, & also wrote to F. Stephan a detailed account of all, enclosing copy of Pratt's letter, & a slip from the Bismarck Tribune, to show the sentiment here against Pratt. Stephan will be ready to meet him if he attacks us.

Tuesday, Aug. 7th

. . . Council at 9 A.M. I watched with the glass, & noticed that the Commissioners were rather excited, & gesticulated a good deal. Old White Bull spoke, then John Grass, & then Gall. I went to dinner, & passed the council just in time to hear Gall say that this was the last council & now they would go home. A big yell of approbation followed. Everyone repeated "we'll go home now," & yelled in various keys, & all stampeded. Major McLaughlin called them back, & told them he would give them bread before they left, & then they all scattered again. I thought I would have to get Mrs. McLaughlin out, in case the Indians should send a shower of old bones, sticks, etc. at the Commissioners, but they omitted this part of the usual proceedings of the regular stampede. The Agent thinks the Commission will leave soon, as they have completely failed.

Wednesday, Aug. 8th

. . . Went to the Mission. Left word for Agent with Two Pack's son to meet the Commissioners at Mission at 8 A.M. tomorrow, to take them to Cheyenne Agency. Told F. Martin of their coming. He wrote to Agent a very guarded letter to say that he had sufficiently answered the Commission through the Agent. I brought up the letter. Stopped at H. Agard's in returning.

A young man of St. Joseph's Society has "stolen" a girl & wants me to marry them. Reminded him that he had broken the rules, & disgraced the Society, & referred him to F. Martin.

Stopped at Wm. Halsey's & took supper, & then came in. Met Agent at Post Office, reading a severe article against Pratt from the Bismarck Tribune (quoted from New York Tribune). He says the Commissioners have changed their minds, & will council again here, next ration day.

Thursday, Aug. 9th

. . . Rode to Douglas' & to Fort Yates. Saw Quartermaster, & got him to order blacksmith to shoe Pinch. Lost my dinner waiting to get it done; but they are really very kind to do it at all, as they are very busy. They refused pay. A mule got loose, & I ran it into the blacksmith shop, on Pinch, & caught it. Sister Mechtilde[151] came with People's team from Mandan, with orders for my sister Emma Halsey, & Sister Anselma[152] to come to Zell. Emma had gone with the other girls for cherries, & I hunted them up on Pinch, & sent Emma & the 2 sisters in [on?] in the buggy. F. Bede & Emma went to Halsey's to take leave, & I arranged to get Coles' wagon & harness, to use with Pinch & F. Bede's horse, & take them to Parkins to meet People's team (which left at noon) tomorrow morning.

Friday, Aug. 10th

Harnessed up Pinch & F. Bede's horse, but Pinch threw himself down, & wouldn't go, and, after many trials, we had to look for another horse. None could be got, at any price, & just at the last moment, when I was about to take them up with F. Bede's horse & a single buggy, I got Willie Cadotte's horse by offering $5.00.

[151] Sister Mechtild Decker, a teacher at St. Benedict's School at Fort Yates.

[152] Sister Anselma Auer, OSB, a seamstress at St. Benedict's.

We got off at 8 A.M. Mist, & cold. I was sick on the way, but we reached Parkins, via Wells, at 12 M. just in time to catch People's team. Took dinner. Gave Emma a dollar to get lunch, etc. on the way. Lent Sister Anselma $10.00 so they would be sure to have plenty, in case of accident. Gave Emma my last advice, & good-by kiss, & saw her safely off. She is now, with Josie & Annie, in the care of the Sacred Heart of Jesus, to whom I have given them.

I rested some time at Parkins, & then went to Wells'. In unhitching, F. Bede's horse got away. We caught him again, with much trouble. I got worse. Diarrhea & pain in bowels. Got some laudanum [a pharmaceutical preparation of opium] from Mrs. Givens, & checked it a little. Wells is busy cutting hay.

Saturday, Aug. 11th

Took some more laudanum. Pain less, but still weak & sick. Mr. Wells hitched up for me. Drove to Agency. Commissioners still here. Prepared to say 1st mass tomorrow but, possibly, may not be able.

Sunday, Aug. 12th

Unable to say 1st mass at 8 A.M. Too weak. Heard mass. Mr. Wm. Halsey promised to bring me photo of young Spotted Tail to have copied. I hear that he is dead, but letters from Rosebud, from Big-Turkey & others, do not mention it.

Monday, Aug. 13th

Said mass at 7 A.M. Still weak & sick. Took Epsom salts & laudanum. Emeran wants to go to Crow Creek, to see his mother, who is dying. I borrowed $40.00 for him, on my account, from Mr. McKenzie, the bookkeeper at Douglas'. He crossed the river tonight, & will go by stage to Bismarck tomorrow. Cautioned him to say nothing about Commission.

Sisters went to Mission. Sent Emeran's trunk by Coles' team to Mandan.

Tuesday, Aug. 14th

. . . Went to Scott's & had photo taken. My mother just wrote to me & wants some. Received letters from Bertha & F. Willard.

Got a photo of Red Cloud from Coles'. Wanted to go to Parkins, but unable yet to ride.

Wednesday, Aug. 15th

Feast of the Assumption, B.V.M. Said mass at 7 A.M. F. Bede sang High mass at 8 A.M. Met Judge Wright at Coles', & he afterward, called me in to talk with the other Commissioners. I explained to them why we could not interfere either in word or writing, in order to avoid trouble with press & Indians. Exonerated half-breeds, "squaw-men,"[153] Agent, & all from blame, & pointed out the fact that the real opponents of the bill are all Indians over 35 or 40 years old who voice their sentiments through the 4 chiefs, Gall, Grass, Mad-bear, & Big-head.

Recommended breaking all chiefs, & leaving Indians in districts under boss-farmers (white). Explained that the Indians feared not the loss of land,—but the way opened to civilization by the bill. For all I know, there may have been a clerk, inside, taking down my words in short-hand. However, as I spoke only my real sentiments, as I have always held them, & gave real facts, they may write what they please. I also told them how I had been abused by their opponents for my civilizing efforts, & told the story of the rescue of Hunka-win at Cannonball, & the complaint, on that account, made to Inspector Pearson. They seemed to understand my position.

F. Bede got package from Benziger,[154] containing pictures for banners, scarfs, badges, rabbis [the black detachable shirtfront worn by priests below the collar], crucifix, etc. & Roman collars.

Thursday, Aug. 16th

. . . F. Bede went to the Mission. Sister Gertrude made me two cinctures, & fixed my rabbi & Roman collar, & band for crucifix. Got Postal Card from Emeran. He left Bismarck for Crow Creek at 11:45 P.M. August 14th. Met Sister Mechtilde. Her account of Sr. Hildegarde, Mistress of Novices, gives me more hope for the safety & perseverance of my dear sisters Josephine, Annie, &

[153] White men married to Indian women, who resided in the camps.

[154] Benziger Brothers, a religious supply house in Chicago, Ill.

Emma. May God give them abundant grace to understand & be understood, & to persevere.

Friday, Aug. 17th

. . . Commissioners are trying to get Indians to come in a few at a time & sign. Only a few come. Rev. F.[ather] Oster,[155] of Clontarf, Minn. came tonight, & went to Agent's house. He is after boys for Clontarf.

Saturday, Aug. 18th

. . . Was called by Giles to the school to see sisters from Zell. As I went I was tortured by a terrible presentiment that Josephine was with them. Sister Gertrude met me to tell me that it was the case. The poor child had the usual severe attack of homesickness, desolation, & temptation against vocation, and, not knowing what she said, wrote to Mother Gertrude & the Bishop, asking to return. She claimed that she never wanted to go, but I & Sr. Gertrude urged her. The letters, & copies of letters, she brought back show this.

Her return breaks my heart. My race is surely still under the curse, & on my account my poor sister suffers. I don't blame her for her wild statements in her delirium & frenzy. She kept silent, & no one watched her, till too late. Had they let her become calm before deciding. Had they sent her to the Bishop, or sent for me, all would have been settled. I treated her kindly, soothed her, & gave her time to become calm. She seemed afraid that I would feel her trouble as keenly as she. She is worn & tired, & has suffered terribly. If she is lost, there is no hope for me.

Sunday Aug. 19th

Said mass at 9 A.M. & preached on Gospel. Talked with Josephine. She is now calmer, & can begin to understand the whole affair. She explained everything to me, & wished me to tell the Bishop that she wants to try again, & to stay here with the Sisters, who know her, as an aspirant, like Mary Schöulé. I began writing

[155] Father Anatole Oster was seeking students for the St. Paul Industrial School in Clontarf, Minn.

to the Bishop, taking Josie's statements point by point, & proving them to be incorrect, & contradictory, & the result of the temptation & desolation, & exonerating her from all blame, & begging him to sanction her remaining here as an aspirant, & to encourage her. I offered my life to save Josie's soul & vocation, & also my whole being as a sacrifice, that God might strike me, & spare my sister.

Monday, Aug. 20th

. . . Gave Mrs. Holley information about Indians. Finished letter to Bishop, & one to Sr. Hildegarde, & mailed them. Received from F. Stephan, copy of school contract, & from F. Willard $300.00 to pay fare of boys to his school. Saw Agent. He says I must get an order. He told me a lot of stuff about Frosted. Doubt it.

Tuesday, Aug. 21st

. . . Called on Agent & showed him F. Willard's letter. He probably has reconsidered, as he sees no difficulty now in my taking boys. He & Faribault got 19 for F. Oster.

I went to Mission & explained matters to F. Martin, & told him about Josie. . . .

Wednesday, Aug. 22d

. . . Told Frosted what the Agent said. He denies part, & explains part plausibly, & went to see the Agent about it. Scott brought up 6 more photos.

Part II
The Second Standing Rock Journal
August 1888–April 1889

O Maria sis mihi propitia
Iyuha wowaunyelo + Le ta wimacaša
Jesus susheca kin akan wanna icipaweh omakatanpi
A. M. D. G.

[O Mary be merciful to me
Who am part of the + total sacrificial victim
Jesus, appearing now at this season nailed upon the cross
For the greater glory of God]

Journal, & record of
daily routine of Mission work.*

Say to your sister "Thou hast obtained mercy."
Osee (Hosea)
C. II. V. I

* The second journal runs from August 23, 1888, to April 13, 1889. The quote in the bottom right-hand corner is from Hosea 2:1.

At Standing Rock Reservation, DT, 1888

Thursday, Aug. 23d

... The Agent & [George] Faribault got his boys (19) together, taking some who had intended to go to Rensselaer, Ind.[1] I said nothing, because I couldn't very well, & F. Oster couldn't understand it. The Agent insists that I shall take John Bain. It looks like a trick to set me at variance with F. Martin, & I refused. He claims that John was not to be sent to the Mission. Mac [McLaughlin] is a rascal.

I went to Cannonball, helped F. Oster at Parkins, after going to Wells' hay ranch, & then returned to Wells'. Killed rattle snake near Beaver-holes. He jumped at me from a bank. All asleep. Camped out. Cold & fleas, not much sleep. F. Oster was to start in the morning at 1 A.M. to catch 9:45 A.M. train at Mandan.

Friday, Aug. 24th

Met John Brown again (met him first last night). He promises to look up boys, but don't do much. I spoke to some, but none are willing. Can't do much without the Agent. Arranged for boys to come to Parkins, but none came.

Saturday, Aug. 25th

Went again to Parkins, & had dinner there. Sick, weak stomach. Gave Mrs. Holley some points on Indian customs. John Brown, by advice of Indians, backed out. Went with Wells to dances at Cottonwood's & Big Head's camps & hunted up boys around there. Got about 10 to promise.

Absolved, anointed, & gave scapular to Ida, daughter of Nagó-Kapa, dying. Got back in time for supper at Wells' ranch. Going & coming stopped at school, & got letters from Givens to mail for them. Heard a story about Givens. It may not be true, but it only shows how sure we are of getting slandered here.

---

[1] Students were being recruited for St. Joseph's Indian Normal School in Rensselaer, Ind.

Sunday, Aug. 26th 1888

Only 3 boys came, & when Mr. Wells, failing to get the team he expected, went & got Bear-Ghost & his team, Bob Brown came along with Johnnie, just as we had started. Johnnie was unwilling. We let him go, but, out of pity for his father, I waited. Perhaps God may make someone treat Josie with courtesy & kindness, out of regard for me, if I pity the anxiety of a relative for a relative,—& I know well how to feel it.

After a while John came along. I went back, & brought him behind me on the horse, & he got in the wagon all right. Brown overtook us, & gave me an order for $15.00 from Wells, the proceeds of the sale of John's horse. We got in all right.

Killed a rattlesnake. Can't find Agent. Gave boys supper at Pleets, & camped them at F. Bede's. The note I sent by Charging-thunder to F. Takukokipešni (to have someone go to Flying-by's camp for boys who want to go with me) he kept some time before showing it to F. Martin. F. Bede says I had better take John Bain. I don't see how I can, especially since Giles went to the Mission (sent by F. Bede with best intentions) & mixed things up. Couldn't expect anything else. He means well, but don't know. F. Bede says it's all right, & he & Sr. Gertrude will explain it. If that's the case I may risk it, but I don't like it. I am sure it's a trick of the Agent to set us at variance. The Agent advised me to get away before ration-day, so Hampton [school] wouldn't get my boys; & now he tells Giles & F. Bede that I do wrong in hurrying.—The hypocrite.

Monday, Aug. 27th

The Agent advises me to wait till ration day, & promises me at least 10 boys. To avoid misunderstanding I will wait. Went to the Mission with Mrs. McLaughlin, & returned with her. Sisters, F. Bede & children have gone there for a picnic.

Tuesday, Aug. 28th

Went back to Mission, & arranged for Paul to aid Wm. Halsey in freighting the boys to Mandan. Returned in afternoon with picnic party. Telegram from [Father] Stephan. Must leave with boys at once. Took leave of Josie & gave her advice regarding desolation, etc.

Wednesday, Aug. 29th

Sr. Gertrude received a letter from the Bishop [Marty]. He wants Josephine to go to her father. He is deceived, & I fear that some wretch is influencing him. May God have mercy on us. When a Bishop tries to cast the sheep to the wolves, what can we do? I fear that God seems to refuse my petition. I am lost. My God, I can do no more. Do the rest for me. Save my sister. We perish. We wish to serve you but alone we cannot. Help us. I am determined to fight this, with God's aid.

Started, after arranging with the Agent & Sister to send Josie to Avoca,—taking leave of Josie, & getting a lock of her hair, & advising her to look to Sr. Gertrude for my wishes during my absence. We took 7 boys in two wagons. Went to Wells & arranged to get a relay for Miss Mary on Monday. Josie may go with her to Avoca. Stopped over night at Parkins.

Editor's Summary: August 30, 1888-September 9, 1888

Father Craft and his group of seven schoolboys traveled by wagon to Mandan, DT, where they caught an 11:45 A.M. train on August 30, reaching St. Paul, Minnesota, the next day about 5:00 P.M. Other passengers were apparently not always civil to a priest traveling with a group of young Indian boys, as reflected in a terse journal entry: "Silenced an impudent fellow." As they waited for the evening train to Chicago, Craft went to confession at the cathedral in St. Paul, which may or may not have had anything to do with the confrontation on the train. However, the next day in Chicago, as they awaited the train to Rensselaer, Indiana, he sought out Benedictine, Jesuit, and Franciscan priests to again hear his confession: "I want to take advantage of my trip to secure all the direction & graces I can. I am sure I am on the right track, & I hope God will not let my imperfections spoil my work."

He agonized during this trip over the fate of Josephine, not knowing whether she was still at Fort Yates, had been taken to Avoca, or had returned to her parents. He wrote, "I must hear at once what has been done, & if Josie is safe beyond the reach of Pharisees & other saints. I learn that [Father] Stephan wants me to visit the Indian Territory for him. I would, willingly, but duty to my sister, under present circumstances, goes first. If she is safe, I go; if not, I don't."

Advised by a telegram that "Josie still at Yates," he met Father Stephan in Chicago on Thursday, September 6. Father Stephan had already arranged with Bishop Marty to have Craft transferred from the Dakota dioceses to the BCIM. Craft was to be reassigned elsewhere—anywhere but Standing Rock. In his journal, Craft wrote, "I refused flatly, & told him I could not leave my sister in danger, but if the Bishop would sanction her efforts to save her soul & vocation, I would be ready for anything."

After Craft pled his case regarding Josephine with Bishop Marty later that same day, Marty reconsidered his position, as evidenced by the following journal entry Craft made: "He [Marty] understood it, gave his hearty approval & blessing to our efforts for her, & said she could be an aspirant at Yates or Avoca, as she liked, & authorized me to say so in his name. I at once accepted the transfer with thanks."

Having established a fragile peace with Father Stephan, Craft returned to Standing Rock to await his next assignment, which was to establish a mission among the Arickara, Mandans, and Gros Ventre tribes on Fort Berthold Reservation. First, though, he was to deliver Josephine Crowfeather and five other postulants to the School of the Holy Child Jesus at Avoca, Minnesota.

At Standing Rock Reservation, DT, 1888

Monday, Sept. 10th

. . . Left in stage at 7:30 A.M. Reached Winona at 6 P.M. Crossed river, & got here about 8 P.M. Josie the first to come to meet me at F. Bede's. Agent wants me to take girls to [the school at] Avoca [Minnesota]. Of course I will.

Tuesday, Sept. 11th

Prepared to leave with girls. Borrowed back $50.00 I gave to Sr. Gertrude. Gave Josie her books & rosary. In the afternoon, F. Martin came. In the evening Mrs. Van Solen & 4 girls came. Claudia wanted to go. Josie anxious for her. Very reasonable, but was deeply grieved to think of leaving Claudia here in danger. She's right. I promised to try to get Major's [McLaughlin's] consent, & succeeded by offering to pay if the U.S. Government refused. While I was contriving in pagan style, Josie was before the Blessed Sacrament crying & praying, & there I found her. Said a Hail Mary & prayers to Jesus, Mary & Joseph with sister in thanksgiving. Mrs. Van Solen, Lucille, & 4 girls took supper at Sister's, & will sleep there. We start in the morning. 4 girls & Claudia will be examined in the morning. I got Josie examined alone today, as she is different from the rest, as my best sister, & a chosen spouse of Christ.

Editor's Summary: September 12–October 10, 1888

It took four days for Father Craft and his entourage of a half-dozen young Indian women to reach Avoca, Minnesota. Josephine Crowfeather and her sister, Claudia, were joined by Mary Black Eyes, Jane Moccasin, Bessie Yellow Bear, and Alice White Deer. They were in very protective company: "I had often to remind inquisitive passengers that the girls must be treated as ladies, & when they saw me determined to punish insolent curiosity, they were quite civil."[2]

They were met at the Avoca train station by several Indian students that he knew from Standing Rock and Rosebud reservations. Craft found the atmosphere of the school "quite refreshing. There is a spirit of order, and a spirit of charity. English, Irish, and Amer-

[2] Craft journal, 14 September 1888.

ican Sisters. I have every hope for Josephine."[3] He wrote in his journal for September 24, 1888, that as he celebrated mass that morning, the Feast of Our Lady of Mercy, he "seemed to hear—or rather feel—a voice speaking from the tabernacle the words of the text, 'Say to your sister, "Thou hast obtained mercy."' " He was encouraged by the prospects of success for his postulants at Avoca.

He stayed for several days at Avoca, counseling his aspirants and helping them to accommodate to their new environs, before returning to Zell to clear up any misunderstandings over Josephine's earlier return from the convent there.

Arriving at Fort Berthold on October 2, Craft reported to Agent Jones, who arranged for a council with members of the Rees, Gros Ventres, and Mandans tribes, whom Craft found to be "more docile than the Sioux." The Indians knew of Father DeSmet, who had baptized many of them, and had long sought Black Robes, or so they said. Craft promised that the Bishop would send a priest in the spring, and that he would return to introduce the new priest, but for now he needed to select a site for the mission. Crow Heart, Sitting Bear, Bad Gun, and Good Bear spoke for the tribes. "All fairly howled with delight," Craft wrote. They selected a site on the Little Missouri Bottom, where Craft drove a stake into the ground to mark the place where land would be claimed for the mission.

Pleased with the results of his trip, Craft wrote Bishop Marty and recounted the positive response he had received from the Indians and the Protestant agent (Major Jones) to his plans for a mission. He also encouraged the bishop to assign a permanent priest without delay.[4]

At Standing Rock Agency, DT, 1888

Thursday, Oct. 11th

. . . Looked at, & priced sleighs & sleigh runners for F. Bede. Went by stage from Bismarck to Winona, & crossed over to Yates. Had supper at school.

[3] Craft journal, 15 September 1888.

[4] Craft to Bishop Marty, 9 October 1888, Sacred Heart Priory Archives.

Friday, Oct. 12th

. . . Returned $50.00 to Sister Gertrude. Called on Mrs. McLaughlin. Emeran came in from Grand River.

Saturday, Oct. 13th

Said mass at 7 A.M. These 3 days masses are to be a triduum[5] for the aspirants, & most especially, for Josephine. Wrote F. Stephan,[6] Rev. Mother Sup. at Avoca, Emma & Annie [Pleets], Josie & Annie [Gaudreau], Bertha, Sec. of Interior, enclosing receipt for report blanks, Giles, F. Pius, & R.R. Agt. at Eureka, to get the half-fare permit he promised.

Sunday, Oct. 14th

Sang high mass for Indians at 9 A.M. Preached on Gospel of Mass. Feast of Maternity. Went to Crow-feather's lodge, & brought Matilda to the school, to stay till tomorrow, when her father will take her to school at St. Benedict's Mission. I did it to save her from arrest as a runaway scholar,—for Josie's sake. I saw my little "Irish sister" Ada Mary Sweeny, at the school. Mrs. McLaughlin brought her in. We have her at last, thank God.

Monday, Oct. 15th

. . . Matilda went home to St. Benedict's with her father. Gave some tobacco to "Bad Gun" & other Gros Ventres. Showers. Emeran went to Grand River. Would have gone to Cannonball, but Givens did not go.

Tuesday, Oct. 16th

Started with Givens & Bob Brown for Cannonball. Took dinner at Givens'. Got photo of Sister Gertrude from Mrs. Wells for Josephine. Very raw & cold. Wind N.W.

Wednesday, Oct. 17th

Went with Mr. Wells to Parkins. Told Mrs. Parkins to have my horse brought in. Wrote letter to Josephine enclosing photo of Sis-

[5] A three-day service or observance.

[6] Craft reported that his "Berthold trip was a grand success" and requested reimbursement for his earlier trip to Avoca (Craft to Stephan, 12 October 1888, BCIM Records).

ter Gertrude, & sent it to be mailed to Avoca, Minn. by Ed Coles, who was going to Fort Yates. Gave a short instruction in school.

Thursday, Oct. 18th 1888

Instructed scholars in school. Points l. obedience to God & His Church. 2nd Respect for self & family,—both essential to the Indians if they wish for life, here & hereafter.

Mrs. Parkins & Caske came to Givens. Went to see her, & came with her to Wells. Her store robbed last night. At least $8.00 taken. Horse not yet caught.

Friday, Oct. 19th 1888

Went to Parkins for horse. Not yet caught. Met Ahewanka [Frosted], who wanted to find things stolen from Parkins' store. He complained to me that Gus Travasil cheated him out of a house. He is a medicine man, & devil dreamer. I gave him a blasting, & wanted him to give me a shot at him, as he claims to be invulnerable. He wouldn't "stand fire," & I laughed at & ridiculed him.

Saturday, Oct. 20th

Went to Parkins. Democratic caucus. One democrat (Bob Brown) present. Chairman, Secretary, & delegates to Convention appointed. I paid Parkins $11.00 on account. Horse caught & was quite wild. I quieted him, saddled, & rode to Wells'.

Sunday, Oct. 21st

. . . Big Wanagiglepi in "Two-Bear's" camp. Only 4 came to Mass. After Mass Waga told us that [George] Faribault had heard, & told the Indians, that 16 Crows were on the way here to fight, & that the Sioux must defend themselves. I suspected that it was Ahewanka, & not Faribault. I told the Indians that I would go with them, if it was a true report, but I doubted it, & would investigate. The police said, when I asked them, that it was not Faribault, but Ahewanka, who had a dream, & prophesied. Two soldiers from Yates knew nothing of it.

I told the Indians not to listen to that devil-dreamer, & explained what the consequences would be, if they crossed into the white-man's country, armed. I advised them to send scouts, & even offered to examine the country myself. They wouldn't listen to me, & all went out on Cantepeta [Fire Heart] creek, to give Ahewanka a sweat, & hear more prophecies.

I started after them at night to make another effort to get them back. I could not find their camp, & learned from two half-breeds that it was three miles further, & over a rough country; so I gave it up, & returned to Wells. They expect to see Crows early tomorrow.

Monday, Oct. 22d

Went with Givens to Parkins. Givens wrote a note to Faribault for instruction, &, as the Indians seemed less likely to return, he telegraphed. Faribault answered by wire, saying that there were no Crows,—he never told the Indians so;—& asked Givens to hold them. Givens replied that he had no one to send after them, & that all had gone. The next message came from the operator at Yates, saying that Faribault was in the Commanding Officer's room in consultation, & he would soon wire again. Then the Com. Officer wired Givens, asking how many had gone,—armed or not,—& where. Givens answered,—gave the desired information, & said there was no danger. Com. Officer replied that he would send a detachment at any rate. Faribault then wired Givens to tell the Indians the troops were coming, & order them in. Scott, the operator, wired again in the evening that the 2 troops of cavalry were on the way. I went back with Givens & Mrs. Parkins & returned with them. Wells came also. Maj. Brown, & Lieut. Steele, & the cavalry arrived after dark, & Crazy-walking, & Tunkan-wicaša, (Police) with them.

Just before the soldiers came, a few Indians returned, but most are still out. Ahewanka is still sweating, dreaming & promising. I interpreted for officers. Brown told Crazy-walking to find out number still out, & where; & report early in the morning. He asked me to aid him as interpreter, etc. I returned to Wells'. Crazy-walking went to Red-fox's house (Zatela's).

FIGURE 11. Sioux dancers.
Photograph by D. F. Barry. *Denver Public Library, Western History Collection, Call No. B-574.*

Tuesday, Oct. 23d

Started early for Parkins on horseback. Rain for a few hours,—then clear. I interpreted for Brown. Crazy-walking reported that all had sneaked in during the night, on hearing of the arrival of troops; & that Ahewanka & 8 others were still out. Brown would have gone after them, on hearing that they were about 8 or 10 miles away, but I advised him to look for them at the Red Fish camp. He sent Crazy-walking to send police for Ahewanka, to arrest him if found. They soon brought him, but had let him keep his arms. Brown ordered him disarmed at once. I took breakfast with officers, & then with soldiers. They then left for Yates, with Ahewanka under guard,—& so ended the "Crow War."

The Agent will raise Cain when he returns, about the troops coming,—but this exposure is very beneficial to us, & our work. I went to Wells, &, after dinner, I went to Mrs. Van Solen's.

Wednesday, Oct. 24th

Said mass in school, at Mrs. Van Solen's, at 9 A.M. Preached on Angels, self-respect, etc. Gave pictures to children. Left at 1 P.M. & came to Agency. Put up horse, & got mail.

Thursday, Oct. 25th

. . . Went with Dr. Caskie to see Mrs. Galpin & Nape-luta-win,—both quite sick. After dark the chiefs returned from Washington, via Eureka. Father Claude[7] is coming here on a visit. Called on Sisters at the school. Agent returned via Mandan.

Friday, Oct. 26th

. . . Wrote to Rev. Mother Anthony, S.H.C.J. [Sisters of the Holy Child Jesus] & sent by registered letter $20.00 on acct. for Josie's school expenses, & $1.00 for Josie. Called on Agent at office. Paid Coles $35.00 ($20 cash & $15 order on Wells), & borrowed $1.00 in cash for Josie—a bill to mail with the $20.00).

Saturday, Oct. 27th

. . . Frosted is told by Agent & [George] Faribault that he must either move the Standing Rock,[8] as he said he could, or he will be sent to the military guard-house with ball & chain. If he can move it by his devils, he will be free, & paid besides. He says he can & wants his singers. They will be sent for. . . .

Sunday, Oct. 28th

Said mass for Indians at 9 A.M. Attendance small. Changed to winter time hereafter. Mass will be at 10:30 A.M. for both whites & Indians. Went to St. Joseph's Society meeting at Wm. Halsey's.

---

[7] Father Claude M. Ebner, OSB (1849-1904), served beginning in 1877 at Fort Yates, Fort Totten, Devil's Lake, and Woonsocket (S.Dak.).

[8] Standing Rock is a pedestaled boulder in the vague shape of a woman and child, for which the reservation was named.

Monday, Oct. 29th

... While talking to the Indians in Coles' store about "Frosted," Spotted-bird, the brother of Crazy-man, said [George] Faribault told him I had called out the military & asked to have the Indians disarmed & dismounted. It may be false, but as all know of it, I had to speak to the Agent. He was angry, & spoke impudently to me. I gave him a "blasting." He called for the Indian, who said he heard it from "Crazy-man." Faribault, when found, denied it, & began a quarrel. I gave him a severe "overhauling," &, in answer to his complaining that I once threatened to have him arrested, I said I intended to do so, if he annoyed me any further, & that I had plenty of evidence. I exposed him to the Indians in the office, who heard his noise & told Major Brown. I have had enough of their insolence, & will now crush it. I gave an order on Douglas for provisions, etc. for Emeran. Received letters from Josie, Annie [Gaudreau], & Bertha,—& Bishop. "Frosted" sang, & tried to move the Rock, but failed. He will be ironed.

Tuesday, Oct. 30th

... "Crazy-man" & his brother were called up today & examined. Spotted-bird sticks to his story. Crazy-man denies it, & says his brother misunderstood him; but he shows hesitation & insincerity. I refused to talk with Faribault, except through the Agent, because he is a blackguard, & an enemy of the Church. Spotted-bird got two weeks in the guard-house for raising the trouble, but I still believe the story. The time has come when we must crush these wretches, who have annulled our work for 12 years. Their tricks cannot deceive us now. The Agent & Faribault, in this case, tried a game of "bluff" with me, but failed. I received a letter from Maj. Jones of Berthold, & answered it. "Frosted" ironed, with ball & chain, & turned over to the military.

Wednesday, Oct. 31st

... Received a letter from Rev. Mother Anthony, S.H.C.J. Josie lost her rosary, Bertha better. Answered, promising to send rosary. Wrote to Muhlbauer & Buhle, Chicago, for one, or, if they have

FIGURE 12.
Frosted, wearing prison uniform and in irons.
Photograph by D. F. Barry.
Denver Public Library, Western History Collection, Call No. B-516.

no sister's rosary, such as I ordered while there (but never got it). I told them to send 2 fifteen decade rosaries, like that lost, & also 3 Imitations, like the one I gave Josie. I wrote also to the Bishop, & to Rev. F. Wolfgang, O.S.B. Bismarck, D.T. & sent Maj. Jones' letter to the Bishop. Had Pinch's shoes set by F. Steinmetz.[9] Boat Batchelor came & returned to Bismarck. Just heard that Kemp & Ryan are discharged, & a man from Chicago, & Joe Primeau take their places. Stewart mended my boot. Sent Chief's coat & leggins to F. Stephan via Chicago.

[9] Frank B. Steinmetz, the agency blacksmith (*Annual Reports*, 1892, 365, 832).

Thursday, Nov. 1st All Saints'

. . . Wrote to F. Stephan,[10] Wm Tiwanzilan, & Josie, Annie [Pleets], & Bertha. F. Claude left for Devil's Lake, via Cannonball & Mandan. . . .

Friday, Nov. 2nd All Souls'

. . . Wrote to F. Willard,[11] Mr. Courtis, & Mr. Gahin, the R.R. Agt. at Eureka. Began an article on the prospects of the Church in christianizing & civilizing the Indians. I feel very weak. I am under a continual mental strain. If the other priests were brave, determined, soldiers of Christ, with a grain of the martyr's spirit in them, I would feel easy; but when I see them fawning upon the enemies of God's Church, & not daring to whisper even to themselves the slightest protest against Satan's work; I feel infinite loathing & disgust; with serious apprehension for the future. They won't help me; & their cowardice may even turn them against me. They forget God & souls, in their anxiety to secure their positions, pay, & peace. . . .

Saturday, Nov. 3rd

. . . Wrote article on Indians for Bishop. It's hard to generalize. He wants an article on all Indians. I would rather confine myself to the Sioux; but there are some things I know of all; & of these I can safely write.

Sunday, Nov. 4th

. . . Went to see my cousin Lizzie Two Packs, & found that she died two days ago. They should have sent for me. [George] Faribault is to blame for all. It is he, who for jealousy & spite against the Church sets the Indians against us. God sees it, & will in good time deal with the case. At least, Father Martin, on my information some

[10] Craft tells Father Stephan that he has sent the "chief's coat & leggins" he promised, and gives an account of the "Crow War" (Craft to Stephan, 1 November 1888, BCIM Records).

[11] Craft's letter refers to some of the attacks made to drive him from the reservation: "Every single trouble I had was started, not by Indians, but by whites on the Agency" (Craft to Willard, 2 November 1888, BCIM Records).

weeks ago, visited Lizzie, & gave her the Last Sacraments. I went on to the Mission, & would have returned, but my horse became lame, & I had to put up for the night. I don't feel at home here. F. Martin is afraid of getting into trouble, & is not in sympathy with my efforts. A fine spirit for Christian priests. Where would the Church have been had the martyrs acted so?

Monday, Nov. 5th

. . . Rode back to the Agency. Found a message from Mrs. Parkins. Mrs. Galpin sick. Will go tomorrow with butcher's team, as my horse is worse, & I can't get butcher's team today.

Tuesday, Nov. 6th

Said mass at 7 A.M. As today is election, I said mass with this intention, viz. that God would direct the election in the way most conducive to Josie's safety, & to the safety of our missions. The elections have much to do with all this.

Went on to Parkins. Took the Blessed Sacrament. The Sacred Heart, my Chief & Commanding Officer, is excellent company. I realized more on this trip, regarding ways & means of getting along, than ever before. Jesus teaches without noise, but solidly & lastingly. Gave blessing to camps, missions, & all on the way. Special intention, for Sister Josie, & her vocation. Gave Mrs. Galpin Holy Communion as viaticum,[12] & anointed her. Took dinner at Parkins. Polls in store. Voted Republican ticket,—for the first time, though I always voted Democratic before. It's my first vote since I wore a cassock, &, perhaps, since I became a Catholic. It would be consoling if my first Republican vote should be for a Republican victory,—especially in view of my intention at mass this morning.[13]

Went on to Wells'. Wells & Givens went to polls, but didn't vote. We persuaded Gus Traversil to vote Republican. He had his

---

[12] Holy Eucharist for the sick.

[13] Craft's Republican vote was likely cast in support of a change of administration on the reservations and especially against Agent James McLaughin, who could be expected to lose his job in a Republican takeover. McLaughlin, however, proved immune to the politics of change, and Craft would be severely disappointed in his hope that government-imposed problems on the missions would improve.

ticket taken away, & so can vote.[14] His vote avenges the loss of the ticket, by the bye.

Wednesday, Nov. 7th

Came back to Agency. Received letter from Rev. Mother St. Anthony, enclosing one from Josie. Beads found, thanks to St. Anthony. Rev. Mother will take the $20.00 I sent as full pay for one year's music; & wants to keep Josie free of charge for the Sacred Heart, as I have given "All" for the Sacred Heart.[15]

Thursday, Nov. 8th

. . . Wrote article for Bishop. Telegrams came in stating that the Republicans have won. News, so far, from New York, Indiana, & California. McLaughlin furious. Agency people say that he will now have to apply to Catholics for aid,—hence his rage. God judges better than men. If election reports are true, the persecutions against us here must cease.

I answered Rev. Mother's letter, thanking her, & proposing that I should pay for Josie, while I live, &, if I die, she shall take care of her, as I don't want her to be a Government scholar. I wrote also to Josie.

Friday, Nov. 9th

. . . Wrote article for Bishop. Groomed Pinch. Old [George] Faribault is evidently getting alarmed. Wells came down today & I saw Faribault talking to him in the store (Coles').

Afterwards Wells came to me, evidently to feel the way, & told me that Faribault was talking of the trouble he had with me, denying all charges, & saying that Indians opposed to him had deceived me. I told Wells that lying wouldn't do. I had plenty of evidence, & would receive no explanations. I required that Faribault should undo all the evil he had done against the Church, & give back to us the confidence of the Indians & our good name of which he robbed us.

---

[14] Perhaps Craft means that someone stole Traversil's "ticket," or list of candidates that each party distributed, but he was still eligible to vote.

[15] Rev. Mother St. Anthony to Craft, 2 November 1888, in the author's possession.

I fear that Fathers Martin & Bede are plotting something against Josie & me. Much that I see & hear goes to confirm this view. They persecuted Claudia on my account, & may try to annoy Matilda. They may rest assured I won't stand it. They can't get me removed, & needn't try. . . .

Saturday, Nov. 10th

. . . Wrote article for the Bishop. Wrote letter for Arron, to Mark & Wallace Wells. Wrote to F. Jerome[16] to let him know what I said to Bishop about St. Meinrad's taking Fort Berthold. Received a letter from Bishop & mother, & a 15 decade sister's rosary from Mühlbauer & Behrle. It is for Josephine. I blessed it, & said a whole rosary on it for her. F. Bede assures me that no one will do anything to annoy Josephine or discourage her in her vocation. I shall not, however, relax vigilance. It's too bad to have to fight our own party, but if they league with wolves to kill my sheep, they must share the fate of the wolves. There are certain people who, like the dog in the manger, want the whole earth though they can't hold it all. They are jealous & prejudiced, & try to destroy others secretly. To maintain an erroneous opinion, they care little how many souls they destroy. Vanity blinds them to law & reason, & selfishness makes them cruel to others. Having once said (to hide their own faults) that Josephine has no vocation, they try to bring every influence to bear to discourage the poor child, & destroy her vocation, that they may justify themselves. Satan can do no more. But God exists, & will not let them succeed.

Sunday, Nov. 11th

F. Bede went to Mission for F. Martin's name's day. I said both masses 1st 8 A.M. 2nd (high) 10:30 A.M. Confessions & communions of St. Joseph's & St. Mary's Societies. Some went to confession last night. Touched with my rosary, Josie's rosary, to make it a relic of European holy places. Baptized child of Frank Longie.

[16] Craft wrote to Father Jerome Hunt, OSB, confirming his suggestion that St. Meinrad's Abbey take charge of the new mission at Fort Berthold (Craft to Hunt, 10 November 1888, St. Meinrad Archabbey Archives, St. Meinrad, Ind.).

Packed up & sent (registered mail) the sister's rosary to Josie, as a present from the Sacred Heart & me. Sent it care of Rev. Mother St. Anthony, S.H.C.J., & wrote to her & Josie. Took Anselmine Wipehinwin & Carrie Taziwin to Sisters' school. Emma Archambeau returned to school. She feels she is in danger, from her mother's deviltry, & despair gives her a small spark of courage. Gave Benediction of B.S. . . .

Monday, Nov. 12th

. . . Wrote article for Bishop. Got laudanum from sisters for Mrs. Prange. F. Jerome sent $15.00 by P.O. order, in payment of John H. Strait's store bill at Coles. John gave it to him to send.

Tuesday, Nov. 13th

. . . Wrote & finished article for Bishop. Received from Mühlbauer & Behrle "The Blessed Ones of 1888" I sent for containing life of Blessed Sister Josephine Mary of St. Agnes. Her life & trials resemble Josie's in some points.[17]

Wednesday, Nov. 14th

. . . Copied off & sent article to Bishop,[18] with letter, advising him to let F. Jerome direct Fort Berthold, informing him of Emma Archambeau's return, & showing up the meanness of the Primeaus & also of Faribault, showing how now, as well as in past years, such people had caused our failures, aided by cowardice & mutual jealousy of priests, & suggesting that if we are firmly united, no power can hurt us.

I packed up & sent Josie's book, with letter referring to Bl.[essed] Sister Josephine Mary's call, & her answer to the Holy Infant, & suggesting that Josie, as she is called in the same way, should answer as her holy patron did, especially when Our Lord gives her the holy kiss of peace & love in Holy Communion, & also before the Blessed Sacrament.

---

[17] Written by Hermann Koneberg, OSB, *Blessed Ones of 1888* contains biographical sketches of four religious persons who had recently been elevated to the level of "blessed" by Pope Leo XIII.

[18] Bishop Marty incorporated Craft's article in one of his own ("Indian Problem and the Catholic Church").

—I wrote on the fly leaf.

> The Sacred Heart of Jesus
> Through his lieutenant
> Wanbli-cinca-aglahpaya
> Sends this token of His holy love
> To her whom He has chosen
> First of the nation,
> Josephine Mary of the Sacred Heart.

And also crossed the names of Josie & her patron, as I do our initials, & wrote, in diamond form, on the cross,

> "The Heart of the Holy Child Jesus
> Calls you, sister, as He called her.
> May He give you grace, sister,
> To answer Him like her."

Thursday, Nov. 15th

. . . F. Bede seems too much inclined to take [George] Faribault's part. The shepherd in league with the wolves. To all the information I give him, he only answers by defending Faribault, though he admits knowing of his opposition. I am now quite sure that the Indian relative question was talked of by F. Martin & B. Prange, & that F. Martin's intention was to get the Bishop to remove me,—but secretly, so as not to appear in it. Barney says he (Barney) mentioned getting the Bishop to give me an easier place, as I was suffering too much. F. Martin answered that he would do nothing against me, & feared that I might trace it to him. If he didn't advise it, he is cunning enough to lead to it, by drawing out & letting impetuous Barney do what he ignorantly thinks is for my good, while he pretends to advise against it, knowing it will go on, & he can say he didn't do it. Macbeth's excuse "Thou can'st not say I did it."[19] Oh no, of course not; but he would cause it.

I have every reason to suspect these men. I never raised the national question, nor hated religious orders. I have tried hard to maintain peace, but it's useless. They want all for German Bene-

[19] Shakespeare, *Macbeth*, 3.4.50.

dictines, of their own house, & are jealous of all others. They attack me secretly, league with our enemies, persecute my sisters, & wish to fill the places more active & zealous men should have, while they paralyze the work of others. I never tried to get them out, & never will, but they deceive themselves if they think God don't see these things. As others have left for the same cause, so will they, if they continue thus, & I, whom they plot against, will hold my seat in the saddle, & my red relations, in much well earned peace. They will probably give me trouble, but I won't yield. God knows my position, & will surely aid me.

Friday, Nov. 16th

Started at 9 A.M. & reached St. F. de Sales Mission at 5 P.M. Road slippery, though snow not an inch deep. Horse jolted & stumbled & slipped very much. Afraid of the road. I had to use the spurs cruelly, to get along. The sum of my meditations on the way touches the bottom of the Indian question. The Indians will remain as they are—or worse—as long as those in charge of them can make money out of them. There is too much to be made by buying cattle, & too much chance of corrupting squaws. When Gov. stops this, we will have some chance to Christianize & civilize the Indians. Until then, [George] Faribault, Joe Primeau, & other reprobates will stand in our way. We need <u>apostles</u> rather than priests, if priests are not to have more courage than these manifest. It would be of great benefit to them, to read & meditate much on the Lives of the Saints. They might then fear God rather than men.

Saturday, Nov. 17th

Wrote yesterday with a quill pen. Blots too much. One "Wašicun wicohan" [white man custom] it is better to lay aside. The hardness & acuteness of the new ideas requires sharp steel to commit them properly to paper.

Emeran held school. Attendance about 35. All did well. Announced mass & blessing of the house & Mission for tomorrow. Dance at Antelope's, & in the evening at Flying-by's. Tried to find out if two girls who stopped here on their way to the dance had any desire to rise above their present condition. They pretended not to understand, though my ideas were expressed in the plainest Dakota. They had the same expression I had noticed in others, where diabolic influence was certain. That is, though cheerful & frank up to the moment I questioned them, they at once put on the usual "look of blank stupidity, scarcely concealing a look showing intelligence, mixed with fear & uneasiness, such as devils are supposed to have in presence of something sacred." The devil isn't going to yield without a fight; & we must trust in God & Mary to crush him. Played on organ, said rosary, prayers, etc.

Sunday, Nov. 18th

Feast of Dedication of the Basilica of Sts. Peter & Paul. Said mass at 10 A.M. About 50 present. Emeran played organ &, with Indians, sang Indian hymns during mass. Before mass, I blessed the house & out-buildings, & then, with the cross, I blessed the missions & people. One young fellow wants baptism, but he must be instructed & fix up his Indian marriage.

Explained in sermon the "Foundation" of Spt. Exerc. [Spiritual Exercises] of St. Ignatius,[20] why we were made, etc. Talked with Flying-by, Swift Cloud, & young men about whites, who, for the purpose of cheating the Indians, set them against the priests.

Monday, Nov. 19th

Saddled up & rode to Jack Carignan's school, reached there at 2 P.M. Spoke to the scholars. Though all seemed glad to see me, they have sadly changed for the worse. High Bear came, & tried to get credit for the good deeds of the Yanktonnai Chief of the same name. It won't do.

Tuesday, Nov. 20th

About 35 scholars attended. There has been a great falling off in attendance. The children would do well, but the parents are in

[20] A series of meditations on religious truths written by St. Ignatius Loyola in the sixteenth century.

the way. I gave no religious instruction, as the scholars are evidently not well disposed to receive it.

Wednesday, Nov. 21st

Some of the Indians already starting for the Agency. Small school attendance. Martha Hinšawin reported dead, & then not dead, but dying. She is with her mother & uncle on a hunt, near Pte-na-tapi.

Thursday, Nov. 22d

Only 5 scholars came. Young Bull-Head, who stopped here last night, & left today for the Agency, tells me that Geo. Faribault, in presence of Grass, Crazy-walking, himself, & others, told Takukokipešin, the Farm-school policeman, to tell F. Martin that he would no longer aid in getting back runaway scholars for the Mission. It's so plain that this wretch is fighting the missions, & yet Frs. Martin & Bede will persist in taking his part against me.

Friday, Nov. 23d

Left Jack's at 10 A.M. & reached Agency at 8 P.M. Warm & pleasant. The horse seems stiff forward, & stumbled & jolted terribly. I fairly had to carry him on the bit. Tired out, & more worried than tired.

Saturday, Nov. 24th

Didn't say mass. No preparations in church. Too cold. I would say mass in the chapel, but don't want to—"justify suspicious fears."

Mrs. Galpin worse. Mrs. Van Solen & Hermanie Cournoyer & Louis Primeau went up. I tried to get a horse, but failed. Mine is too lame, & F. Bede took his to the Mission today. I learn that Emma & Annie [Pleets] will take the white veil [at Zell] on the 8th Dec. Called at the school, & left pipestone for Mrs. Wells.

Sunday, Nov. 25th

Said first mass at 8 A.M. & preached (on the necessity of expecting suffering, 3 kinds of peace, & following Christ crucified) at 10:30 A.M. Mass. After mass, read letter from Emma Halsey to her father. Borrowed F. Bede's horse & rode to Parkins. Mrs. Galpin went to confession. Seems easier. Talked with Rosa & Hermanie Cournoyer.[21]

Monday, Nov. 26th

Mrs. Van Solen manifested a spirit of malignant, diabolic envy, on hearing that Emma & Annie would take the white veil. She declared they would not persevere, & said that all sisters were driven to enter convents by love failures, etc. in the world. I rebuked & silenced her. She also tried to show that I was inimical to the Indians. At breakfast, the whole family, Mrs. McLaughlin included, seemed anxious to prove that we never could convert & civilize the Indians, & need not try. Those who had little to say, lent the aid of look, laugh, etc. to the tirade against Christianity & civilization. It only teaches us what we have to expect here.

I rode to the Agency, leaving Parkins at 11 A.M. & arriving at 5 P.M. Horse hard trotter, but got used to his pace.

Tuesday, Nov. 27th

Did not say mass in the Church. Found no water there. Could have got it, but all was cold as Benedictine charity—as I have found it, & I concluded to wait another day. Said rosary in church, walking, & went to breakfast.

Looked for Indian trinkets to send Mother. Wrote to her, advising her to get Fanny[22] to make a retreat,[23] to decide about a vocation. Received letters from Josie, Rev. Mother St. Anthony, acknowledging receipt of rosary, etc.

Wednesday, Nov. 28th

. . . Bought Indian trinkets at Douglas', & also two black silk handkerchiefs for Josephine, my sister. Rose Cournoyer called. They seem somewhat afraid about their tirade against priests & sisters. Explained to her the state of affairs here.

---

[21] Rose Cournoyer was a teacher at Number 3 Day School on Standing Rock Reservation (*Annual Reports*, 1889, 167, 401). Craft usually wrote it "Rosa." H. Cournoyer was an assistant teacher at Yankton Agency Boarding School in 1892 (*Annual Reports*, 1892, 869–70).

[22] Fanny was Father Craft's younger sister, who lived with their mother in Milford, Pa.

[23] A "retreat" is a temporary withdrawal from everyday secular pursuits to draw closer to the divine through prayer, meditation, and amendment.

I learn at the Fort that Sitting Bull, alarmed at what he had done against me, would have confessed who incited him, had not McLaughlin sent him off with a pass on a visit. That was, no doubt, why he silenced Bull before the Inspector, the rascal. Called at school & arranged for Stewart to take package to Mandan for Cramsies.

Thursday, Nov. 29th

Thanksgiving Day

Sang high mass at 7:30 A.M. Only 4 present beside school children & sisters, viz. Dr. Caskie, Mrs. Kappel, Mrs. Bourke, & Rose Cournoyer. Wrote to Josie, & Rev. Mother St. Anthony, & sent black silk handkerchiefs to Josie, & an "Imitation" each to Bertha & Annie [Gaudreau]. Rec'd. letter from Rev. F. Jerome enclosing P.O. Order for $15.00 from Wm. Tiwanzilan, to pay his bill. Packed up Indian trinkets to send to Mother. Went to Fort & gave McNider address of Emma Halsey to trace package sent last Sept., but never received.

I hear that Long-feather is dead. Died of hemorrhage of lungs, near Pine Ridge Agency, while on a visit. Though he was a treacherous wretch, I grieve to think he died so. His unprovided death is due to the efforts of Geo. Faribault & Joe Primeau to set him against priests. May God forgive him & not visit on the poor tool the vengeance due to those who set him on. I shall be satisfied if God forgives me as freely as I forgive poor uncle Long-feather.

Friday, Nov. 30th

Did not say mass. Filled out & sent to Mr. Gahin at Eureka, D.T. application for half-fare permit on C.M. [Chicago, Milwaukee] & St. Paul R.R. for 1889.

Left package of Indian goods for mother at the Sisters, to be sent, via Mandan, by Mr. Stewart. Rode to Cannonball via Mrs. Van Solen's school. No one there. Reached Wells' after dark. Finished letter to Bishop, which I began at the Agency. I refuse to consent to suppress revelations of Gov. misdoing.

Saturday, Dec. 1st

Went to Parkins & borrowed Mrs. Van Solen's key to get my vestments. They seem to regret their tirade against priests & sisters. However, I wouldn't go in. I went to Mrs. Van Solen's & got vestments. Went to see Eugene who is said to have measles. He is well, & if he had them, it can't be detected now.

Sunday, Dec. 2d

Said mass at 10 A.M. Only 8 Indians came,—among them J. High Bear & S. Two Bears. Went to Parkins with Mr. Wells & returned key. Though invited, I refused to go in. A priest must maintain his dignity. These worthy people have brought themselves to believe that they were necessary to our existence, &, like the low brutes they are, they try to degrade us, & trample on us. Their day is over, &, with God's help, I propose to let them feel it.

Monday, Dec. 3d

Feast of St. Fr.[ancis] Xavier, Patron of the Cannonball Mission

Said mass at 9 A.M. using wine grown & made here from our wild grapes. About 40 children & one man (Old Frank Wakan-inyanka [Runs Holy]) present. Gave an instruction on St. F. Xavier. Went to Zatela's, & saw Annie. Ordered her to get well. Sent her tea & sugar by Zatela. Stopped at Parkins & asked about Mrs. Galpin. Sunka-cikala [Little Dog] brought Coles' horses as a relay.

Tuesday, Dec. 4th

Went again to Zatela's & took cough medicine for Annie. She is much better. Directed Zatela to bring Spotted-Tail's children from Rosebud. Stopped at Parkins. Coles passed on his way to Mandan, & took dinner at Wells. The weather still continues warm. Ice on Cannonball scarcely bears a horse.

Wednesday, Dec. 5th

Rode to Parkins, & saw Mrs. Galpin. She is weaker, & suffers much. Mrs. Capt. Harmon is with her. For unlimited "cheek," I think that family bears away the palm. Mrs. Parkins wants me to say mass there, so they can all go to communion. For several reasons, I won't. They never come to mass here. Such favors are granted only to good Catholics who are capable of appreciation, & these people have manifested such a spirit of malignant enmity towards Sisters & priests, as to put them without the circle of those we consider good Catholics. It has been too long the custom here to consult the wishes & the convenience of such people, until they consider themselves entitled to our service, & treat us with contempt; imagining, perhaps, that if we don't make ourselves their slaves, a note to the Bishop will enlist him in their service, & bring us to our knees in short order. It is time to teach them their mistake, & give them a sharp reminder that they are not our masters.

Besides all this, their wicked desire to keep the Indians in their present state, that they may profit by their necessities, is enough to unfit them to receive any sacraments,—unless their dispositions undergo a very great change, which, at present, don't seem at all likely. It is hard to forget their conduct, some years ago, in decoying an Indian girl into their house, locking her in, & sending for a depraved, diseased, white man, who could not get her otherwise; & closing their ears to her cries for help, while he ravished, ruined, & diseased her, causing her death shortly after. Nothing can be too severe for such wretches; &, now that I know their evil dispositions, I shall not make it too easy for them to profane the sacraments. They must change towards God & His Church, before I change towards them.

Mrs. Galpin is too sick to confess, & puts it off till my return next Monday or Tuesday. Returned to Wells', & prepared to go to Agency.

Thursday, Dec. 6th

Went to Agency, starting at 11 A.M. & arriving at 4 P.M. Came by telegraph road. Spiritual desolation & mental pain & anxiety torture me so I can hardly pray. If this is, as I believe, God's acceptance of my offering for my sister's safety, I thank Him heartily for it. In that case, "Amplius Domine amplius" [More, O Lord, more]. May He give me assurance that it is for her, & patience to bear it,—& then it can't get too severe to please me. As Lieutenant of the Sacred Heart, I fight for my sister, the Bride of the Sacred Heart, whom He chose first from the nation that chose Him as its last & greatest Chief. The harder & more painful the fight, the better I am pleased,—so all the wounds fall on me, & I conquer in the end. As He gave His blood for her, so I give mine, even to the last drop.

An Inspector is here—a Col. Malette. F. Martin came, & returned at once. Rumor that Kemp & Ryan reported to the Agent.

Friday, Dec. 7th

Said mass at 9 A.M. Had to prepare everything, & then the cold made me numb, & sick, & slow. I went to the school to get hosts, & said mass in church. Intention first for my sister Josie, who will be received as a child of Mary at Avoca tomorrow, & second, for my sisters Emma [Halsey] & Annie [Pleets], who will take the white veil as novices at Zell, D.T. After mass I took the maniple [a long silk band worn over the left forearm of a priest at Mass], to be mended, to the school. Told John Pleets that he & George must receive [Holy Eucharist] tomorrow for Annie, our sister. Merril tells me that the charges against the agent are for employing known bad characters, specifying Joe Primeau, Sport, & Geo. Faribault. Unless the present inspector differs much from others who have been here, the rascals will escape. However, if God wishes to expose them, & punish them for annulling the work of His Church, & destroying so many souls, they can't well manage to evade His vengeance.

Received Telegram from Mrs. Parkins. Mrs Galpin worse, & wants to see me. Will get butcher's team & go tomorrow. They could have foreseen this, as I did, & saved me a long trip at a busy time. Perhaps Satan, who inspired their attack on priests & sisters, would like to stop what I expect to get by saying mass tomorrow. If so, he will fail. Mr. Wells came in. I received a letter from Annie

Gaudreau, my sister [at Avoca], enclosing a hymn to the Sacred Heart, taken from the Messenger of the Sacred Heart. It is a love song, to the melody & in the spirit of "Meet me Tonight." Instead of being out of place, by contradiction of words & melody, it is professedly & openly a love song to the Sacred Heart, & is, for us, most appropriate & proper. I shall take care to meet little sisters there very often, as it is about the only place where those who love the Sacred Heart can meet in peace. We are not of the world, & our meetings & conversations should be neither in nor of the world. In the Heart of Jesus we can meet in peace & learn to love each other with the love of the Sacred Heart,—the love of sacrifice,—that helps to temper, & form & harden us, as fire tempers & forms & hardens good steel, that we may do & suffer much for Jesus & for each other, & neither bend nor break in all our battles for the glory of the Sacred Heart. Went to confession to F. Bede.

Saturday, Dec. 8th—Feast of Im[maculate]. Conc[e]pt[ion]. B.V.M.

Said mass at 8 A.M. Principal intention for my sister Josephine, second for Emma [Halsey] & Annie [Pleets], etc. Today Josie becomes a child of Mary, & Emma & Annie take the white veil. Josie is not left out,—God's ways are not the ways of men. F. Bede sang high mass at 9 A.M., & had the Immaculate Conception Sodality take their veils & read their act of consecration for the first time. I did not stay to see it, as I had to leave for Parkins at 9 A.M. I reached there at 12:30 M. Mrs. Galpin sleeping or unconscious. Woke when I came, & went to confession. I would not take dinner, but rested & fed the team, & left at 3 P.M. & reached the Agency at 7 P.M. Used butcher's team & Welch's military ambulance wagon.

Sunday, Dec. 9th

Said mass at 9 A.M. Lila confessed. F. Bede sung high mass at 10:30. I preached on Immaculate Conception explaining also Mary's exemption from "debitum proximum et remotum contrahendi originale peccatorum" [the proximate and remote debt of contracting (incurring) original sin]. Inspector Malett is a Catholic & went to mass.

Monday, Dec. 10th

. . . Sent goods from Coles' & Douglas' to Emeran. Those from Coles charged to Emeran, & those from Douglas' charged to Catholic Indian Bureau. Met Inspector, & gave him my views on the Indian question. Introduced him & Major Brown to Wm. Halsey. Inspector won't do much,—none of them will. It is a general whitewashing affair. Our appeal must be made to the people, who are, really, the Government. Called at McLaughlins to see Hermanie Cournoyer, whom I found there, & after enquiring at Primeau's. I wanted to ask about measles at Mrs. Van Solen's. From her account, it is not measles. From the conversation at McLaughlin's, I should judge that all the talk against Germans, religious, etc. has emanated from there. They seem anxious to degrade the servants of God, to be the slaves of His enemies. I gave them much sharp, sound advice, & talked chiefly on spiritual matters. Poor Rosa & Hermanie came here with the best intentions, but they are fast being spoiled & turned against their faith & its representatives. May God & His Holy Mother protect them & defend them against Satan & his allies, who seek to pervert these poor little ones of Christ. If all Catholic Pharisees on the Agency had been plunged into the Missouri or the sea, or into the depths of hell, with a millstone about their necks, things would now be in a better state. We expect the world to hate us, who are not of it; but it is hard to see our little ones perverted & turned against us. May the Sacred Heart of Jesus interfere & save them, before it is too late. I have told F. Bede of all this, but he is too weak & fearful,—& besides, has too little love for a secular priest. He fears even that his brother Benedictine of another house, F. Jerome, may get credit for some of the work done here. Had he & F. Martin more manly honor & priestly grace, we could do much here; but they fear men rather than God, & this, with their jealousy & suspicion, betrays God's Church to the enemy. I am determined to fight for God's honor; & though according to the rules of worldly "prudence," my course no doubt, seems rash & foolish; & there is every chance that the Bishop & my brother priests will turn against me & plot with the enemy to destroy me; still, I can't believe that God will allow them to succeed, even for a time, as I fight His battles, & trust to His honor for my safety. He has ordered my advance; he holds my reserves & overlooks the field. Can He see me wounded, surrounded, fighting desperately to keep His colors from being disgraced by this enemies' touch,—& yet withhold aid, while I am cut to pieces, & His colors carried off & dishonored? Such conduct in man would be everything that is low & base & dishonorable, & will God act so? Impossible. He may withhold aid to give me the victory, as the father of the Black Prince did,—through love & wisdom; but He surely will order up the reserves if He sees me too hard pressed. If I, His poor soldier & Lieutenant, hold His honor so sacred as to give up my life & my blood for it, & do desperate things at His order, trusting in His honor to aid me, will He regard it less? Perhaps, even now, He is striking the enemy; though wounds, & weakness, & blood, blind me as I do not see anything far off. O modicae fidei! Et quid dabitasti? [O you weak in faith! Why did you doubt?][24] En avant Santa Maria. [Forward for St. Mary.]

F. Bede tells me Sr. Gertrude wants to see me about altar linen, etc. I'll go tomorrow. Telegram from St. Paul. Storm coming. We only got a high N.W. wind & low temperature.

Thursday, Dec. 11th

Said mass of the Sacred Heart for Josie & also Annie [Pleets] & Emma [Halsey] at 7 A.M. Called on the school & got altar-linen from Sister Gertrude. Wrote to Muhlbauer & Behrle, F. Jerome, Josie & Annie, & F. Pius[25] at Crow Creek. I find that the Inspector has changed his plan, & will visit Crow Creek first. Rosa Cournoyer's talk against the German Benedictines there has, no doubt,

[24] Matt. 14:31.

[25] Craft's letter to Father Pius Boehm, OSB, warns him of a possible visit by Inspector Mallet (Craft to Boehm, 11 December 1888, St. Meinrad Archabbey Archives.

reached his ears. I must be beforehand with them, & therefore I wrote to warn F. Pius. B.[rother] Nicholas [Enz] came from the mission. F. Bede received $10.00 from F. Martin, sent, at their request, by Mother Gertrude, from Yankton. It is the money I gave Sr. Anselmein, & with which she paid Josie's fare back from Zell. F. Bede knew I would refuse to take it, & therefore offered it in presence of others, hoping I would take it to save "giving him away." I joked him off until the others left, & then told him I would not take the price of the sister's blood, as it would be so, if she should fail to persevere. He left the money on the table, & I also left it there, & there it may lie till some one steals it, if they will. I told him to send it back. Brother Nicholas has trouble at the mission. They're all queer. Today Rosa & Hermanie were to go to Goose's camp. I hear they went.

Wednesday, Dec 12th

Did not say mass. Too cold in church. I don't mind the pain, but should not risk my health. This morning the money still laid on the table. At last, F. Bede, finding I would not take it, sent it to F. Martin. I wrote to Rev. Mother Gertrude, & explained the whole affair. Their espirit de corps is confined to their order, & don't extend to the whole Church. They plot against me, & persecute my poor sister, while they might be better employed in maintaining the dignity of the priesthood against the low wretches who try to trample on them. . . .

Thursday, Dec. 13th

F. Bede went to visit Adele Cadotte. She seems to be dying. I will delay sending the letter to Rev. M. Gertrude. I don't like to let them see at Yankton the discords existing here. Frs. Martin & Bede may yet come to their senses. If they don't, it will be time to write. If they could forget jealousy awhile, & resolve to defend God's interests instead of slavishly submitting to God's enemies,—nothing could stop our prosperity. I rode to Wells, & brought up Givens mail. Said rosary on horseback. Left Agency at 10 A.M. & arrived at 4 P.M. Went with Mr. Wells in buggy to Parkins.

Mrs. Galpin worse, but does not care to confess, as she can remember nothing, as she tells us. I will see her tomorrow. They want mass said in the house. I refuse, telling them that we must protect our Lord from insult, & not allow Him to be used as a convenience,—as He puts Himself helpless in our hands. Where there is faith & reverence, we do not fear insults for him; but where the reverse is manifested, as in slandering His clergy, we must stay strict, & withdraw what we could otherwise grant. In the Catholic Church we do not allow the laity to override & degrade us, as they do in the Russo–Greek Church. They listen with exterior submission, whatever they may <u>feel</u>.

I returned with Wells from Parkins. Mr. Stewart came from Mandan, with a white woman. They went to Givens'. Stewart brought for me the blank application for half-fare permit on N.[orthern] P.[acific] R. R. Went with Wells to Givens' & got blank from Stewart. Agnes Comes-last came with her mother to beg tobacco, & stole a pen-knife.

Friday, Dec. 14th

Gave instruction to scholars, on prayer & mass, & announced mass for Sunday. About 50 present. Rode to Parkins'. Mrs. Galpin worse. Gave her plenary indulgence (in art. mort.) & left holy water for her. The other side is becoming paralyzed. She seems to recognize no one.

In the evening "Crazy-man" came & told a bear story of "ye older time," & showed scars on his leg where a bear bit him.

Saturday, Dec. 15th

Went to Parkins to see Mrs. Galpin. Coma has fairly set in. She moans, but her face expresses no consciousness of pain, & the increase of the paralysis shows effusion in the brain is already far advanced. Gave her the blessing for the sick. Returned to Wells & cleared up the school room for mass tomorrow. Cauwape brought back the pen-knife that Agnes stole. Walking-bird's children are capable of much good, but they are being destroyed by evil influence. It's hard to think that parents would deliberately corrupt their children, but here we see it.

Sunday, Dec. 16th

Said mass at 10:30 A.M. About 100 present. Preached on Advent. Coming of Christ at mass, & again when he calls us at our death. Developed a big discourse on death. All took it well. Things are gradually on the mend. The return of the Indians to a right way of thinking, seems to be in direct proportion to the degree of their falling out with [George] Faribault, whose ways & views are becoming more clear to them.

Went to Parkins to see Mrs. Galpin. Slowly getting weaker. Susan Primeau is there. Took no notice of her. These wretches, with Faribault, have been the cause of all the late troubles with the Indians, & have caused many to die without the sacraments. Mrs. Wells went to sit up with Mrs. Galpin. I could not allow Agnes Comes-last to enter mass with the rest. She has not yet made amends for the insult to the picture of the B.V.M.

Monday, Dec. 17th

Said mass at 7 A.M. & cleared away the altar. Mrs. Wells returned from Parkins. Went to see Mrs. Galpin. Still growing weaker. Coma. Wells worked at & cleaned the well & pump. Made out a list of scholars, & their tickets to enable them to get something in the issue. This day school business is a great humbug, as far as any real benefit to the children is concerned.

Tuesday, Dec. 18th

Finished & sent off a list of scholars for the Agent. Mr. Wells went to Fort Rice, & I took the school for him. Dismissed at 2:30 P.M. & went to see Mary Aniwin. Measles. Gave her some beef & tea. The men of the family were making a sweat for her. I went to see Mrs. Galpin. Blessed holy water for her, & gave her the last absolution. She was near death today. They sent for Mrs. Givens to help lay her out, but did not send for me. I went without being called. These people are <u>superficial</u> in all they do,—in their affections as well as their religion. Their one end seems to be to do just enough to satisfy public opinion. That seems to be their God, & from it they will probably get condemnation instead of the reward they expect. Wells returned.

Wednesday, Dec. 19th

I learned that Mrs. Galpin died at 9 P.M. last night. So she got the last absolution just in time,—but no thanks to her surroundings. God overlooks all. It seems as if He calls someone before Him to report, whenever His Church is attacked here. Remained quiet today to rest horse for trip to Agency tomorrow. . . .

Thursday, Dec. 20th

Rode to Agency. Left at 11 A.M. & arrived at 2:30 P.M. Passed Parkins' family bringing in Mrs. Galpins body. F. Bede went to & returned from Mission. Called on sisters to see if F. Bede had left word. Told them of Mrs. Van Solen's & the others' talk against sisters, & how I stopped them. Sister Adele thinks it's not the right way to do. She don't believe in defending ourselves & our Church.

So I have defended the "German Benedictines" from their enemies, & get no thanks. Never mind. I shall continue. It's God's cause more than theirs, & He will approve it. Frosted told me [George] Faribault would go to St. Joseph's meeting to say something,—probably unpleasant. Wakan-yuha told him. I told Wakan-yuha to say to Faribault that St. Joseph's was neither a police nor a work society, but a Catholic society. The priests are its directors, & without their order, Faribault must not go there. If he persists, I will inform the Agent, & if he don't stop it, I will go to the Commanding Officer at Yates.

I learned afterwards that F. Bede had consented to let Faribault go there to say that he was not opposing the society. I protested, but he won't listen. Faribault's intentions are to hurt us. The young men know it, & will think F. Bede is aiding him, & I must confess it does look as if he aids him against me & the Society through moral cowardice. F. Martin, his superior, is, of course, responsible. Their cowardice, with their jealousy, will, as of old, lead them to yield God's interests to His enemies, & try to join those enemies in driving all not of their house & order from their place, that they alone may have all. As they act towards F. Jerome & others, so I see they act towards me. I won't go, & God must sustain me, & open their eyes to the folly they are guilty of. To keep enemies from thinking that we differ in views, I sent word to Wakan-yuha that F. Bede would be at the meeting to watch Faribault, & that it would be all right. If he said anything that F. Bede could not understand they must tell me & I would explain to him. May God expose & defeat the plots of His enemies. I will fight as well as I can for Him, & trust to Him to aid me. . . .

Friday, Dec. 21st

Last night I got the Ordo[26] from Muhlbauer & Behrle. I wrote to George Peoples, enclosing application for ½ fare permit on N. Pacific R. R. asking him to identify me at the ticket Agent's office. I wrote also to G. W. Gahin at Eureka, thanking him for ½ fare permit. I sent to F. Kerwick some Indian trinkets bought at Angevine's. I rode to Cadotte's to see Adele. Very weak. May die at any time. She seems happy & resigned. Wrote letters for her & Nick to her sister, Mrs. Harriet Dupuis, at Cheyenne Agency. Came back to Agency, & wrote address to letter & sent it off. Gave Zatela, who came with Mary, an order for tripe, etc. at butchers. He promises to give me a full account of his view of Indian customs. Met Wells, just come in for his cattle trial. Instructed him how to give a form of oath to the Indians, which, in their present state, they would be likely to regard. [George] Faribault is trying to pose as the champion of the Indians, & hold Wells & everyone else up as their enemies, to gain his own ends, & keep them from exposing his buying of branded cattle, & other vagaries. Explained this to Wells.

[26] A list of offices and feasts for the liturgical year.

Saturday, Dec. 22d

Hermanie & Rosa Cournoyer & Rachael Faribault came to F. Bede. I explained to them the stand I have taken towards the Primeaus, Faribault, Mrs. Van Solen, etc., & Rosa's meanness in causing the inspector to go to Crow Creek prejudiced against the German Benedictines. I explained to them the Sacrament of Penance, & exposed the hypocrisy of those Catholics who go to the sacraments while continuing to slander priests & sisters, & seriously injure them in the opinion of others, & yet never think of either contrition or making satisfaction. Both seemed ashamed.

High Bear came with Goodwood's rejected wife. Referred him to the Agent. Peter Hehaka-ouzinca & Leo Hehaka-gi came up. Gave medal of St. Benedict to Peter's little girl. Met Mary Mad Bear, with her mother & sister. She seemed glad to see me, & came to shake hands quite cordially. Borrowed $7.00 in cash from Douglas, & got my bill, & that of C.[atholic] Ind.[ian] Bureau. Wrote to Muhlbauer & Behrle (registered) & enclosed amount of bill in full, $4.75, & also wrote to Director of Apostleship of Prayer & Editor of Messenger of Sacred Heart, Woodstock, Md. (registered) enclosing $2.00 for Messenger for one year, to be sent to me till further notice, & asking directions for aggregating person & societies to Apostleship of Prayer, & recommending intentions. 1. Vocation & perseverance for Josie [Crowfeather], Annie [Pleets], Giles [Tapetola], & Emma Archambeau. 2. Removal of obstacles to their vocation. 3. A particular intention,—all about Josie's vocation, & money to bring her through. My offering for her. That she may die rather than lose her vocation or fail. That she may never return here, except as a sister—persevering. Giving her to the Sacred Heart as His spouse.—In fact, all my intentions for her. 4. Removal of obstacles to the conversion & civilization of the tribes of the Sioux nation. 5. Spiritual & temporal welfare of six families: Crowfeathers', mine, Pranges', Wells', Wm. Halseys', & Pleets'. 6. Perseverance of two novices, Emma & Annie.

I gave Crowfeather 3 undershirts for Josie's little brother. His eyes are very sore. I told him to stay either at Police Quarters or at Sport's, & I would get the doctor to treat him; & if he should fail, I would get the Post doctors. He will let me know tomorrow what he will do. I met Ida, Hohekte's wife. She says Martha is getting better. Met Wells again. His trial was to come off at 2 P.M. [George] Faribault is trying to defeat him, & help the guilty party, & the Agent sides with Faribault. Plenty of corruption here, & little else. Met poor old Primeau. He noticed I treated him coldly. I told him why,—the conduct of his family towards the Church, & me, especially. He protested innocence. I don't doubt him, but would rather F. Bede would be his confessor for the future, for decency' sake. However, if the poor man insists, I won't refuse him.

Howard Coles, a Protestant, says there are only two real Catholics on the Agency,—men who try to do their duty & don't slander their priests, & those two are Barney Prange & Dr. Caskie. It seems Protestants see pretty clearly, & are more Catholic than some Catholics. Fire call sounded at 6 P.M. Fort bake-house on fire, but soon put out. Herr & F.[rank] Steinmetz came up as usual.

Sunday, Dec. 23d

Said 1st mass at 9 A.M. F. Bede sang high mass at 10:30 A.M. I preached on Epistle, showing identity of the spirit that presumed to judge & condemn Christ & His Apostles, & now acts in the same way towards His church. At 1 P.M. St. Joseph's Society met. I protested again to F. Bede against allowing [George] Faribault to go. He took Faribault's part like the cowardly traitor to the Church that he has ever shown himself. I intended to go, & expose Faribault, but if I do, F. Bede will take his part openly, & thus make matters worse. I concluded not to go, & told F. Bede so, telling him why. I went to tell the Society I would not go, & I saw there John McLaughlin. He has no right there, & goes as a spy. I told them that if I went I would give Faribault a tongue-lashing & put him out. F. Bede allowed him to go & would be with him. I therefore could not do so, & had better not be present. Besides, as a priest I could not submit to the indignity of sitting to hear a discourse from a well known enemy of the Church,—an insolent layman & slanderer of priests, whom we all knew as such. They agreed that I was right. I told Mr. Halsey to post F. Bede as to Faribault's talk. It turned out just as I expected. F. Bede says that Faribault asked what he had ever said against the Society, & none but Frosted answered him. He said the Society had grown less, because they got no help from Agent, etc., & advised them to go ahead without expecting any help. It is plain that he meant to show them that they would get none, but their enemies would. Frosted answered him very sensibly, that, while they formed the Society chiefly to save their souls, still the secondary object was their temporal advancement. Government & its employees had certain privileges, & aids, & offices to give, & it was the intention of Government to give them to those only who deserved them; & who deserved them if not the members of the Society, who had bound themselves to cast off old ways, & become civilized, & had actually done so. Hitherto the old "dance & superstition element" had been aided by Faribault & the Agent, & the Society discouraged. This is wrong. Frosted deserves much credit for his action. Faribault did not attempt to reply. F. Bede in telling me of it, pretended not to have understood Frosted's speech; but I heard it all afterwards from Frosted & others. I proved to F. Bede how he must be fully aware that Faribault had slandered & tried to injure me, & was bound to reparation, & that, as his confessor he should hold him to it, & defend the interests of the Church & God, if he had any manliness & priestly grace left. He has to admit it all, but still strives to excuse Faribault. If all were like F. Bede, there would be no martyrs, & soon no faith, & no Church. Called at school & asked Sr. Gertrude about book for Barney. Warned her against the Cournoyers.

Brought from Barney to F. Bede the formula of the consecration of the Dakota nation to the Sacred Heart, the oath of allegiance, etc., read last New Year's, which we will renew at high mass on Christmas. Frank Steinmetz, Herr, & an Irish soldier came up to F. Bede's in the evening. Herr brought F. Bede a turkey. F. Bede visited Adele Codotte. Sinking. I will take her communion tomorrow. Crowfeather did not come. I fear, from all I see, that F. Bede does not like to have F. Martin here too often, & deceives him as to the real state of the Agency. F. Martin should examine into the conduct of his subordinates, & his natural shrewdness, if not common prudence, would surely lead him to change their course. These good people will yet have a terrible row amongst themselves, & disgrace the mission as in the past. I fear there is little use in aiding & defending them. Barney Prange & his wife were at F. Bede's this afternoon.

Monday, Dec. 24th

Took communion to Adele Cadotte. Dying, but cheerful. Told her that as her uncle & her brother in the Sacred Heart, I would do all I could for her; & if God would let her send me word in some way, I would say masses for her, or suffer for her, as far as He wishes to release her from Purgatory. I also went to see Winyola, wife of Ho-waste, in the Hunkpati camp. Very sick, but won't let me do anything for her. Promises to think it over, & let F. Bede & Sr. Gertrude do something for her when they can come to see her. I found Crowfeather in his tent, beyond the Fort. His eyes are better. If he does not soon recover he will come again & remain here for treatment. Heard confessions until time for midnight mass. Went to midnight mass & staid till after consecration.

Tuesday, Dec. 25th 1888 Christmas

After mass, slept till 6 A.M. F. Bede said his masses at midnight & at 6:30 in church, & at 7:00 in the school. I said mine at 7:00 & 7:30, consecutively (rather later, owing to F. Bede's being later than he intended), & sang high mass at 10:00 A.M. Preached (in Sioux) on Nativity, showing how our Lord preferred the gift of the hearts & little lambs of the poor, to the gold, etc. of the rich Magi. He was announced to the poor shepherds by angels, but to the Magi by a star only. We too are poor & have only our hearts & the lambs of the Sacred Heart (the children) to offer. We will first do as the shepherds did, & lastly will offer the gifts of the Kings—the last "royal chieftainship" of the Dakotas. Then we read & renewed the consecration to the Sacred Heart of last January, with the oaths of allegiance, & the transfer of the chieftainship from me to the Sacred Heart. Then I announced, formally, that the Sacred Heart of Jesus was now our "Royal Chief." In opening the sermon, I addressed the Indians as the "Nation of the Sacred Heart," & announced to them, as the angels did, a great joy, in the birth of Christ long ago at Bethlehem, & again today, on the altar, at mass.

Our societies came in full force. Took dinner at the school, & again at Barney's. Ellen Brown gave me a pair of cuffs & stockings. Dr. Caskie gave me a writing desk. Jack & Mrs. Carignan & Maude came to Pranges', & Mrs. C. & Maude stayed there. Received from Mother a bag worked by Fanny for Josephine, & a New Year's card. I offered all my masses for Josephine.

Wednesday, Dec. 26th

Perfumed bag, & sent it with letter to Josephine, & the card to Annie Gaudreau. Wrote also to Mother & Miles Gibbons. Met Joseph LaCroix, Mr. Wells' nephew. Mr. Wells went home. Went to school & took up express package for Sister Mary Mechtild. Visited children sick with measles, & one with erysipelas [an acute skin disease]. Tried to persuade Maude to receive [Holy Eucharist] on Feast of Holy Innocents [December 28]. I hear that Rosa Cournoyer was crying bitterly in Church on Sunday, & at midnight mass. I will willingly forgive her, & aid her in every way, if I can see my way clear to it. I would do much for her, if I could only trust her. She will yet find it to her interest to cast off the enemies of the Church, & come to us for aid & sympathy. Frank Steinmetz was at Barney's. Talked till late, & came back to F. Bede's at 11 P.M. Said rosary & went to bed. . . .

Thursday, Dec. 27th

Adele Cadotte died at 6 A.M. F. Bede went up after her death to say the prayers for her. I hope she is safe, & that I can aid her if she needs it. Hermanie & Rosa Cournoyer seem to have gone to their school. I don't see them around anywhere. Visited children at the school, with Dr. Caskie.

Friday, Dec. 28th

Visited children at the school with Dr. Caskie. Some cases seem to threaten catarrhal pneumonia. Frank Steinmetz came up in the evening. At 9:30 P.M. Topuna came with a message from Mrs. McLaughlin that Ed Kangi-ska [White Crow] was dying, & wanted to see a priest. He has hitherto refused to marry rightly, & now, though dying of consumption, his case is doubtful. However, I went, leaving our chance of success to our Commander, the Sacred Heart. I found him well disposed. His wife hesitated, but finally yielded. Mrs. McLaughlin instructed her in Pleets' house, while I heard Ed's confession. He was very deaf, & I had to send everybody out. I was very reluctant to send his sister out, as she had the measles, but I had to. I then called all in & baptized the wife, & married them, & then anointed Ed & gave plenary indulgence, in art. mort., & gave him the scapular, & a picture of the Sacred Heart. So four sacraments were given together. Baptism, Penance, Extreme Unction, & Matrimony. I got back in time to say the Rosary, at 11:30 P.M.

Saturday, Dec. 29th

Ed Kangi-ska [White Crow] seems much better. Sits up, & seems not so deaf. Heard his confession again, & gave him Viaticum, & received him into St. Joseph's Society. We buried Adele Cadotte at 10:00 A.M. I sang requiem high mass, & was much disturbed by the shouts & yells of Indians & soldiers slaughtering the beef close by, for the "big Killing." Knowing their custom well, I could see in imagination the rush to cut out the tongues, when all the cattle were shot down,—the steers, with tongues cut out, or half severed from the throat, long before dead or senseless, rising, mad with pain, & charging their tormentors; until several better aimed shots brought them down, & put an end to their torments. It was not a pleasant distraction. In the cemetery, some old squaws started the usual camp yell. I stopped them, & explained that we should pray for with hope,—not yell with despair like pagans, especially as she was not like others.

After the funeral, Ed Kangi-ska died. I got in in time to give last absolution. I went for a coffin. He will be buried by St. Joseph's Society tomorrow afternoon. The society men dug his grave. I visited the children at the school, with the doctor. Mrs. Carignan & Maude went to confession.

Sunday, Dec. 30th

Low mass, with Exposition [of the Blessed Sacrament], Rosary, Te Deum, Act of Consecration & Homage to Sacred Heart (St. Gertrude's), & Benediction, all for Sacred Heart. We anticipated one day, the closing exercises for the Pope's Jubilee. I gave a short instruction on the Sacred Heart. Explaining that as our Lord reserved the devotion to the Sacred Heart as a last effort to gain men, in their last days, so the Sovereign Pontiff reserved these devotions to the Sacred Heart as a last effort to gain souls at the close of his Jubilee, the whole object of which was to bring us to a sincere reception of the Sacraments.

Visited the school with the Doctor, some cases of catarrhal pneumonia. Called F. Bede & got him to anoint one. He hesitates to anoint the others, saying others may laugh if he does it so soon. I explained to him that the sacrament is to cure the body too, & the rule is to give it, while there is yet time to benefit by its healing effects, & that we should go on without regard to the contrary views of the world.[27] It won't do to delay & regard what others say, & thus deprive our little ones of spiritual & temporal benefits. Mrs. Carignan & Maude & all the Cadottes except Willie & wife received at mass. I heard the confessions of Cadottes, & told them to offer the indulgence for Adele. In the afternoon we buried Ed Kangi-ska.

[27] In 1991, some hundred years later, the Catholic Church clarified the sacrament of extreme unction to encompass the healing of the sick, incorporating a ceremony for the seriously ill that takes place in church.

Monday, Dec. 31st

I said mass at 8 A.M. in honor of Sacred Heart & according to His intentions, & gave plenary indulgence. Emeran served & received. Barney & Mrs. Prange also received. Wakan-yuha's child died today. I caught old Red Fish giving his medicine, & protested quite strongly, yesterday, but they refused to listen. I let them know what I thought of it. In the evening, Wakan-yuha came to beg a candle. He seemed to be drunk, & could scarcely articulate. The Doctor left medicines here for him. Emeran took them down to his house. He came again this morning to say the child was dead.

Emeran received his pay. $300.00 for 6 months. I took his check to Douglas' & paid what I had got for him, $97.42, & gave him the balance, $202.58. I borrowed of Douglas $2.25 & paid Angevine in full. I went to the school in the morning & saw children, & got medicine from Doctor. He was reluctant to give it. I talked as if he was perhaps out of it, & offered to buy it in Bismarck. That bought it. It's plain the poor get less sympathy & care than the rich,—except for priests & sisters. I went to Hunkpati camp & baptized a child that had measles. I went again in evening to see children. F. Bede anointed Cunegunda[28] & gave her Viaticum, after which she was much better. She has great devotion to the Sacred Heart. Sacraments are the best physicians. I went again at 8:30 P.M. to see children. All better, Cunegunda weak, but improved much.

Tuesday, January 1st, 1889

I said mass at 9 A.M. & wished all a Happy New Year, in the name of the Sacred Heart. Benediction[29] of the Blessed Sacrament after mass. Last night there was a dance in the Agency Council Hall, given by Agency employees. I notice that Mrs. Clement, Maude Carignan, & Mrs. Prange did not dance round dances. I went to the school & helped take care of the children. Cunegunda

[28] How Black Bear's daughter came to be called Cunegunda is a mystery. St. Cunegunda was an eleventh-century Bavarian saint with patronage in Lithuania, Luxembourg, and Poland. She sponsored a monastery for Benedictine nuns in 1025, so the name may stem from the Benedictine sisters at Fort Yates.

[29] A ceremony during which the priest exposes the Holy Eucharist for public adoration.

is growing worse, but may improve. Case of catarrhal pneumonia in lungs filled with tubercles. Gave pledge from now to Christmas eve next, to John Hughes. Frank Steinmetz was at Barney's at dinner. Cadottes want masses said for Adele. We gave the $2.00 Nick gave us to old Mr. Cadotte as a New Year's gift, & will say the masses without honoraria. I wrote to Josephine.

Wednesday, Jan. 2d

Said mass for Adele at 7 A.M. Went to the school & took care of the children. Black Bear, (Cunegunda's father) came twice to see her, & wanted her to take Indian medicine. She, & we all, refused. His visits excited her very much. We advised him as kindly as possible to go, & let her rest, but he would not, until she herself insisted on it. She was much weaker after his visit. She slept a little after the Blessing for the Sick, which I gave her. I set up with her until 11:00 P.M. F. Bede gave her viaticum again, & consecrated her to Our Lady of Perpetual Help. I vowed 7 masses to the Sacred Heart, according to His intentions, if He would cure her, leaving it to Him to do as He thinks best, & most for her good. . . .

Thursday, Jan. 3d

Went at 7 A.M. to see Cunegunda. She had a hard night & is restless & delirious. Her father came again. I coaxed him away with an order for coffee & sugar, but let him in on the doctor's recommendation & his promise not to stay long. He staid too long again, & she had to tell him again to go. She sank rapidly after this. She was too weak for more opiates. I heard her confession & gave her a Plenary Indulgence. She named the girls several times. The sisters left me with her. I was about to give her brandy & water, & her pulse was imperceptible. She called to me "Be quick, Father, please be quick." I saw she was dying, after I lifted her higher on the pillows, & instead of giving the brandy, I called the sisters, put on the stole, & after repeating an act of contrition, & "Jesus, Mary, & Joseph help me" as a penance, I gave her the last absolution, & said the prayers for the dying. I sent for F. Bede. He came before she died. She passed away quietly & happily at a quarter before 11

A.M. I thought before she was too sick, of having her take her vows, as she has a vocation, but, fortunately, Sister Superior had already allowed her to do so yesterday, giving her the name of Sister Mary Aloysia, at her own request. I added "of the Sacred Heart."

How shall I thank our Lord for His kindness? May He help Josephine, too. Sister Mary Aloysia promised to ask it when she sees our Lord. I had recommended to her all my intentions, & all affairs here. She remembers me, I know. Hardly had she passed away, when F. Bede was called to see [George] Faribault who is very sick. He seems alarmed at his wicked conduct towards the church, & me especially. I reported her death to the Agent, & took her measure, & went to Barney for a coffin. Sister Gertrude called me over to prevent her father, grandfather, & grandmother from carrying off the body. I stopped them. Her father went to the Agent, but got no satisfaction. He came back, & I gave them a little lecture, & pacified them, & all shook hands, & parted better friends than ever. I fast today for sister. To do some penance for her, & also to thank the Sacred Heart for His great mercy to her. I swallowed the matter she had coughed & vomited.[30] It don't seem to nauseate me. I ought to be proud to do something for my sister, the bride of my Chief, the Sacred Heart of Jesus. So, sweet sister,—the first "Lily of the Sacred Heart" the New Year gave Him,—blooming in the midst of winter's snow, far whiter, purer, & holier than snow or earthly lilies. Ven.[erable] Sister Mary Aloysia of the Sacred Heart of Jesus, OSB, rest in peace in the eternal happiness you have gained, & pray for poor brother, still fighting hard & desperately for the Chief & his Church.

Dr. Caskie wants to intercede for George Faribault. I'll gladly overlook his misdeeds, if he atones for them & <u>when</u> he atones,—

[30] Separating Father Craft from his contemporaries was an aberrant penchant for penitential sacrifice that defies any modern-day understanding. His medical training may have given him some assurance that his digestive system was stronger than the contaminated cuspidors (he repeats this sacrifice on Jan. 11, 1889), or perhaps he was influenced by the publicity given to Louis Pasteur's experiments with vaccines. But when he later writes of resolutely "kissing little brothers' and sisters' sore eyes," some with ulcerated and broken corneas, we can perhaps identify with the tradition of kissing an injury to make it well.

but not till then. As a priest, I must not only fight for the Church, but must have sense enough not to let the enemy gain by fraud, what they can't by force. May sister pray for my success. Mr. Herr & a friend from the Fort stole up here, in spite of the military quarantine against measles. Black Bear came to ask me to write two letters for him. I filled a pipe for him & consoled him.

Ven. Sister Mary Aloysia of the Sacred Heart, OSB, took her vows at 12 years of age, as did Sisters Agnes & Cecelia, & offered herself as "a sacrifice of holy love," almost with her last breath. Her death seems to give consolation instead of sorrow, & strengthens my faith in the Sacred Heart. I loved her as my sister, but infinitely more when I saw her devotion to the Sacred Heart, & learned that she was His bride by religious consecration. Surely she is with me in the Sacred Heart. The Heart of Jesus unites those who love each other for His sake & in Him, far more closely than anything in the mere natural order, &, now that she seems nearer to me than before, & I love her more than ever, & feel that her happiness is mine. I am certain that the Heart of Jesus has done this. I keep the picture of the Sacred Heart which I gave her, & which she kissed so fervently when dying. It seems to bring me nearer to Jesus, &, in His Holy Heart, to my sweet sister. She is not dead to me. She does not even sleep. She has passed from a life of sympathy with me & my work here, to the more active life of intercession for me with Jesus, Mary & Joseph in heaven. "Say to your sister, 'Thou hast obtained mercy.'"[31] Sweet sister in the Sacred Heart, remember brother, from whose hands Jesus received your spirit. May he accept Josephine & me, as He has accepted you.

Friday, Jan. 4th

Brought black antependium[32] & Holy water vase & aspergil[33] to the school. F. Bede sang requiem for sister in the school chapel at 7 A.M. I served. I afterwards said mass for her also in the chapel.

[31] Hosea 2:1.

[32] The curtain or tapestry that covers the entire front of the altar.

[33] An aspergillum is the metal or wooden rod that is used to sprinkle holy water as the priest blesses the altar, congregation, or both.

Before requiem mass I sat by the body & said a rosary for sister, & then helped the sisters put the body in the coffin, & carry it to the chapel. We laid her out in the school room, that her relatives & the children might see her. I gave her a last kiss, until I meet her again, & then went to see that no mistake was made about grave or box to enclose the coffin. Sure enough it was made too short. I sent White Crow with a hammer to the cemetery, to be ready to avoid delay. We had to knock out the foot of the box to get the coffin into it. I served at the funeral. . . .

Saturday, Jan. 5th

Visited children at the school with the Doctor. Indians getting their beef. Dr. Caskie wants to make peace in the Faribault case. I insist that [George] Faribault shall withdraw his threat of making attacks on me, & apologize for it, & then say in presence of Crazy-walking, Wm. Halsey, Mad-bear, Victor Frosted, & High-bear, that he is sorry for the past, & will not attack me or any other priest or sister,—thus committing himself to a non-aggressive policy. I am sure he won't do it, but they seem to think he will. F. Bede said in presence of Dr. Caskie that I ought to give up my Indian relatives, because such men as Faribault don't like it,—though he admits I am right. He also says that the Bishop don't like it. I resented it sharply, & took an oath not to give them up, to make matters stronger. I also told F. Bede, after Dr. Caskie left, that I didn't like his & F. Martin's conduct towards me, & that I expected that they would either remain passive, or would attack me. F. Bede said that Faribault intended to make foul charges against me. I at once told him that all hope of settlement was now ended. I would defy Satan & his allies, & trust to God, & would also leave his house & lodge at the garrison, as I cannot stay where I can't be in harmony with others.

Sunday, Jan. 6th

F. Bede went to the Mission with Barney. Melda McLaughlin[34] & Rosa Cournoyer came for confession, but F. Bede, not recogniz-

[34] Marie Imelda McLaughlin, 16-year-old daughter of Agent McLaughlin.

ing Melda, put them off. He is afraid now about it. Serves him right. I said both masses (9 & 10:30 A.M.). Preached on feast, & regarding the offering of our hearts to God. I suggested that they should first be purified by the Sacrament of Penance. I visited children at the school. All better. Dr. Caskie reports that [George] Faribault denies all, refuses to retract, or to take a non-aggressive policy, & threatens to make charges of immorality against me if I attack him. He says I, as a priest, have more to lose than he, & should fear such charges. I will teach him that the innocent fear nothing, & that God is with me, & said so to Dr. Caskie, saying that if priests were as anxious to condemn Faribault's course as they are anxious to counsel fear, he would abandon his course. I said that I would now listen to no propositions, but would expose Faribault at once. The Dr. said that mud thrown would stick. I pointed to the crucifix & told him that the wounds & bruises & "uncomeliness" of our crucified Lord are now His brightest ornaments in heaven.

F. Bede came back. He says that he & F. Martin will keep out of this affair. I answered that a passive policy while still dealing with Faribault meant to all men real hostility, & I should quit their house at once. He said it would look bad for them. I answered that they had not spared me, who had spared nothing to defend them in cases of less gravity. They are jealous & suspicious, & would rather see me hurt than help me, that they may possess all. Since they envy me my miseries, they shall have them tenfold, & yet I will not go away.

I heard yesterday that Isnala-wica is back, & that my little sister Ptsanwanyakapi,[35] daughter of Chief Sinte gleska [Spotted Tail], is dead, & also the other children for whom I sent. I rejoiced at Sr. Mary Aloysia's death, but I deeply grieve at theirs. She went to eternal rest, but they, I fear, died unbaptized. May God pity the poor little orphans. I would have taken them, but I was too late. It seems all Benedictines are alike. The Bishop selected the day of

---

[35] Ptsanwanyakapi, which means "White Buffalo," was, coincidentally, also Josephine Crowfeather's name in Lakota.

little Paul's death to attack me; & these attack me about my relatives, when I am heartbroken at their unhappy deaths. May the Sacred Heart, my Chief & Commander set all this right. I have done my best, & will not stop. . . .

Monday, Jan. 7th

Sent by Flying By provisions to Emeran at Grand River. Saw Isnala-wica, & learn that Spotted Tail's children are really dead. Had I been there all would have been well. Those who advise me to abandon my relatives will not care for them. What I don't do, won't be done. If they have no manliness, I must keep mine.

Miss Maude Carignan went to Winona. I began moving my clothes, etc. to Barney's, & when Maude goes to Grand River, I will stay at Barney's while at the Agency. I will stay at Douglas' when Barney has no room. I spoke to McNider to secure lodgings, etc. when needed. It's not safe for me at F. Bede's. He has joined the enemy through cowardice & jealousy, &, to keep the peace, & give God time to settle matters, I had better keep away.

Thursday, Jan. 8th

Children at school all better, & I need not see them any more. I will go to Cannonball as soon as I write some letters, & get all my things moved to Barney's. Soldier came to me at F. Bede's for instruction. Hairy Chin came to say that Indians want my help about land.

Wednesday, Jan. 9th

Dr. Caskie is getting sick. Took Crow-feather to see him, & got medicine for his eyes, which we are to call for tomorrow. Maude went to Grand River. She came back from Winona this morning. I finished moving my things from F. Bede's. I asked the Sisters to make an eye-shade for Crow-feather. I stay at Barney's tonight.

Thursday, Jan. 10th

Began letter to the Bishop. Went with Crow-feather to see Dr. Caskie. Dr. sick in bed, but had put up medicine. I took to the school medicine put up for children. Some still weak, sore throats. I went again to see Dr. as most of the medicine was out, & Sr. Frances asked me to get more. I left a list, & offered to act in his place & let him rest. He can't think of anything tonight, but will answer tomorrow. . . .

Friday, Jan. 11th

Went to Dr. Caskie's. He had filled out direction on list. Mrs. Caskie gave me the dispensary key, & I put up the medicines. I gave John Pleets Epsom salts for his child. Indians wanted medicine for measles. Explained, & gave advice. Went to school & attended children. Gave Crow-feather his eyeshade at the Police quarters. Went again to the school in the evening. As a penance, to obtain from God the recovery of my sick sisters & cousins at the school, I swallowed the pus & mucous from the basin containing it. I got from Hospital Steward medicines not in Agency dispensary.

Saturday, Jan. 12th

Called at John Pleets' to see child. Sore throat. Hard to swallow. Recommended poultice of fat pork. Visited Dr. Caskie, & got medicine for him from the dispensary. Visited children at school. Black Tomahawk came to see Dora. I gave him some tobacco from the store. F. Bede met me in Post Office. He asked me which mass I would say tomorrow. I told him I would hear mass [i.e., attend mass rather than say, or celebrate, mass]. He seemed very anxious to have me say mass at the school, saying that no one would know it. I answered, in Latin, that I feared, not Agency people, but <u>him</u>, & would abstain from all further interference in his affairs, as he has joined the enemy against me,—that I would defend him if necessary, but would give him no excuse to hurt me. Finished letter to Bishop. Sisters think of having a retreat.

Sunday, Jan. 13th

Heard mass at 9 A.M. in gallery in church. Visited scholars at school. Two girls have an erysipelatous flush & swelling on face. I painted it twice with Cinct. Iodine. The children seem timid &

reserved with me, though I treat them kindly. Still they seem to like me. With F. Bede, they romp & play familiarly. Of course, gravity & reserve on my part may account for it, but it seems the devil tries to draw them from those who are their true friends, & lead them to trust those who would not suffer the least discomfort to save them. The older Indians have found this out, & are changing towards me; but the younger ones have yet to learn it. N'importe, the dead are mine. We know each other well now, & are safe from misunderstanding & separation.

Monday, Jan. 14th

Visited children at school. Hard work removing diseases set in action by measles. F. Bede wants me to bury Aleck (Cadotte's child), so he will have more time to go to Mission for F. Martin &, on my refusing, he repeated his old excuse,—"no one will notice it." I repeated, emphatically, that I was not deterred from action through fear of Agency people, but was merely attending to my own affairs, & keeping out of his, & that I visited the school merely as a physician. He buried the child before leaving. I will give them no further chance to attack me.

I gave castor oil to McLane for his & Sport's children. Also salve & Iodide of Iron (syrup) to Ida Cankula. Visited John Pleet's child, & read & wrote a letter for Mrs. Howard, to her brother. Visited Mrs Caskie, & asked after Dr. & sent an Indian to cut his wood. Wrote to Emeran & sent his mail by Frisking Elk. Wrote to Bishop, & sent the Koran I captured some time ago.[36] Goose had a woeful tale to tell about his son-in-law, Wanikiya, who had made outrageous charges against him. He takes his own physic & finds it bitter. Gave cod-liver oil to Eagle-man. Talked with Hairy Chin & the other chiefs about land question. I tell them I will advise them if they will all do just as I say, trusting to my judgment.

I have an idea that God may intend that I or someone should found a congregation of Indian Sisters. I will do my part, if I find

[36] Where or how Craft would have acquired a copy of the book of Muslim revelations is unknown.

it is His holy will. Like all other incepta it will have hard struggles with poverty, & God's assistance, as a reward of faith, will be abundantly given. It seems to begin in heaven, before starting on earth, since so many of our best have gone.[37]

Goose got drunk, shortly after I saw him, & got in the guardhouse. Received 1st (Jan.) numbers of Messenger of Sacred Heart, & Pilgrim of Our Lady of Mercy.

Tuesday, Jan. 15th

Wrote to my sister Josephine, to tell her of the deaths of Cunegunda & Adele. I wrote also to John Brown. F. Bede returned from the Mission. Received a letter from Annie Gaudreau. Visited Charles Rabbit at the Police Quarters. Has had hemorrhage of the lungs, & also has tried to shoot himself, but only succeeded in splintering a rib. Gave him cod-liver oil, cough medicine, & cotton batting. He denied attempt at suicide, & said he shot himself accidentally while picking up a Winchester to shoot a rabbit. He certainly hit the wrong "Rabbit," but it looks like intent,—perhaps to gain sympathy, as the wound is not serious. I visited the school & attended to the sick. About a dozen cases on hand, but all doing pretty well. All the effects of the measles. Gave castor oil to Nick Cadotte. Called on Dr. Caskie. Better.

Bought at Douglas' 10 yards of blue cilicia for Sr. Gertrude, & ordered 10 more of pink for Bismarck. Heard new reports of scarlet fever at LaGrace (from McNider). F. Bede has contradicted what I said to F. Martin about scarlet fever. I told him what I heard today; & that if F. Martin should let any of the Russian children into the school just now, Agency people would at once charge him with introducing the disease here. He seemed alarmed. I am now quite confident that it is to his absurd & malicious jealousy, that all the troubles here, from the charges against me, to the bad treatment

[37] This is the genesis of the founding of the Congregation of American Sisters, led by Josephine Crowfeather as Mother Catharine Sacred White Buffalo and joined by Claudia Crowfeather, Nellie DuBray, Jane Mocassin, Susie Bordeaux, Mary Black Eyes, Alice White Deer, and others. It would consume Father Craft's life for the next decade.

given to my poor sister Josephine, & also Faribault's bad conduct,—can be safely attributed. I hope God will teach him & those deceived by him, what a grave mistake they have made, before more mischief is done. I received a letter from Rev. F. Pius, of Crow Creek. He says the measles is past & also the Inspector, & thanks me for my aid. Thank God I was in time to save his mission. I could aid these here even more, were it not for their absurd jealousy. Gave apples to the sick children. Snowing & blowing hard from N.W. Issue [of government provisions] ended.

Wednesday, Jan. 16th

Snow & high wind from N.W. Up to yesterday & day before, the weather was unusually warm for this season. Still it is not as cold as so high a wind would lead us to expect. Visited school. All patients better. Sr. Gertrude has a sore throat. Examined it, & recommended greased cloth tied on, & gargle of sol.[ution] of chlorate of potash, (weak).

Examined Charles Rabbit's wound, & gave him more cotton. He is going to Hunkpati camp, so I won't venture to cut on it. An abscess has formed from the burrowing of matter under the shattered rib, some splinters came away, but more are there, &, probably, some pieces of cloth. An opening should be made in a depending part. Gave Eagle-man cough medicine for his children. Also to a man from Flying-by's camp on Grand River. Sent mine & Josephine's & Annie Gaudreau's names with $2.00 by Barney to Sr. Gertrude at Yankton to be aggregated to the Perpetual Adoration. Wrote to F. Dewey, S.J.[38] & sent intentions to Apostleship of Prayer for Feb. 1889, & asked information as to the aggregation of persons, societies, & missions, & offered my services here, if needed, to further the work of the League of the Sacred Heart.[39]

Thursday, Jan. 17th

Dr. Caskie better, will be able to attend school. I visited school, all better. Copied out formula of Benedictine vows. Wrote to Annie

[38] Raphael S. Dewey, SJ, editor of the *Messenger of the Sacred Heart.*

[39] The worldwide membership of those who profess devotion to the Sacred Heart.

Gaudreau & John H. Strait. Dr. Von Classman & wife called at Barney's. They want to send their children to Sisters. Agent & sister's object. If they take some they must take all; & the Fort children are too bad to bring among our Indians. Agent called at school.

Friday, Jan. 18th

. . . Visited school children. All better. Little Anastasia Papan is weak, & may not live long. Little sister promises to remember my intentions if she goes to heaven. Promised Sister Frances to get oranges for the convalescents. Met Dr. Von Classman, & explained why children from Fort could not be taken at Sister's School. Dr. Caskie went to visit school. I made a last visit, & started for Cannonball. I promised to return Monday for my mail, & be ready to attend sick if Dr. Caskie gets sick again. I left at 1:30 P.M. & reached Wells at 5:30 P.M. I hear that Bob Gaudreau is better. Will see him tomorrow. Joe LaCroix put up my horse. Went with Wells & family to supper at Givens.

Saturday, Jan. 19th

Ed Donahue came for steer he won from Wells on election bet. His horse fell, narrow escape. Visited Bill Zahn's[40] child. Measles over, & convalescent. Gave Sacred Heart cards. Pinch lame. Went with Wells to Parkins. Bob & Caske better & out in store. Bought ½ dozen oranges. . . .

Feast of the Holy Name of Jesus

Sunday, Jan. 20th

Prepared for mass. It took a long time to warm up the school room. Began mass at about 12 M. About a dozen attended. All gone to the Agency for rations. Cottonwood talked about Dr. Bland's[41] Land Bill, & says the Indians have not yet decided what to do. He seems opposed to Faribault & guard-house. Yuzuzupi came to borrow Wells' buggy. He says the Agent received a letter from Rev.

[40] William Presley Zahn, a veteran of Custer's command who had married an Indian woman (Vestal, *Sitting Bull, Champion of the Sioux*, 281).

[41] Dr. Thomas A. Bland of the National Indian Defense Association.

M. Superior at Avoca, that Bertha is worse, & will return. He acts queerly, & seems afraid of me, & afraid I may interfere. He soon became ashamed of it, but I suspect all is not right. I fear the Agent & the Primeaus are plotting mischief; & I always fear they may try to injure Josie too. I recommended the affair to the Sacred Heart, & He must aid me against His enemies. I vowed to the Sacred Heart to recommend Bertha to the Apostleship of Prayer, for a religious vocation, & perseverance in it, & safety from temptation; if, on reaching the Agency, I find that she will remain at Avoca; & also that Josie is safe,—I will go in tomorrow. . . .

Monday, Jan. 21st

Went to Agency. Left Wells at 10 A.M. & reached Agency at 3 P.M. Saw Agent, & learned that Bertha is really sick, but may, possibly, be too weak to come back here. Offered to go for her, if necessary. Gave oranges to Sister Frances for the sick. She asked me to see them, but I did not, so as to avoid a racket with F. Bede. I went up again to ask Sister Gertrude if Bertha could come to the school if she should return. I met F. Martin. Civil, but said nothing about F. Bede's racket. I wrote to Rev. Mother St. Anthony, saying that all would be satisfied if Bertha should not return, & offering to go to Avoca for her, if they wish her to return. I wrote also to Bertha, & also to Rev. F. Dewey, S.J. with badge, calendar, directions, etc., & authority to begin work. I met Bertha's mother on the way here, & promised to enquire about Bertha. I received a letter for Yuzuzupi from Bertha in my care.

Tuesday, Jan. 22d

Went with Dr. Caskie to visit sick at school. Anastasia Papan sinking fast. Went to Police court to enquire for copy of Council Fire. Got toe caulks for Wells from Frank Steinmetz. Called on Scott to give directions for telegrams sent here for me. Bought red ribbon at Douglas' & put it on my badge of the Sacred Heart.[42] Talked with Major Brown, at Douglas'. Learned that F. Martin

[42] A cloth emblem distributed by the League of the Sacred Heart.

is aiding F. Bede, either ignorantly or willfully. Don't know which. Our enemies on the Agency are trying to hurt Fathers Martin & Bede, & get them to attack me, so I won't defend them, & the foolish men have walked blindly into the trap. Answered F. Dewey's letter, & asked for badges, etc. & to have my name registered.

Wednesday, Jan. 23d

Called at school to see Anastasia. She will, no doubt, die today. Her mind seems clearer as the end approaches. I asked her again to pray for Josephine & all my intentions. I left the Agency at 10:30 A.M. & reached Cannonball at 3 P.M. Told the school children to come tomorrow, to hear about League of the Sacred Heart. Wells is drawing ice. I hear that F. Martin is beginning to open his eyes. He, probably, sees that F. Bede has been deceiving him, & imprudently leaguing with his enemies against his best friend. I leave the whole affair to the Sacred Heart. If they seek to make amends, I shall let them off from making amends for all personal injuries; but I will strictly exact reparation in Josephine's case. They must undo all they have done against her vocation, & agree to aid me in aiding her, if she & I require it. As a Bride of Christ, & as my sister, her safety is more important, & her cause more sacred to me than my own. Blessed my badge of the League, & made holy water for Wells. I began to make the "morning offering" to the Sacred Heart.

Thursday, Jan. 24th

Announced again to children about the League. I want them all here tomorrow. Wells finished drawing ice. I went to Parkins & telegraphed to Rev. Mother St. Anthony to let me know by telegraph if Bertha is worse & she wishes me to return, & I will come for her. Mrs. Parkins offered me $10.00 for my former visits to her mother, Mrs. Galpin. I explained that we could not receive money for sick calls. She then offered it for the mass & funeral. I refused saying that I was aiding F. Bede, at his request, as he was sick. She said she would see him. I told her she might, but would probably find that he would not take the money. These people have no idea of honor or decency. Sport stopped here on the way to Mandan to meet Major & Mrs. Cramsie. I told stories of spiritual things. I remark that Wells & others here don't care to hear of such things. They would be glad if God & His law were out of their way; & look upon me & other priests as intruders to be criticized & found fault with because we represent God & His law. They hope to excuse their own bad acts, by finding real or imaginary faults in us. . . .

Friday, Jan. 25th

I forgot to record last night that I learned from Sport that my little sister Anastasia Papan died as I departed, on Wednesday, January 23rd. Fast. Dispensations B.V.M. at St. Emerentianal, just after I had taken leave of her. Only 5 or 6 years old, she passed at once to heaven, to join little St. Emerentianal in celebrating the feast of our Mother. The Sacred Heart, whose image on my badge she kissed so fervently last Tuesday, will welcome little sister & return her kiss of holy love & peace. Again I say to my sister "Thou hast obtained mercy."

Yesterday was warm & melting; weather today is cold, with high wind. Only 5 scholars came. I explained to some of the League, & the Morning Offering, which I had translated into Sioux yesterday, with Bob Gaudreau's aid. Satan may kick his best, but I will succeed in destroying him. Last night Yuzuzupi, hearing that some Eastern scholars [Native American students from Carlisle or Hampton], with the body of another [dead person], were waiting at Mandan, thought Bertha was dead, & came to enquire. I explained that the whole affair was, probably, an outrageous lie, & was founded on the single fact that I had sent a telegram yesterday. I hear that the Indians will have some kind of ceremonies for Bertha. They think she is dead. I will try to keep her from dying in their camps, & will take care that if she returns she goes to the Agency school. It's too bad that after we have trained one in Christianity so long, they must be turned over to Satan at the moment of death, just when we should reap for God the fruit of our labors. It is all done "to avoid noise & trouble," & is the very way to ensure the annulment of all our work.[43] I, for one, will fight against it, & trust to the Sacred Heart to sustain me. If we fear men, we can never do anything for God & souls. I rode to Parkins, to see about my telegram. Met Bob outside. He said he had forwarded it to [Fort] Yates, & it would be sent from there, & he would let me know if an answer should come. I rode back, & got here before dark.

Saturday, Jan. 26th

Went with Wells to Parkins. Telegram came by Indian from Parkins sent by Sport from Mandan so we went down to Parkins. Wells to meet Cramsie, & I to look after my telegram. No answer yet. Cramsie & wife came, passed Parkins', we overtook & came back to Wells with them. They took dinner, & then went with Sport on to Agency. They know about the letter F. Bede wrote to prevent John & William from coming here. I tried to explain it, but it is evident that F. Bede has let his jealousy get the better of his judgment, & has written a very unkind letter to F. Jerome. I don't want to bear the responsibility of it, as I am entirely innocent of it, & would not be guilty of ingratitude towards F. Jerome; as his young men were really of great service to us. Tomorrow I shall announce the establishment of the League of the Sacred Heart. Satan has good cause to fear it, & will probably kick. Let him kick. God is more powerful & will see us all safe through.

Sunday, Jan. 27th

Said mass at 10:30 A.M. Less than usual came,—about fifty. One man came in with his hat on, talking loudly. I gave him a lecture on decency. All behaved well. Announced formally the establishment of the League of the Sacred Heart. Explained the League.

---

43 Avoiding "noise and trouble" was apparently a guiding principle for all factors on the reservation, but especially among the Benedictine missionaries and sisters who operated schools on the reservation. Their salaries were paid by the federal government, and great pressure and criticism had been brought to bear to end this unconstitutional merger of church and state. Craft's vision of engaging Native American priests and sisters was fueled by the prospects of waning influence of foreign-born missionaries.

All understood my explanation, but found it hard to grasp the idea, which is too high for those used to crawling on the earth. They will soon get it. I will explain more clearly to Promotees whom I shall select, & set them to work as soon as possible. Very few girls were present. Red Hail has been opposing the school, because the Agent did not do much for the Yanktonai children in the issue. Wells gave him a scolding.

At mass I laid on the altar the intentions I had sent to the Apostleship of Prayer, & also other intentions,—the principal for the successful establishment of the League, & for Josephine, Bertha, Annie Gaudreau,—especially for Josephine.

Monday, Jan. 28th

Rode in to the Agency from Cannonball. Called at school to ask about children. Received a letter from F. Stephan, enclosing check for $184.31 to pay Douglas, but none to pay me the $46.93 I advanced, & sent receipts for. Also received a letter from Rev. Mother St. Anthony, telling of Bertha's illness, asking for a mass, & asking me to get Bureau to send them money. They have received none since August, & are borrowing at 10 pr. ct. interest, & are in great distress. It's a pity Catholics have less care & charity in dealing with each other than in dealing with the world. I received also a letter from John Brown, & one of his teachers, & also the Little Messenger, S.[acred] H.[eart] Received Handbook of the League of Sacred Heart.

Tuesday, Jan. 29th

Called at school, & saw the sick children. All improving. Talked with Sr. Adele, & left message for Rev. M. St. Anthony for Sr. Gertrude, asking prayers for Bertha. Left box for hosts. F. Bede stood by while I talked with Sr. Adele. I had little to say to him. He has acted like a traitor to God & the Church. I paid Douglas $184.31 for F. Stephan, & got receipt. Clerk promises to lend me money if I need it. . . . Met F. Martin in Douglas' store. Talked politely. He invited me to the Mission. I answered, of course, politely, but as insincerely as his conduct towards me. I shall avoid danger & him. I am, no doubt, welcome at the Mission; & so is the fox to the trap. I shall trust in God to save Josie & me, & will make no terms with God's enemies & those who aid them. Maude Carignan called. She stays at McLaughlin's. No proper place there for her. . . .

Wednesday, Jan. 30th

Went to school to get hosts & visit sick children. Agent & Cramsies visiting school. I will go up later. Sister Adele seems to be watching so that I can't see Sister Gertrude. Their watching is in vain. I do not intend to see her. I would like to ask her to pray for Bertha, & give her the "Morning offering" & get her to say it with the children, but as they seem to suspect me of plotting against them, I will leave them to suffer from their fears, & will do nothing to endanger the peace of the poor sisters, who seem to have much to suffer for having more wit & more charity than the rest. . . .

Visited school in the evening. Sr. Adele gave me hosts, aided in dressing Carrie's arm. Maggie wants vocation, & wants to go to school where Josie is. I will recommend her with intentions for March to the Apostleship. Cold, high wind from N.W. Something like a blizzard. Snow blowing.

Thursday, Jan. 31st

Wrote to W. C. Courtis at Rosebud & asked for copy of Bland's bill, & asked about Spotted Tail's children,—if dead or not. . . . Left Agency at 12:00 M. & reached Cannonball (Wells) at 4:30 P.M. I seemed to travel slower than usual. In the evening I happened to think that it might be necessary to have the Bishop's permission to establish the League here. American Bishops have given their consent, but I want to be quite sure. It's no harm to ask, so I wrote to Bishop to ask permission. I will get a chance to send the letter tomorrow.[44]

[44] Father Craft's papers include a Latin document, dated 1889, establishing the League of the Sacred Heart, Apostolate of Prayer, as a pious association in the Diocese of Jamestown (in author's possession).

I begin to think again that it may be necessary to found a community of Indian Sisters. No one pities the Indians, except a few Americans. The German element is not disposed to make sacrifices for them, or to give them spiritual advantages. There are some holy souls, whom God seems to call to perfection, but Government schools, & Government salaries, & the fear of losing them;—& also jealousy of anyone & anything outside of their own selfish views, on the part of the German Benedictines, puts it out of the question to do anything to save them, unless it be done independently of German Benedictine influence. I would gladly do for them (the Benedictines) what they are unable or unwilling to do; but their jealous fear leads them to destroy all around them, & makes it too dangerous to aid them. This, & the probability that we will, sometime, lose Government aid,—& the necessity of doing something for God & souls rather than for Government pay, makes it evident that a start should be made to found our own Indian communities.[45] May the Sacred Heart of Jesus guide me, & teach me His will in the matter. I would be glad to make any sacrifices for the work—for Josie's sake.

Friday, Feb. 1st

Read Handbook of League. Sent off letter to Bishop, & one for Wells to Dr. Caskie for medicine by "Crazy-Man." Taught some children who came, the morning offering in Dakota. No school. Nearly everyone gone to the Agency to get rations & the blankets not given in the annuity issue. Little Shana came to sell a frock & get flour, sugar, & coffee. James Cekpa came with his aunt to sell shoes. Mrs. Wakute-wakan [Sacred Shooter] came to sell shirt. Young man came for coffin for child, not yet dead, but don't care to have it baptized. Instructed him about baptism. It changed him a little, but not much.

[45] Many of the missionaries who staffed the government schools were employed and paid by the federal government. Father Martin Kenel, for example, was paid $720 for the year 1888; Sister Gertrude, $720; Brother Nicholas Enz, $480; and Sister Adele Engster, $480 (*Annual Reports*, 1888, 60).

Whooping-cough suspected in camps. How much I could do with a community of Indian Sisters! They would gladly submit to strict discipline; & for love of God, under the rule of charity, would make many sacrifices, & suffer much to save their people. Under present rules, the Indians will never amount to much,—with few exceptions. But under Jesus' guidance, & carrying out the practices of the Church, they can arrive at high perfection. I could find enough, even now, to begin with. I think there must be something in it. If Jesus has such a design, He may be sure I will do all in my power to make it succeed. May He tell me what He wants me to do, & give me grace & means to do it. I count on the suffering & am ready for it. The means I want are God's means, not the world's. Hitherto we have had too much worldly aid, & too little of anything in accordance with God's views,—& for that reason, we have not had success. I would like to see things managed according to God's views for awhile. All the success <u>we</u> should want would be sure to follow.

Saturday, Feb. 2d Purification B.V.M.

Warm, light wind, snow melting. Wells made hay-rack. I rode to Parkins. Parkins came from Bismarck. Got my bill made out. Over $15.00. He has made some mistakes in charging to me what Wells has paid. I am charged also for meals & lodging for Giles & Paul & Mrs. Halsey on the trip with school boys for Rosebud to Mandan. It's <u>just</u> perhaps, but it looks exceedingly <u>small</u>. However, I now know what I owe; &, after paying what I owe, <u>less</u> the amount unjustly charged, I won't do much more trading there. In the evening, I put up & arranged the altar in the school-room. I will say mass early tomorrow, & go to the Agency. Wrote out intentions to be sent to the Central Director of the League, this month, for March. I will lay them on the altar during mass tomorrow. . . .

This Agency is a very bad place, & the class of people have utterly gone in depravity. The whites are far worse than the Indians. I shall do my best in spite of their opposition. I have nothing to fear. No one can hurt me, permanently, unless through the Church. I have made up my mind to save my soul in the Church, by adhering to the rules of honor & rectitude. Either the Church will maintain me in this, or it will not. If it will, I have nothing to fear, as the only power to condemn me, sustains me. If it will not, I still have nothing to fear, as, in that case it would clearly not be an infallible Church, &, consequently, incapable of aiding by approval, or hurting by condemnation. I speak, of course, of the Church in toto, & not in part. Not a single bishop, but the judging authority of all. I mean to extract strict conformity to Christ's wish, in dealing with the world, & Christ will see me through. Tomorrow's gospel speaks of His sleeping while His apostles were fearing shipwreck. Even so now, He will not desert us. He is with us,—that is clear, & if we doubt it will only be to hear him say "O modicae fidei, ut quid dubitasti?" ["O you of little faith, why did you doubt?"] So why doubt at all? If He is with me, what can I fear? & I would be a fool to doubt that He is with me. All I have asked is according to His commands & counsels, & I am willing to suffer & die to gain it. He can't refuse me. He whose last thought on the cross was for the Holy Mother who stood by Him to the last,—He will not be indifferent to my efforts to save my sister who alone stood by me in my hardest trial.

Sunday, Feb. 3d

. . . Rode to Agency. Started at 11 A.M. Stopped on the way to see a case of what seems like abscess forming on the humerus, in Mato gli nazin, aged about 40. He wants his daughter to return from Hampton. Reached Agency at 4:30 P.M. Called at school to see Sr. Gertrude. I think of going to Avoca, & want to see if she wishes to send any word there. Told Major McLaughlin that I may go, & will let him know if I do. He wants me to see Melda safely on the way to St. Cloud.

Monday, Feb. 4th

Indians get their blankets. Met Jack Carignan. Measles raging at Grand River. . . . Telegraphed to M. St. Anthony at Avoca that

I would gladly come if she or Bertha needed me. Told Major McLaughlin that I can't go yet. I will wait for telegram. . . .

Tuesday, Feb. 5th

Saw Cramsies & Melda McLaughlin off, & took breakfast at Major's. Mrs. McLaughlin denies using "Honi [*sic*] soit qui mal y pense" ["If you are thinking bad thoughts about me, I hope bad things happen to you"] in an insulting way at Parkins,' & says it was Mrs. Van Solen, who, it seems, knows French. It may be my eyes & ears deceived me. I hope so. Melda forgot her satchel, & the boys followed with it. I telegraphed to Parkins' to have them wait for it. Got dispatches for me & Major from Rev. Mother St. Anthony, saying that Bertha died on Sunday at 5 P.M. The very day I laid the intentions on the altar, & hers with them. God heard me, as seemed best to Him, & took her. She is safe now & won't blame me for saving her. In heaven they know all & thank there, though they blame here. Went to school & told Sister Gertrude about Bertha. Wrote to Rev. Mother St. Anthony to answer her telegram, & also to Miss Zathona-waštawin at Hampton as her father requested. Promised M. St. Anthony money for Josie's tuition. . . .

I fear that Mrs. Van Solen has been writing against me to the Bishop, & that the priests here will sustain her. If I <u>must</u> fight, I may console myself that I am persecuted for Jesus' sake. I know well that for no other cause do they hate me,—the laity through malice, & the fear that their Pharisaical hypocrisy will be unmasked, & the clergy through cowardice, or jealousy, or both. I am sure I can attribute most of my troubles here to F. Bede. May God forgive him, & open his eyes. May God help me to save my soul, as I cannot sneak to save it, & without His aid it seems impossible to beat back my persecutors. If the Bishop uses his power to attack me, I am lost. Innocence does not save here. Above all may God do what He will with me, & save my poor sister Josephine & her vocation. . . .

Wednesday, Feb. 6th

Blessed badges of the League, & made out certificates of League for myself, Barney, & his wife & mother-in-law, & opened Register of the League, dating it Feast of Scholastica, February 10th. Dated certificates the same, except Mrs. Capell's, which I dated March 3rd so we can get Plenary Indulgence on the day of admission. Went to Douglas' & borrowed $21.50. Got Pinch shod by Frank Steinmetz. Cole's man did not tell me when he left, & Pinch got no feed nor water from Tuesday morning until this afternoon. Got from P. Office postal notes for $31.00 & sent them in a registered letter to Rev. M. St. Anthony. $30.00 for Josie's school expenses for quarter ending Dec. 31st 1888, & $1.00 for Josie's pocket money. Called at Mrs. McLaughlin's, to see about getting her to act as Promoter of the League for the woman's society. She was dressing to go out, & did not see me. Excused herself, etc. . . .

Thursday, Feb. 7th

Fed Pinch, wrote to Mother, Fanny, & Josie & Annie [Gaudreau], & told all of them about the League, as I also told Rev. M. St. Anthony in yesterday's registered letter. Started for Cannonball at 2 P.M. Before starting called on Mrs. McLaughlin. She don't care to introduce the League in the woman's society, & don't care to join herself. Thinks she may have joined long ago. Warned her against using Protestant hymns & prayers, or in any way joining heretics "in sacris."[46] Called on Dr. Caskie & got medicine for Mato-hdi-nazin. (liniment).

At the fork of the telegraph & river roads I doubted whether to go by river road & baptize Frank Gates' child, or to take the shorter way & baptize the child on my return, as it was getting late. I left it to the Sacred Heart to direct the horse, just as He wished me to go, & dropped the bridle, & used the spur. Pinch turned from his usual course (the telegraph road) & took the right hand road, towards Gates'. I came to another fork, & again left it to the Sacred Heart

[46] A canon law term prohibiting Catholics from participating in the religious ceremonies of other churches.

to decide, & dropped the bridle. Again Pinch kept the road towards Gates'. Baptized the child. No one there but Mrs. Gates & the 3 children, & one girl in the next house, who, however, did not come in. Named the little one Josephine Scholastica, & named as sponsors my two sisters Josephine M. Crowfeather & Scholastica Mentz. The little one seemed to enjoy it, & laughed continually.[47]

Stopped at Tatanka-hokšina's to see sick children, passed Mrs. Van Solen's without stopping, & went to Leo Otaapapi's to see sick children. My little cousins gave me a very affectionate greeting, which took away all fatigue & heartache for some time. Gave them a quarter. Stopped at Mato hdi nazin's & gave him the liniment. His arm has broken, & is now less swollen & painful. Reached Wells at 8 P.M. Givens & family & Bob Brown at Wells for supper & card-party. The Indians blame Wells & Givens for stopping a dance. Heard of a rape. Recommended to Wells & Givens that the Indians should make an appeal to law, &, failing, as they likely would, to get legal redress, should defend their families by armed force, if necessary, as the laws of God & man allow them to do. There is an evident disposition among Agency people to hush up such things; & until the laws are in force here, but little can be done. May the Heart of Jesus hasten the advent of law, order, morality, & decency, & the removal of all who delay this, & persecute & slander His priests for trying to hasten it.

Friday, Feb. 8th

Not many scholars came. The Indians are angry at the stopping of their dance, & show it in this way. Howard Coles came from Bismarck with his store freight. He reports scarlet fever at Bismarck. He met Indians on the way up there. Of course they will bring it [scarlet fever] here. Black Bull came to see if the Agent was com-

[47] Father Craft's earlier training as a Jesuit seminarian surfaces regularly in his journals. It was St. Ignatius of Loyola, founder of the SJ, who first dropped the rein of his mule at a fork in the road on his way to Montserrat in March 1522, leaving God to lead the way. Craft's frequent use of St. Ignatius' spiritual exercises, the voice he "felt" coming from the tabernacle on September 24, 1888, and the dream records on August 18, 1889, all mirror the experiences of Ignatius Loyola, the great mystic of the Catholic Church.

ing. This evening dance in Two Bear's camp. Drums beating defiance. Howard Coles threw out hints about my formerly going to dances to instruct Indians. Gave him the rules of the Church with regard to such things, & shut him up. Wrote out new intentions.

Saturday, Feb. 9th

Howard Coles started for Agency. Agent McLaughlin & Lieut. Smith stopped at Givens' on their way to the Agency. Took dinner with them. They report scarlet fever at Bismarck, Mandan, Fort Lincoln, & Heart River, & Small-pox at F.[ort] Buford. Crazywalking stopped at Givens to hear about dance disturbance. Wells interpreted for him with Givens. . . .

Sunday, Feb. 10th

It seems that the ill feeling of the Indians against the school has extended to the church. Satan is, probably, kicking against the League of the Sacred Heart. Very few came to mass today. Before mass Caddy came to see Mr. Wells & answered me angrily & insolently when I saluted him. I gave him a severe reprimand for his folly & injustice for blaming me for other's quarrels, & then Mr. Wells put him out.

I said mass at 10:30 A.M. Before mass I gave badges for Mr. & Mrs. Wells, James, Frank, & Joseph, with the formula in the Handbook, & then repeated with them the promise against secret societies, & the act of consecration for promoters, & appointed Mr. Wells a promoter. During mass I laid intentions on the altar, adding five more for Mr. & Mrs. Wells. Mr. & Mrs. Wells confessed before mass, & received during mass to gain indulgence. Wrote out morning offering in Sioux for Catka, & gave it to "Wapaha." High Bear came in the afternoon. He says he has nothing to do with the "old-time" & "dance" party. Much could be done for him if he would give up his attachment to old ways, & follow us sincerely. . . .

Monday, Feb. 11th

A few more scholars came today, but the strike is by no means over. I wrote out morning offering for Mr. Wells to teach the children, & prepared them for it. I went to see Frances Ihawin [Smiling Woman] in Waga's camp. I baptized her three years ago. She is now dying of consumption. It is a "devil's outfit" of the Red Fish type. The stepfather Sinte-sna-mani [Rattling Tail Walking], is "dead gone" in "devil worship" & "stone-throwing." The sick girl (age 13) laid on the ground, & near her were the stones for their incantations, & the medicine-drum with the horned demon painted on it. Before it were the wild sage, the tobacco board, & other things used in the incantations. Here, where in that part of the house set apart for sacred things, the orthodox Indian rules would require that all should be clean & orderly,—all was dirt, darkness, squalor, & disorder. The poor child was just conscious enough to receive the sacraments, & would soon be beyond the reach of evil. Always "simple"—almost idiotic, sickness had left her but little reason. She probably never knew what sin was, & would soon be safe from knowing. I scarcely knew whether I could give her the last sacraments. I left it to the Sacred Heart of Jesus to dispose her. He is too anxious to save not to do all He can to aid my efforts. I asked her if she wished to receive the sacraments, & while waiting for her answer, explained them. She answered "Hau" [yes], the only word she had spoken for some time. I did not send the family out, but ordered them to stand back, & after putting on the stole, tried to get through with her confession. Finding that she could not speak, I thought it best not to attempt to hear her confession, especially as she was not in a condition to remember anything. I repeated an act of contrition, & prayers to the Hearts of Jesus, Mary, & Joseph, & gave her conditional absolution. I then anointed her, gave her the scapular, gave the blessing for the sick, & the plenary indulgence, in art. mort. It was all I could do. An attempt to hear her confession would only have confused & disturbed her, & I was positive it would be useless. I took every precaution, in case she should need absolution, but it is probable that she will go to heaven like a baptized infant. God has His own ways of lifting one to heaven from the greatest depths of misery. De profundis clamvi ad te

Domine. [Out of the depths I cry to you, O Lord.][48] Out of the depths of "devil dreaming," superstition, ignorance, savage degradation, misery & squalor, the miseries & danger of poor little Frances have cried out to the Heart that could not refuse such pleading, though He will be deaf to the elaborate petitions of worldly Pharisees. The Heart of Jesus saves in strange & unsuspected ways. If thus He snatches souls from the jaws of hell, & even keeps them pure in the midst of corruption, as He did Catharine Tegakawita [*sic*], the Lily of the Mohawks, how can I doubt that He will save & sanctify & take as His spouse my Josephine Mary, the Lily of the Sacred Heart! Perhaps my blood & my sufferings may help to plead for her. If violence is to take heaven by storm I shall spare no violence, especially if I am to suffer.

Crazy Man & Black-bull came in the evening, & gave names of those opposing school. Wakute-wakan, wife & daughter came & got lamp oil. Wells & I sent word to all the Indians about scarlet fever. Wakute-wakan reports that all the police were ordered in to the police court today for some business—he did not know what.

Tuesday, Feb. 12th

Came to the Agency. On the way I stopped to see Frances Ihawin. She is much better. Storm started from southwest, as I reached the bridge at Beaver-holes, & lasted all the way to the Agency. Found letters here from F. Dewey, F. Stephan, Rev. Mother St. Anthony, Josephine, & Annie [Gaudreau]. Diplomas of Aggregation & Local Director also came. F. Dewey sent bill, & 3 mass intentions. F. Stephan said he had sent money to Avoca, & will send to me, & would aid me all he could. Rev. Mother said the money came, & spoke of Bertha's happy death, offering her sufferings & death for her parent's baptism.[49] Josie wrote before Bertha died. Josie thanked me for all I had done for her, & wrote me a

[48] Ps. 130:1.

[49] Mother St. Anthony wrote to confirm the death of Bertha (Anthony to Craft, 6 February 1889, in author's possession).

beautiful letter, & sent me her Reward of Merit card. Annie gave particulars of Bertha's death, & sent a letter for Bertha's mother.

Henry Mulhern dying at the school of tubercular meningitis. Visited him & Lizzie Schöule,—case of inflammatory rheumatism. Doctor had gone with F. Bede to Mission, & returned at night. 30 cases of measles at Mission. Went for Doctor to relieve Henry. He gave him twice a hypodermic injection of morphine, 1/4 gr. each. I held his arms to prevent struggles. He had a good rest after,—the first since Sunday. He will certainly die. His parents are visiting him.

Wednesday, Feb. 13th

Visited Henry morning & evening. His father is with him. Gave him scapular of Sacred Heart. Dying, conscious, slight delirium, but less pain. Towards evening his sight failed. F. Bede gave him all the sacraments. Met F. Bede, but scarcely spoke to him. I want him to feel what I think of his cowardly, treacherous acts towards me. . . .

Thursday, Feb. 14th

Henry Mulhearn died at 5:20 A.M. Went to school & found him dead when I got there. F. Bede & Dr. Caskie went to Mission. Heavy snow storm in afternoon but not cold. . . .

At night, after getting the mail, I heard that a prisoner was dying in the guard-house. Went & found it was Ite gi kiza, in for some squaw scrape & screaming with pain in bowels. It looked like case of intussusception [bowel obstruction]. Put on hot water poultices, & sent for Dr. Von Classman, Military Hospital Steward. He thought it might be rupture of liver. Gave hypodermic injection of morphine & dose of castor oil. He consented to be baptized, &, as he seemed to be dying, & promised, before witnesses to obey & follow the Catholic Church if he recovered, I baptized him (using water only, as I had nothing else with me), & afterwards gave him extreme unction & the scapular. He seemed easier at 10:30 P.M.

Friday, Feb. 15th

Heavy snow storm. Went to Hospital & got castor oil & laudanum for Joseph Ite gi kiza. Gave him 4 tablespoonsful plus 20 drops laudanum. Went to school. Lizzie better. Was requested to bury Henry, as F. Bede had not returned, but he & the Doctor got back at 1 P.M. Went to see Dr. Caskie. He went with me to see Ite gi kiza; gave calomel & ipecac. Case probably impaction of feces. Doctor was called again at night; patient fainted. Gave hypodermic injection of morphine. The calomel & ipecac. had produced vomiting. Some blood in it. Relieved. Looks now as if he was over his sickness, & was perhaps malingering to escape guardhouse. F. Bede buried Henry today.

Saturday, Feb. 16th

Storm cleared up by noon. Indians came for issue. Sent Cardigan jacket to Crowfeather by Paul Kill-eagle. Ite gi kiza better. Bowels acted. Threw out hints of suspicion as to malingering. Dined with Dr. Caskie. Went to school to see about photograph of Cunegunda for Black-Bear. Got pills for Barney.

Sunday, Feb. 17th

Heard mass at 9 A.M.. Rode to Mission, & to Crowfeather's, & back to Mission. Stopped at young men & women's society meeting. All, or nearly all at school have measles, but are recovering.

Monday Feb. 18th

Said mass at 7 A.M. Visited sick scholars. Dr. Caskie came. Visited sick scholars with him. Very cold.

Tuesday, Feb. 19th

Started for Grand River. Very cold. Saw Victor Frosted & wife at Paul's. Went on across the hills until I found the road too bad, ravines full of snow. Owing to circling about & turning round drifts, I could not reach Grand River till after midnight, if I should proceed. I therefore turned back & returned to the Mission.

Wednesday, Feb. 20th

Said mass at 7 A.M. Saw sick scholars with Dr. Caskie. He & Sport returned to Agency. 2 cases of diphtheria, but mild. All from bad health. Agent & Barney came. Wa ali & Pehinšakiya talked with Agent. Agent & Barney returned to Agency. Wa ali's daughter Susie came to school. Francis Takukokipešni advised me, in jest, to get my father Crowfeather into St. Joseph's Society. Good bit, but it's just what I am trying to do.

Thursday, Feb. 21st

Said mass at 7:30 A.M. Visited sick scholars. Matilda (Kušlaptecela's girl) has pneumonia. Ordered Laudanum poultices. Wa ali came. Instructed him about Church & advised him to join St. Joseph's Society.

Friday, Feb. 22d

Said mass at 7 A.M. Visited sick scholars. All better. Rode to Agency, intending to go to Cannonball. Received Little Messenger, & letters from Josephine, Rev. M. St. Anthony,[50] & B. Joseph O.S.F. [Order of Saint Francis] (Clontarf) & also Rosary sheets, & calendar for March. Called at Dr. Caskie's to tell about sick.

Saturday, Feb. 23d

Awoke about 4:30 A.M. Heard F. Bede talking with Barney. Heard my name. Called to Barney, & he & F. Bede said F. Martin sent for me or the doctor, as Matilda was dying. Threw some grain to Pinch. Woke Dr. Caskie. Arranged for him to go with Sport. Barney got me some coffee. Saddled. Asked Sport to hurry. Sent word to Caskie by Barney, as I heard no one up at Caskie's when I went there again. Reached Mission at 8 A.M. (Started at last call for reveille). Met Matilda's father, & learned she died at 5 A.M. this morning. Rode on to Mission. Found her dead (of pneumonia), & Agatha, Agnes, Annie [Pleets?], & Augustina worse. Scrofula, weakness, & pneumonia. Dr. Caskie reached here just before 12 M. Visited sick scholars with him. Matilda's body was moved to church, & the 4 bad cases put in Sister's parlors. I sat up with them, to keep the parents from annoying them too much. I

[50] In her letter, Mother St. Anthony acknowledges receipt of the $30.00 for Josephine and advises Craft that White Blanket's daughter, Mary, is dying (Anthony to Craft, 11 February 1889, in author's possession).

learn that Agatha is my sister [a relative through Craft's adoption into Spotted Tail's family]. Gave F. Bernard Badge of League for the 4, & I gave badge & certificate to Agatha, & enrolled her in the League. F. Bernard gave badges to others. We said the offering with them. Black Lightning & wife rather troublesome, but soon reasoned them out of it. Sat up all night with the 4 sick. F. Bernard gave them the last sacraments, & F. Martin & I prepared Agatha for death, & said last prayers for her.

Sunday, Feb. 24th

. . . Visited sick with Doctor. Matilda's funeral after high mass at 9:30 A.M. Agatha better. She says she will die. I preached at the funeral. Black Lightning & wife are talking too much to Agnes, & tiring her. Warned them about it. Agatha's mother is very good, & prudent & reasonable. Rested till midnight, & then relieved F. Bernard in watching sick.

Monday, Feb. 25th

. . . Parents of Augustina, Annie, Agnes, & Agatha here. Agatha's & Agnes' mothers usually remain all night. Towards morning Agatha's pulse failed, & we had to use ammonia (carb.) & digitalis (tinct). I was up again all night with the sick.

Tuesday, Feb. 26th

. . . Agatha rallied towards sunrise. She seems sure of dying, but is happy, &, though suffering, very patient. She confessed again. Black Lightning troublesome. Gave him a lecture, & left him to himself. If Agnes dies, it will be his fault, & I want him to know it.

Henry Agard's child was buried today. It died at home (3 years old). A Yankton mixed-blood (perhaps John Lamont) disturbed the young men at Agard's who were praying for the dying child, & fought with one of them. Police afraid to arrest him.

Sat up again to nurse sick children. Dr. Caskie went home in the afternoon. Sent letter by him for Josephine, & Rev. Mother St. Anthony.

Wednesday, Feb. 27th

Agatha died this morning at 3 o'clock. At 12 midnight, F. Martin called me, just as I laid down. Agatha's internal abscess had broken in the cavity of the chest, & some matter was discharged through the bronchia. Collapse, body cold, pulse ceased. Gave doses of Carb. ammonia & digitalis (8 drops) and repeated it until the pulse could be felt. She said she would die, & named all around her,—her mother, F. Martin, me, & Sister Rhabana. When asked who I was, she said "Tiblo," & when asked my English name, would only smile & answer "Tiblo" (brother). She told who was in the next room, & their very position, saying "it seems as if I see them." Then she said "Wanna Wanna" (Now Now (I will die)) She armed herself with the cross which she always held, kissing it frequently, & making the sign of the cross, & kissing her badge of the League. She then rapidly sank. I put my crucifix to her lips. F. Martin gave last absolution & said the prayers for her. Sr. Rhabana prayed with her in English, & I said with her an act of contrition & the "offering" of the League in Dakota. I held the crucifix before her; she fixed her eyes on it for the last time, became comatose, & died with a smile on her lips, & so quietly that we could scarcely be sure she was gone. It was just 3 A.M. when we are sure she must have ceased to breathe. The poor mother cried, but quietly, so as not to disturb the rest. F. Martin & I got her over to F. Martin's room, while F. Bernard & I carried the body to the church & laid it on a bier before the altar. After the sisters had dressed & laid it out, I gave little sister a goodbye kiss. We all said mass for her in the morning. In the afternoon we buried her, & also a child of Bear-face's son-in-law. So now the first Associate of the League enrolled here, has gone to be our intercessor, with Bertha & Mary Xavier. I preached her funeral sermon.

Boy returned from the Fort & brought my mail. Letters from Bishop, Mother, Josephine, & Annie [Gaudreau], & letter from Annie, in my care, for Bertha's mother, enclosing photo of Bertha. Visited sick. Black Lightning's people came. I told them to keep away from sick room, & talk with F. Martin. I met Supa-ohotonna, one of the same of the same outfit, & told him the same. I warned them again in F. Martin's room, that I would abandon the case if they troubled me again or disturbed the patient, or even entered the sick room. They did go there, & I abandoned the case, & wrote to that effect to Dr. Caskie. I first appealed to F. Martin to keep them in order, or to order the police or Sport to do so. He is afraid, & don't even want me to act. He says he will keep them from taking the child away if he can, but ain't sure if he can. Such weakness & want of Christian manliness, as would lead a shepherd to let loose the wolves on his sheep, is too disgusting for me. I can't see such things, & if I can't keep Agnes safe I won't see her hurt, or aid those who injure her. Neither will I stay here with my hands tied by regard for F. Martin's rights & views, & thus lead those who now respect, & fear to attack me, to once more have the hope that they may do so with impunity. Now that I have the peace of victory, I will go with that peace, & not lose it by association with the timid & cowardly.[51]

Thursday, Feb. 28th

Did not say mass. Too late when I got ready. Fixed everything for the sisters to carry on the care of the sick under Dr. Caskie's orders. I shall go to the Agency tomorrow. I feel sad to leave the sick in such a state, but F. Martin is responsible. He will neither act nor let me act. Emeran came in the evening. Explained the League of the Sacred Heart to him. He wants us to see if Gertrude would obey a husband rather than her relatives. He fears her grandmother is troublesome.

I gave Sport my opinion of his talking in a friendly way to those who act like Black Lightning's family. He should let them see that public opinion condemns them, & then they will fear to do wrong.

[51] The medical quarantine over outbreaks of measles, scarlet fever, and other illnesses, imposed at Fort Yates and in the schools in January, became increasingly difficult to sustain as the Indians sought to fight the diseases with their own medicine.

Friday, March 1st

Said mass of reparation, & for intentions of the Heart of Jesus, (Votive S. Cardis Jesu) at 7 A.M. I enrolled Emeran in League, gave him badge & certificate, & named him promoter. F. Martin & I talked to Gertrude Yaperwin. She promises, if she marries, to obey her husband, & not listen to others. Emeran will propose to her. I arranged to stay today, & go in with F. Bernard & Emeran tomorrow. Emeran gave Waanakšin, Black Lightning's son, a sound blasting, & laid his misdeed out in good style. I would not address him directly, out of contempt, but told him through Emeran, that what I said last summer I meant & still mean, viz. I would drive 3 balls through the head of anyone who would insult a sister of mine, & Waanakšin should think equally of his sister, Agnes, & not disgust those who try to save her life. He is heartily ashamed. Had F. Martin shown so much spirit, we would have had no trouble. Team came from the Fort with medicines & letter from Dr. Caskie. Sickness in Agency school. Little brother of Henry Mulhearn dying of tubercular meningitis, just as Henry died.

At about 8:30 P.M. Gabriel Naginyaupi died of hemorrhage of the lungs (ruptured blood-vessel). Could do nothing though we tried hard. I gave last absolution & F. Bernard anointed him. Emeran proposed to Gertrude & was accepted.

Saturday, March 2d

. . . F. Bernard & Emeran went to Agency. Wa ali, Gabriel's father, came from Agency. I prepared medicines for the sisters to give to the sick. I take no further charge, as I suspect Sport is inciting the Indians, Agent, etc., & F. Martin is too cowardly to sustain me.

Sunday, March 3d 1889

. . . Preached at high mass at 10 A.M., & read Bishop's letter & Lenten Regulations. Wa ali & his wife came. Gabriel's funeral in the afternoon. Sport came from Agency with Dr. Caskie. Case of croup. Doctor relieved it. Sport reports that I am blamed at Agency for keeping the Indians from troubling the sick, etc. & says that they want to make trouble in the police court about it. He has caused it, if any. . . .

Monday, March 4th

Said mass at 7 A.M. Went with Dr. Caskie to see sick children. I will go tomorrow if Agent comes. He is expected today. Warm, thawing.

Tuesday, March 5th

. . . Visited with Doctor. Agent came. He has heard nothing of Sport's stories. I told him of Sport's conduct. Dr. Caskie & Sport went to Agency. F. Martin offered me money for my services. He knows better. I refused as well as I could without quarreling, but he won't get a chance to act so again. I left before the Agent. Reached Agency at 7:30 P.M. Agent came just after. Visited the school, saw Sister Gertrude. I will see my sister Lizzie Papan tomorrow. Dr. Caskie says she will die.

Wednesday, March 6th

Ash-Wednesday. Called at school. Saw Lizzie Papan. She is quite thin. Went again in afternoon. Saw Sister Gertrude. She showed me a letter from Josephine, regretting that she left Zell, & wishing to return. My horse got out, & I had to catch him. I put him in Barney's stable. Mr. Wells gave us a note from Mrs Van Solen, Wanaksunta dying & wants to see me. Received letters from Wm. Tiwanzilan from F.[ort] Totten, & from F. Wolfgang, O.S.B. inviting me to preach on St. Patrick's day in Bismarck. Wrote to F. Wolfgang declining. Too much to do here. Also wrote to Josephine & Annie [Gaudreau], Rev. M. St. Anthony, Bishop, & F. Willard. I consoled Josie, & advised her to learn more before going to Zell. Asked M. St. Anthony to let me know if any try to interfere with Josie. Asked Bishop for $25.00 per month from this date. Spoke of charity & sympathy for Indians—Indian nature emotional. Pharisees growl if I correct vices, & also more still if I become the equal of God in the person of His poor, dignity, degrading, etc. My Indian relatives' scrofulous ills less offensive than the moral rottenness of white Pharisees. Recommended mission be begun at once, & by Irish or American priest, to teach the German maniacs that we are Catholic in doctrine. Asked F. Willard to get Dr. Caskie retained.

Thursday, March 7th

Finished & mailed letters, & started for Cannonball. Saw Wanaksunta. Not so sick as represented. Gave him the scapular, & advised him to see Dr. Caskie. His wife called me aside to tell me about his bad dreams, & bloody emissions. I pretended not to understand, & referred her to doctor for all medical advice. Reached Wells in afternoon.

Friday, March 8th

Only 10 scholars came. Police watching border to keep off danger of scarlet fever. Mr. Wells & Givens returned. Mrs. Wells & Mrs. Givens had an absurd dispute about a dress. Wells says that Mrs. Van Solen is found out by Agent. Red Fish is deprived of two weeks rations for breaking through the quarantine line & going into camp.

Saturday, March 9th

Rode to Parkins. Overtook Agent beyond Parkin's (in ambulance) & gave him letter to mail for Mrs. Wells. Interpreted for Givens at "Quarantine camp." Swept out class room & put up altar. Instructed Levi Degera & wife about League. Wells & Wakanyuha announced at dance about mass. Antony Ireland (Crazy-Man) brought 2 children for baptism. Told him to come tomorrow.

Sunday, March 10th

Said mass at 10:30 A.M. Before mass baptized Francis Xavier (Gautrelet) & Margaret Mary (Alacoque), the two children of Antony Ireland (Crazy-Man). About 80 to 100 came to mass. At mass I explained League, & spoke about school, & also about scarlet fever. After mass I took names & gave badges & certificates. I admitted 24 to the League. Went with Givens to quarantine camp to see Crow-Ghost. Sick. Disinfected tent with carbolic acid, & let him go home. I offered the mass today as a mass of reparation.

Monday, March 11th

Better attendance today. About thirty scholars. Went to see Atan-sha. Seems to be getting better. Gave him scapular, & admitted him, his sister Helen, & Joseph Akicita to the League. Went to young men's meeting at Wapaha's. Sang hymns & instructed them. They are trying to get new members for St. Joseph's Society. Old element wants to delay, but young men mean business. I am more & more convinced that the Indians must be roused from their vices, & separated from bad whites, & taught self-respect, before we can do much with them.

Tuesday, March 12th

Taught scholars morning offering, & admitted 5 to League. Rode to Parkins. Met Peter Hehaka-ouzinca. He will have another young men's meeting tomorrow. Gave him some tobacco for them.

Wednesday, March 13th

Taught scholars morning offering. Instructed Joe LaCroix about Catholic Church. He seems inclined to go to his duties. All this is the work of the Sacred Heart. I got the League to pray for his conversion over a month ago. He says he has no difficulty now in resisting sin, & feels something he cannot account for drawing him to the Church. Vive le Sacré Coeur de Jesus! [Long live the Sacred Heart of Jesus!] Went to Peter Hehaka-ouzinca's meeting, & instructed young men.

Thursday, March 14th

Sick, bilious vomiting, slight headache. Atan-ho-wašte's daughter came & gave me back a scapular of the Sacred Heart I gave her some days ago, saying "Brother, my father & mother say that as I am an Indian I can't wear this, & they forbid me to take it." Poor little sister. I explained to her that Indians never before rejected God & His badge, & must now have become very bad to do so. I said her parents must want her to perish, if they warned her against the Giver of Life, & I told her to come to me & Mr. Wells if she should be ill-treated at home, & we would send her away to school. I put on the scapular myself, as a reparation to the Sacred Heart, because others rejected Him.

Mr. Wells went to Parkins in the evening. Wells promises to pay medicine man if he cures a patient, but not before the patient can work. I explained to them the difference between white & Indian doctors.

Friday, March 15th

Wrote for Wells note to the Agent to be forwarded to Department, explaining reason for small attendance during last quarter. Measles, etc. Rode to Agency. Received letters from Annie & Cecelia Gaudreau, Wm. Tiwanzilan, & Major Thos. H. B. Jones of Fort Berthold, the letter urging haste in starting our mission.[52] I answered Major Jones that Bishop would do his best to aid his Berthold Indians. I thought it would be a good chance to do something for Josephine. I therefore wrote to Bishop, enclosing Major Jones' letter, & offering to take Berthold if he would give me 2 or 3 Benedictine sisters, & let Josephine & some other Indian or mixed-blood novices make their novitiate with them, under my direction. I also offered to let him use my salary for the sisters' support, while I would live on mass intentions. Before writing I recommended the plan to the Sacred Heart, & consulted Sr. Gertrude as to the possibility of getting sisters, in case Bishop should ask for them. I don't like to leave here, but will make the sacrifice for Josephine. May the Hearts of Jesus, Mary, & Joseph direct this now, & save my sister Josie.

Saturday, March 16th

Issue day. I hear that Joseph Crowfeather's eyes are worse. Got some medicine from Dr. Caskie, & will see him tomorrow. Went with Dr. Caskie to see Joseph Wanaksunta. On the way, saw a row

[52] Maj. Thos. H. B. Jones to Craft, 5 March 1889, Assumption Abbey Archives, Richardton, N.Dak.

between Crazy-Man & White Lightning, over a little baking powder. Finished letter to Bishop, & mailed letters to him & Major Jones. Dinner at Dr. Caskie's after interpreting for him in dispensary, & getting medicines for Wapaha, White Lightning, & others. F. Bede came to Dr. Caskie's for medicine for Mission. Madbear bought green ribbon for his girls in the school for St. Patrick's day.[53] Met Tom Goodwood. He says he didn't send for Protestants, & promises to be with me.

Soldiers caught an Indian dragging a woman by a lariat,—his wife, 14 years old, whom the police helped him carry off by force on horseback to live with him against her will. She threw herself off near the Fort, & he "roped" & dragged her. The soldiers arrested him, put him in their guard-house, & sent a scout to notify [George] Faribault. He was taken to police quarters, & a lot of soldiers went to testify against him. Good.—It's all the result of making <u>brutes</u> judges.[54]

Sunday, March 17th

St. Patrick's Day. Heard mass at 8:30 A.M. Said rosary in church. Met Mrs. McLaughlin & Mrs. Wakan yuha & her mother. They went to communion. I wrote to F. Dewey & ordered 200 badges & certificates of League, & 5 "Handbooks," & also sent in intentions for April. Saddled Pinch, & left for Mission at 2 P.M. Frank Steinmetz rode with me as far as Cadottes. I stopped at Wm. Halsey's & saw children. No one else at house. Kissed little brothers' & sisters' sore eyes. Rode by hill-road to Mission. Will see Crowfeather tomorrow. Too late tonight to put up medicines.

Monday, March 18th

. . . Put up medicines for Crowfeather, & rode up there. Gave medicine & examined eyes. Admitted the family to the League, & gave badges & certificates, & taught them "Morning Offering."

---

[53] The appeal of St. Patrick's Day went beyond Mad Bear, chief of the Yanktonai Sioux. On March 10, 1892, Josephine Crowfeather, Susie Bordeaux, Alice White Deer, Nellie DuBray, and Jane Mocassin sent their St. Patrick's Day best wishes to readers of the *Irish World*, a New York City newspaper.

[54] Craft evidently had a poor opinion of Indian justice on the reservation.

Gave my mother, Crowfeather's wife, my moccasins & also left for her at F. Martin's a dress to be made up for her by Matilda. Met Winkte-yuza. He wants to take his grandchild from the school here to Grand River. Gave him my opinion of him in sharp terms, & rode away.[55] Visited sick school children.

Tuesday, March 19th

St. Joseph's Day. . . . Preached at high mass on St. Joseph. Promised to have a solemn requiem mass for Sr. Mary Aloysia, O.S.B. & my relatives who died in our schools, to teach the Indians how to honor the dead properly. Benedict Gliyunka came to talk about marrying Rosa Edgar. F. Martin told him to call her. He followed her near her house, & went through a performance very like Indian courting, while Jovita Tayahanska did the same for her companion Cinpila. F.[rank] Takukokipešni stopped them. Girls came in the afternoon. We told them we had seen them with the field-glass, & advised them not to follow Indian ways. They wish to marry, Rosa to Benedict, & Placida Cinpila to Francis Aglila. We advised them. They seem to appreciate it. Visited sick children with F. Martin. Little Placida's eye is very bad. The cornea seems to have ulcerated & broken. . . . Told Indians story of Sts. Benedict & Scholastica. The Missouri broke up. Ice running out fast.

Wednesday, March 20th

. . . Sent medicine to Joseph Crowfeather's mother-in-law, by Leo Hehakagi. Visited sick children. Find out that Agnes Wahpiya is my sister. She's all right, but the rest are a hard set.

Tuesday, March 21st

Feast of St. Benedict. Said mass at 6:30 A.M. Preached at high mass on Sts. Benedict & Scholastica. I am trying to get them to help me about Josephine. Admitted Rosa Bearface to League, & made her a promoter. Some school boy wrote a letter to my sister Matilda, but she did not get it. It must be stopped. Matilda, in a

[55] "Wintke" is the Lakota term for "heart of a woman," so Wintke-yuza may have been a male transvestite, which would explain Craft's negative opinion of him.

spirit of mischief may, I fear, encourage such things. I will admit her to League, & when the Sacred Heart teaches her, I will teach her, & can be sure she will listen.

Visited sick children, & gave them pictures. They are improving. Geese are flying north. Wrote letters to Josephine, Annie, & Cecilia Gaudreau.

Friday, March 22d

. . . Admitted Matilda to League. Visited the sick children. Talked with my sister Matilda, & advised her how to act, so as to be respectable & happy & good. Recommended frequent confession, & communion. After dinner, rode to Agency, stopped at Wm. Halsey's. Reached Agency just at dark.

Saturday, March 23d

Visited the school, saw Wells' boys, & sisters Adele & Gertrude. Anselmine is very sick. Cholera morbus, & scrofulous constitution. In collapse. Rallied, but can scarcely recover. She is ready & willing to die. Enrolled her in League, & came up again & brought her badge & certificate. Enrolled Sr. Gertrude in League. Took leave of Anselmine, & recommended Josephine & Annie Gaudreau—especially Josephine to her prayers.

Wrote letters over again to Josephine & Annie Gaudreau, & Cecilia Gaudreau. Wrote to Bishop & F. Stephan, sent a postal note for $1.00 to Josephine. Explained further to Bishop my proposal about Berthold, & told him of Methodist minister being at Fort Stevenson in charge of school. Reminded Stephan of $46.93 due me. (wrote to 41 LaSalle St.) & told him of proposal to Bishop about Berthold. . . . In writing to Josephine, I said nothing about my offer to Bishop about Berthold, fearing to wound & disappoint her by raising hopes that might, perhaps, not be realized. I, also, so informed the Bishop, saying it would be time enough for me to tell her when I heard that he approved my proposal. I told him that all depended on the part of the proposal relating to Indian novices. I said I was sure Josephine would consent. The Sacred Heart seems now to honor Josie, in return for what she has suffered. My poor little Indian sister was neglected, despised, & plotted against, her vocation disputed & doubted. She was treated as no novice was ever treated before,—allowed to return while suffering from desolation & trial. My efforts in her behalf were opposed. Even the Bishop tried to send her to her father, in the camps, thinking that I was at Fort Berthold. Now all shall bend before the Indian Bride of the Sacred Heart. Her decision shall govern missions, & be the condition ruling Bishop's plans; & perhaps the very mission (Berthold) where I was supposed to be out of the way of aiding her, shall be her novitiate, & see her consecrate herself to Jesus; & even, perhaps, obey her as its Sister Superior,—who knows. Only Jesus, her spouse; & may He aid her, & receive her, for His glory & her salvation.

Sunday, March 24th

Saddled up & started for Wells at 2 A.M. Reached Wells at about 7 A.M. Rang the school bell & woke everybody. Said mass at 10:30 A.M. Spoke again of League, & Indian objections to holy things. Went to young men's council (St. Joseph's) at Peter Hehaka-ouzinca's. On the way stopped at Itegikiya's. Heard of a "Capapi olowan" and thought Itegikiya was at his incantations again & went in to ridicule it. Found Zatela treating him for a stab in the left iliac region. Woman he stole once, & was made by Police court to leave, stabbed him for courting her again—so they say. Some think he did it himself. Too dark to examine much. Evidently no danger. Staid at St. Joseph's meeting until near midnight.

Monday, March 25th

Instructed my little sister, Niyaiyohiyawin for baptism & communion. Prairie fires all over, on both sides of Missouri. Warm & pleasant. Queer weather for March.

Tuesday, March 26th

Instructed Children, & told them legends & stories of Our Lord & Saints. Instructed Niyaiyohiyawin again. Went to see High Bear & Itegikiya. High Bear not at home. Itegikiya's wound small,—healed up—has not penetrated beyond the cellular tissue, pulse regular, tongue clear, appetite good. Result of observations—confounded humbug,—did it to himself to get sympathy, or get the woman in trouble. I saw a coat he wore when stabbed, no mark,—a little blood on inside,—he refused to show wound when asked at the time, no knife was found on woman, who was at once examined. He has, no doubt, gone home, & then made a trifling scratch. . . .

Wednesday, March 27th

Went to High Bear's & gave Henry his badge & admitted him to League. Advised him about Indian ways. Fixed cross on Ursula's grave. I put it there in 1884. Passed Juliana Oiyotankawakanwin's grave. Poor sister, where is she. Died in 1884. Not well disposed. Gave last absolution sub conditione. My only hope is that she died in the scapular. After acting so well so long at school, to die in this way. May God, for the love the Sacred Heart, & the souls he suffered to save, prevent such things for the future, & crush under the iron hand of divine justice the wretches who cause them.

Told the children legends & stories again. They seem now to be afraid of the "wakan" [sacred] part of them. One boy noisy & troublesome, & let me know plainly that they didn't want to listen. Continued until I wanted to stop, let the children go, & kept this one boy, & reprimanded him, & when he saw how mean he had been, I treated him kindly. It's the work of the old people.

Crazy Man (Antony Ireland) called me to see his wife. Trifling throat trouble. Won't go till morning. Told him that when all hear me as a priest, I can afford to act as a doctor. His wife,—so he said some time ago, don't want the sina-sapa's [black robe's] ways, & therefore she must not expect me to be doctor only & not priest. Now if he has lied in blaming her for his own slowness, as they often do, he is being rightly served, & will be exposed. He seems disposed to deny what he said before.

Sold my field glass to Wells for $20.00. He will take so much on his account at Coles' next quarter. I'll suffer so much for Josie. School girl had fit. Got pipe from Wolf Necklace for her. Went to Givens' & interpreted.

Thursday, March 28th

Went to see Crazy-Man's wife. Just what I expected,—a grain of corn lodged back of the tongue. Took a spoon to examine,—she was afraid, & I gave up in disgust. A few scholars came. Gave them some pictures. After dinner started for Agency (at 2 P.M.). Reached there at 7 P.M. On the way stopped to see Catharine Mahpiyakoyakena (Waga's). Bad cold. Vomiting. Told them to get from Wells what she needs. Gave her a picture of St. Catharine.

Received badges, certificates, & handbooks of League from Rev. F. Dewey. Also letter from Bishop enclosing checks for $134.70, paying salary of $15.00 per month for 1888, & $25.00 per month, for Jan., Feb., & March, for 1889. He wants Belgian Benedictines for Berthold, but will take my offer if he can't get them. Today, on the way from Wells, I saw the first duck & crows of the season.

Friday, March 29th

Met Emeran. Went to Douglas' & got bill made out. Also got bill from Coles'. Called at School, & saw Wells' boys. James has a headache & fever,—slight. Wells & family came in afternoon. I have made up my mind to go to Sioux Falls & see Bishop, & talk over Berthold matter, & try to send Josie to Zell if possible. That will be an answer to the intentions I sent to the League, & far better than what I asked, if I get it. Jesus knows best. . . .

Saturday, March 30th

Issue Day. Emeran got his pay, & gave me $45.00 for things I got for him at Douglas'. I will go to Mandan with Wells & Mr. Bison (Mrs. McLaughlin's brother). Called at school again. Anselmine Wipelinwin died on Sunday. Holy death. May she pray for us as she promised.

Sunday, March 31st

Heard mass at 8:30 A.M. After High Mass meeting of St. Mary's & St. Joseph's societies in council room. Went there & made them a speech, telling them I was going to see Bishop about Ree [Arickaree] mission. During council Okute's wife sick. Looks like heart trouble. Dr. Caskie attended her, & she improved. Wells won't start today. After council Okute's wife sick again. Sent for F. Bede's oils, etc, & anointed her, while unconscious. She had not her scapular on, so I gave her one. After anointing & attendance of Dr. Caskie, she improved. She & Okute staid at Pamplin's.

Got tea, tobacco, etc. at store, & medicine from Dr. Caskie—for Crowfeather. Called at school, & admitted Lizzie Papan to the League.

Monday, April 1st 1889

Issue Day. Prepared all day to get off. Lectured "Wamahe" (Louis Sitting Bull) on his deviltries at Grand River. Told Mad Bear, Big Head, & young Bull Head about Itay a gi annoying Barney. Met Mrs. Van Solen & the Cournoyer girls. Shook hands with them, but not with her. Gave Rosa a handbook & badge of League. From what they say I think F. Bede has been treacherous enough & unmanly enough to tell what I told him of their past career, for his own benefit & guidance. I don't mind their knowing it, but it was contemptibly mean on his part. I will enquire further. I met Crowfeather's family, got medicine for them, & went to see Crowfeather at F. Bede's, & gave him tobacco. Started for Cannonball at 5:30 P.M. & reached here at 15 minutes to 9 P.M. Will leave horse here, & go with Wells to Mandan tomorrow. Givens brought up my satchel. Very high N.W. wind.

Editor's Summary: Tuesday, April 2, 1889–Friday, May 3, 1889

En route to Sioux Falls to present his plan to Bishop Marty, Father Craft stopped at Avoca to check on the progress of Josephine Crowfeather and his other postulants. The news was good: "Josie is willing to go to Zell, Berthold, or anywhere, so she can be a sister."[56] Also, he found that Annie Gaudreau had a religious vocation as well.

[56] Craft journal, 6 April 1889.

Two days later, Craft visited Sioux Falls, where Bishop Marty readily consented to his plan. Craft wrote, "Josie will go to Zell & take habit as soon as possible, & then go with Benedictine Sisters to Berthold. I can have novices there. . . . He [Bishop Marty] adopts Annie and Cecilia Gaudreau [and] gave me [a copy of the] Benedictine Constitution and Ceremonial."[57]

Bishop Marty's acceptance of financial responsibility for Annie and Cecilia Gaudreau, and especially his presentation of the Benedictine constitution and ceremonial, are important recognitions of the bishop's initial approval of Father Craft's plan for an order of Indian sisters. A series of declarations on the holy rule of St. Benedict, including the directives for rites celebrated by a bishop, this material would provide the vow formula taken by Craft's postulants. Craft could now prepare the foundations for his sisterhood. The first order of business was to get Josephine to the Benedictine Convent at Zell, near Redfield. Father Craft and Josephine Crowfeather arrived at the convent at Zell on April 14th, where she was well received by the Benedictine Sisters. Father Craft recorded in his journal that on Easter Sunday, April 21, 1889, Josephine Crowfeather

> received the habit after the Gospel, according to ceremonial sent by the Bishop. F. Bunning cut her hair according to ceremonial. She received [Holy Eucharist] during mass. After mass I shook hands with her & congratulated her before the congregation, as she had shaken hands with me two years ago, when none but she dared show friendship or sympathy for me. Thanks be to the Sacred Heart of Jesus. May He grant her final perseverance in her holy vocation & to me grace to perfect my sacrifice for her, & may He establish firmly the religious vocations of <u>all</u> Indian & mixed-blood aspirants, & give them abundant grace, & final perseverance.

With Josephine safely at Zell, and soon to be sent to Yankton to take her vows, Father Craft returned to Standing Rock to prepare for his next assignment on Fort Berthold Reservation in what would soon become North Dakota.

---

[57] Craft journal, 9 April 1889.

Part III
The Third Standing Rock Journal
April 1889–May 1890

—All For Jesus—
Sweet Heart of Jesus be our Love,
Sweet Heart of Mary be our Salvation,
Holy Heart of St. Joseph pray for us.
A.M.D.G

Journal and record of daily
routine of mission work.

"Say to your Sister, 'Thou hast obtained mercy.'"*
Osee. C. II, v. 1

* The quote is from Hosea ("Osee") 2:1.

At Standing Rock Reservation, DT, 1889

Saturday, May 4th

Landed at Cannonball, below school, & walked up with Louisa. Went with A. C. Wells to announce mass near dance. Went to Parkins, & went with Wells fishing with Jack Light. Rain.

Sunday, May 5th

Said mass at 10:30. Not many came. Told them about Sisters Josephine, Emma, & Annie [Gaudreau], & Indian Community at Berthold. My little sister Niyauyohiyawin came, but was not fasting. Advised her to go to Sister's school to be prepared for baptism & 1st communion together. Went to Parkins & paid my bill, & bought lariat.

Monday, May 6th

Went to Agency, visited Sisters. Bob Gaudreau & Philip went to confession for their Easter duties in the church.

Tuesday, May 7th

Went to church, heard Philip's confession & gave him & Bob communion at 6 A.M. Wrote to Rev. Mother Hildegarde, & Sisters Josephine, Emma, & Annie, F. Bunning, Bishop (telling that I will go to Berthold in 2 weeks. All about Zell, & asking for the whole novitiate & F. Bunning for Berthold. Telling about Indian disposition towards bill, & that they would hear him, or any he sends.) [and] Rev. M. St. Anthony, Annie Gaudreau, & Claudia [Crowfeather]. Received letter from Rev. F. Dewey, S.J. with 5 intentions & bill. Answered it & promised to say Masses. Paid my bill at Coles' in full. I put $20.00 on Wells' account, to pay for field-glass & paid in full, $82.40. Black Tomahawk wants Dora to be a Sister.

Wednesday, May 8th

Mary Halsey & other children made 1st Communion. Went to school. Gave Dora & Maggie Goodday badges of League, & told them about vocation. They are delighted. Met F. Bede. I will most gladly forgive him, & will also forget, & not watch him, if the Sacred Heart will open a way for me to do so safely. . . . Sold Pinch, saddle & bridle to H. S. Parkins for $50.00 & received the cash. I rode to the Mission, stopping on the way at Wm. Halsey's. Some sickness at the Mission owing to cool damp weather.

Matilda is here all safe. Met my two other sisters from Crowfeather's family at May devotions. Father Bernard has baptized my last little sister Josephine. Thank God. Just what I wanted. He gives them a Josephine in place of the one He took, & now He will surely keep Sister Josephine for ever. Found & destroyed a letter from Hampton [School] to Matilda.

Thursday, May 9th

Anniversary of Paul Tezila's death. Remembered him at mass. Saw Matilda & showed her photos of our two sisters, Sister Josephine & Claudia. She promises to be good, & write to us often. I gave her Sister Josephine's & Claudia's & my address. Went to Crowfeather's & gave him photo of Josephine & Claudia. He says Matilda thinks of marrying Veremund Catka. I returned to the school, saw Matilda & asked her. I put the different states of life before her, prayed with her to God for light & grace to know & do His will, & gave her till tomorrow to decide.

Friday, May 10th 1889

. . . Saw Matilda again. She decided to marry Veremund Catka. Called & questioned Veremund. He says just as Matilda does. He has wanted to marry her for two years. F. Martin & I instructed both separately. They will be married July 4th. Crowfeather came before I had settled about Matilda. Promised to let him know about it tomorrow. He & his wife will come for instruction & join the societies. Rode to Agency. Called at School.

Saturday, May 11th 1889

Met Wells at Coles', bought trunk ($5.00). . . . Went to May devotions in church, & called at school afterwards to meet Cournoyers, but did not see them. Saw Crowfeather & told him that all was settled favorably for Matilda & Veremund, & that they would live near him & help him. Packed trunk & sent it to Wells' by Red Tomahawk.

Sunday, May 12th 1889

Patronage of St. Joseph. Heard mass in church at 8 A.M. Called at school after mass but Cournoyers had gone. Called again after dinner & left message with Sr. Gertrude for Rosa about League. Met Rosa & Hermanie at Coles', paid Coles for trunk & horse feed, etc., in full. Hermanie wants to join my Indian Community. I encouraged her & warned her not to expose her vocation at dances, balls, etc., & told her & Rosa to look to Sr. Gertrude as their friend. Called again at School, & told Sr. Gertrude about Hermanie, & asked her to encourage her & keep her from danger. I promised to enroll all the Sisters (9) in the League.

Rode to Mission. On the way saw Bull Head & Wm. Halsey, & engaged them to look for Theodora, to save her vocation & soul, from danger in the camps. Stopped at St. Joseph's Meeting & sang with them, & spoke about Bishop, & Sisters Mary Josephine, Emma, & Annie. Reached Mission in time to receive Benediction outside, at the close of May devotions.

Monday, May 13th 1889

. . . Rode to St. F. de Sales' Mission. Got Emeran to get his team & go with me to Sina-lutas for Theodora. James Frisking-Elk went with us. Raining. We found her quite ill. (Consumption) The old people objected to letting her receive the sacraments, & wanted her to continue taking Indian medicine. I gave them a blasting, & enrolled her in League of Sacred Heart, & heard her confession & anointed her, & gave her the plenary indulgence, in art. mort. She improved very much. She wants to return with us tomorrow. Staid all night.

Tuesday, May 14th 1889

Theodora much better. Received her as a postulant of my Indian Community. When I proposed taking her with us the old people opposed it. She cried & wanted to go, but would not go, saying they meant to stab me. I laughed at her fears, but she asked me to go for Bull Head. She said it would be all right if he came. After threatening the old people, & making them promise to let her go if Bull Head decided so, we went for Bull Head. He returned late, & we will go down with him tomorrow. If poor Theodora could only have courage enough to rely on me, she would soon be safe. Before leaving, I gave the people a severe instruction on impure conversation in presence of children. Louis Primeau & Agnes Red Eagle came to Bull Head's from Agency.

Wednesday, May 15th

Went with Bull Head to get Theodora. Paid Bull Head $1.00 to stimulate his energy. He rode ahead & got them ready. He thinks it best for me to let her uncle take her to the Agency, & pay him $2.00 for the use of his wagon. I gave them an order for $5.00 on Sr. Gertrude, promising to repay her. I gave so much, to enable them to hire horses. I insisted that they go at once. Sitting Bull came in. I would not talk to him except through Emeran. He acted well enough, & advised them to take Theodora in at once. I advised the Indians to call & counsel with the Bishop before meeting the Commissioners, & to have the Bishop sit with them in council & speak for them.[1] They seem to like the idea very well. We finally got Theodora safely off at 1 P.M. I sent my rain coat with her to use in case of rain. I find she is my sister, through relationship with Bull Head & Halseys. I notified Sr. Gertrude that I had received Theodora as a postulant, so she can take her vows if dying, & receive the habit. She wants the name of Mary Gertrude.

Sitting Bull wanted to make friends. I told him, through Emeran, that I regarded him as the tool of [George] Faribault & the Primeaus, & would be ready to forgive him, if he would make amends decently for slandering me. He said he was sorry for it, but began trying to get me to pay a store bill for him, saying I had promised to do so. I

[1] Craft is referring here to the 1889 Dawes Commission, which will soon arrive to reopen negotiations on the purchase of Sioux lands.

exposed his misstatements, & said he ought to know better than to introduce such stuff, if he were really sorry for his crimes. Emeran got confused & impatient, & I had to speak myself. I then spoke to the crowd, but not to Sitting Bull, saying that he should have the decency to acknowledge his fault, & ask pardon publicly, after such a grave offense, & that I did not care to see him until he made up his mind to do so.—I would like to forgive him, &, in my heart, I really do forgive him; but my position demands a full public reparation, & I really have no right to let it go, & he ought to be man enough to do it.

I stopped to see a sick woman. Also to see Mato-Kaninge, sick. Also Iron Star,[2] Red-feather, Ida Cankula, & Joseph Giuiya. I told Ida to say to Long-feather's children that I forgave them, & would aid them if they wished. The rain kept off till we got home. We stopped at Flying-By's & got bed & crackers, etc. Pinch has been left till today with plenty of hay but no water.

Thursday, May 16th 1889

Still raining. Horses tired. Scholars came. Emeran fears horses will play out, & wants to go to Mission tomorrow. I am anxious to hear from Theodora, but I have put her in the hands of the Sacred Hearts of Jesus, Mary & Joseph, & I trust them & all the holy angels & saints to do their part for the bride of Jesus.

Friday, May 17th 1889

Started with Emeran for the Mission. Very muddy. One horse tired out. Put Pinch in his place. After reaching the Mission & resting horses, went with Emeran's wagon to Agency. Sina-luta had taken two days to get in. He wore my raincoat, & Theodora got wet. She is much worse. I let her rest. F. Bede, not knowing I had anointed her, did so again. Agreed with him that he should give her habit & vows, if F. Martin consented. Got letter from Cecilia Gaudreau, saying that Robert will go to get them in June. Enclosed it to Bishop, asking him to interfere. Wrote also to Rev. M. St. Anthony, Annie & Cecilia [Gaudreau] to prevent it.

[2] George Ironstar, a district farmer on Standing Rock Reservation (*Annual Reports*, 1892, 833).

Saturday, May 18th

Went back to Mission. Agreed with F. Martin about Theodora. He selected in the ceremonial the ceremonials for giving habit & vows, which will be perpetual, as she is dying. Instructed Emeran & Gertrude Yaperwin for their wedding tomorrow.

Sunday, May 19th 1889

I sang high mass at 10:30, & before mass I married Emeran & Gertrude & gave them the nuptial benediction during mass. In the afternoon I went with F. Martin to High Eagle's[3] to young men & women's council, & interpreted for F. Martin. They do much better here than at the Agency. Here the priest rules,—there Catholic Pharisees spoil our work. Sent note & ceremonial to F. Bede by Barney Prange.

Monday, May 20th

Said mass (Requiem) at 6:30. Remembered all my Indian relatives. Saddled up & rode to Agency. F. Bede absent at Goose's camp. He took Lucy to show the way. Theodora worse. Helped nurse her.

Tuesday, May 21st

Said mass at school. F. Bede returned. Theodora wishes to take vows at Zell. Fears the girls will laugh at her hair. It's a temptation. Satan's last effort. Explained to her condition, & prayed to Sacred Heart for her, & let her decide. She decided to take habit & vows at once, & have her hair cut. I questioned her before F. Bede & Sr. Gertrude to make sure of her consent. F. Bede wishes me to officiate, though I would prefer he would do it. He will give her Viaticum. No time to send to Bishop, I don't know where he is, & she may die or get delirious soon.

I heard her confession, & then I gave her the habit with full ceremonies, just as Josephine received it, & for the vows I used the ceremonies for the triennial vows, but used the formula for perpetual

[3] Martin Higheagle, police private on Standing Rock Reservation (*Annual Reports*, 1893, 559).

vows used by these Sisters.[4] I gave her the name of Mary Gertrude. After her profession & receiving the Holy Viaticum from Rev. F. Bede, she was filled with holy joy & peace, & seemed to forget her pains. In the holy habit & black veil, she looks just like Sister Jodacha. The Sisters then removed the habit that she might rest better, & cut her hair close, & gave her one of Sister Gertrude's caps. The first full blood Sioux, Theodora Piicegewin, dies to the world, & becomes by her perpetual vows Rev. Sister Mary Gertrude, O.S.B. May she persevere, & intercede for us with the Heart of Jesus in heaven.

As I began the ceremonies of giving the holy habit, a terrible windstorm arose, but it ceased after her vows. Satan is vanquished, & now may Jesus guard His Spouse, our Sister in His Sacred Heart. Dr. Caskie called & examined her, & directed treatment. He thinks she cannot last more than ten days, if as long. She is resigned to live or die, as Jesus wills, though she asked me what would cure her, so she could live to reach Zell, but she says she will leave it all to Jesus, & be happy in His decision, & obey Sr. Gertrude in all things, & not seek to see her relatives, as she has left them for Jesus, & will only pray for them, & let Him care for them. It is plain, the best plan is, to advise such chosen souls to be generous, & then trust to Jesus to give them abundant grace. At our new Sister's request, I took supper with F. Bede. Went to confession to F. Bede, & he to me.

Wednesday, May 22d

. . . Took leave of our dear Sister Mary Gertrude, O.S.B., leaving her to the loving care of her Spouse, the Heart of Jesus. Took leave of all at the school. Rode to Wells, packed trunk, & got ready to start.

Thursday, May 23d

Could not quite finish packing. Arranged with Wm. Zahn to take me to Mandan for $5.00. Went to see old Red Fish who is

[4] Father Craft recorded the vows of Theodora Piicegewin on May 21, 1889 (in author's possession).

dying. I wish to give him a last chance, for the glory of the Sacred Heart. His wife opposed my entering the tent. I tore the door & went in. I advised the old man. He wavered, & seemed about to consent, but finally said conclusively that he had many devils, & many crimes, & would not receive baptism. After exhausting all argument & persuasion, he started to crawl out. I told him four times. He firmly refused each time. I sprinkled tent & vicinity liberally with holy water. Made the sign of the cross over all. Advised Red Fish to change his mind & send for me,—lectured old Waga, & rode off. Went with Wells to Parkins', & gave up Pinch. Wells related how the Agent [James McLaughlin] sneered at my & Josephine's photo at High Bear's. Told Wells what to say to him. He is a traitor & enemy of the Church, & of anything but his own base temporal interests. We must not attach ourselves to such men, but to God alone.

Wm. Zahn backs out of going to Mandan. I will go by stage. I warned Bob Gaudreau not to go for our sisters Annie & Cecilia.

Editor's Summary: May 24–July 27, 1889

Father Craft left Standing Rock Reservation by stage and traveled via Bismarck and Mandan, arriving at Fort Berthold on May 28. Meeting with the agent Thomas Jones, he found that the seeds he had sown the previous September had fallen on hard ground. The stake he had driven to mark the spot for his new mission on the Little Missouri Bottom had been removed and the land sold to Hall, the Congregationalist minister. In an interesting by-play, the Knife River Gros Ventres, an off-the-reservation tribe that the agent hoped to bring into the agency, asked Craft to place his mission in their camp. Eventually, Craft applied for another 160-acre plot of land—still on the Little Missouri Bottom—on which to build his mission. (Its location today is at the bottom of Lake Sakakawea.) A series of councils with the Gros Ventres, Rees, and Mandans produced grudging agreement over the priest's demands that any school he built there would be well-attended by their children, who would have no vacations during which they might return to their camps. However, parents could visit their children on certain days. Until the school was built, the tribes could continue their traditional dancing and Indian ways. Craft wrote, "It may take a year,—maybe not so long, and as fast as they are able, they must come in as civilized men and women, and good Catholics. I required a sincere renewal of last year's promise."[5]

Craft, though, was essentially a middleman in the construction process. Father Stephan, the director of the BCIM in Washington, D.C., arranged for a contractor named Lexan to handle the project. The building was to be 100 × 34 feet. Craft was not pleased with the building's design, writing that it was "just what I protested against. I can't see why those who have to carry on the work can't be consulted about plans."[6]

Craft envisioned a boarding school for at least a hundred students, a school that he would eventually staff with an order of Indian sisters; Father Stephan planned a day-school served by Belgian Benedictines. None of the signs boded well for the success of Sacred Heart Mission, despite the fact that Craft made his formal application to the agent for 160 acres of land for the school on Friday, June 28, 1889, the Feast of the Sacred Heart of Jesus.

At Father Stephan's request, Craft next traveled to St. Paul, Minnesota, where they arranged for builders and lumber dealers to provide materials for the school. Stephan, though, took the occasion to warn Father Craft against any repetition of the conduct that caused his removal from Rosebud Reservation back in 1883. Moreover, as the leader of the BCIM, Father Stephan was adamantly opposed to Craft's plan for an order of Indian sisters. Craft was taken aback: "I am afraid he [Stephan] will prove an enemy."[7]

For his part, Father Stephan was desperately trying to accommodate a major political transition taking place in Washington,

[5] Craft journal, 15 June 1889.

[6] Craft journal, 26 June 1889.

[7] Craft journal, 3 July 1889.

D.C. Thomas J. Morgan, a Baptist minister and professional educator, had just been appointed Commissioner of Indian Affairs by President Harrison. Although Morgan was a strong proponent of Indian education and assimilation, he would not be a friend of Catholic schools, and Stephan did not want an uproar caused by erratic or misunderstood actions of a loose cannon missionary, well-intentioned or not. Moreover, Stephan, Bishop Marty, Bishop Ireland, Cardinal Gibbons, and most of the Catholic hierarchy in the United States and the Vatican had for some years been carefully nurturing the vocational and philanthropic interests of Katharine Drexel, a wealthy heiress from Philadelphia, Pennsylvania. Miss Drexel was a major benefactor of the BCIM; for instance, she donated $12,000 for the construction of the school at Craft's mission. Only a few months earlier, she had entered the novitiate of the Sisters of Mercy at Pittsburgh, Pennsylvania. The Catholic hierarchy did not want a competitive order of Indian sisters to interfere with their own visions of a separate order of sisters, financed and founded by Katharine Drexel, serving Native Americans and other minorities.

On Sunday, June 23, Father Craft noted that he had written a letter to General George Crook at Pine Ridge Agency, "offering to help the Sioux Commission. (I registered this letter under the name of F. M. C. Basset, so Post Masters won't give away my plans.)" In the course of Craft's return trip to Fort Berthold, he visited his postulants at Avoca, then traveled to Minot, where he arranged for lumber to be shipped to the Little Missouri Bottom. He returned to Standing Rock on July 28, 1889, where the Dawes Commission had already arrived.

At Standing Rock Reservation, DT, 1889

Sunday, July 28th 1889

Arrived at Agency. Wells met me between landing & Agency. Evidently sent to sound me. My arrival caused consternation on Agency. They fear I will expose their tricks to Crook. He [Crook] had told them that some[one] of great experience & influence was coming, & now [that] they see me they understand it & are afraid. I told Wells they need not fear if they behave, but I would not spare them if they didn't. Called on Crook, & arranged plan of action. Will see him again. . . . Commissioners visited St. Joseph's & St. Mary's Societies & were much pleased.[8]

Monday, July 29th

Council at Agency. I sat with Indians. Agreed with Crook to withhold my opinion, & have St. Joseph's boys ready to make a break when time came. This morning mass at school. Commissioners in council spoke very highly of our societies, as the <u>only</u> good thing they had seen.

Tuesday, July 30th

. . . Council at Agency, & again of Yanktonnais alone at their camp. Went to both. Called on Crook & kept him posted.

Wednesday, July 31st

. . . Council at Agency, & Yanktonnai camp. (This last for Indians alone) Went to both. Called on Crook. Wired to lawyer in Bismarck to ask if Gov. could open Reserve without consent of Indians. I did so after consulting Crook, Grass, & Mad Bear.

Thursday, Aug. 1st

Went to council with Blackfeet (Indians alone). Sitting Bull sent Crawler & others to quarrel with Grass. Grass announced that he could do nothing, & they had better suggest something, if they knew better than he. I acted as his counsel. Hanitch [the Bismarck lawyer] sent dispatch the Gov. could take & sell all Reserve without consulting Indians. I showed Indians dispatch, & told them we were outflanked. [Sitting] Bull tries to excite Indians & goes about day & night as a crier.

---

[8] The 1889 Dawes Commission arrived at Standing Rock Agency on July 25, 1889, led by Maj. Gen. George Crook. The other members were Charles Fowler, past governor of Ohio, and Maj. William Warner of Mo., national commander of the Grand Army of the Republic.

Friday, Aug. 2d

Went again to Blackfoot [*sic*] council. [Sitting] Bull's party again tried to quarrel. I made a speech for the first time, saying that we were holding off for better terms, we were outflanked by Gov. & by Indians below [at Cheyenne River, Rosebud, and Pine Ridge] signing, as I heard in telegraph office. This is like a war council, & they should give their views quietly as to fight, escape, or a surrender on good terms. All seemed pleased & ceased quarreling. Called on Crook. Letter from Zell. Emma Halsey dying. Took vows, & is now Rev. Sr. Mary Christina, O.S.B. Walked out to Halsey's & told him.

Saturday, Aug. 3d

Beef issue. Council with Commissioners. Today was appointed for final council & signing if Indians consented. After Crook spoke, the tables were brought out. Grass said he had given his objections, & been clearly answered, & that Indians below were signing, & he also would sign if Crook & other Commissioners would make certain promises. They did so. Antelope & a few others tried to object, but were not listened to.

I was sure that [Sitting] Bull or others would make some demonstration, & therefore I had St. Joseph's boys & those they controlled (about 200) ranged along inside the platform, & on the outer edge, so as to be ready, & instructed them not to sign until I gave the order. I kept my opinion back, & spoke of holding off for better terms. Bull came outside with a mounted party, & just as Grass & Mad Bear rose to sign, they began shouting & running their horses in a circle. A stampede followed, to see what was the matter, but all returned. Grass & Mad Bear then signed, followed by a few other chiefs. [Sitting] Bull then came in, & wanted to speak, but no one would listen to him. He then rushed out calling on all to stampede & follow him. The stampede began. This is just what I wanted. If I could check & turn it in our favor, success was certain.

I called to our boys to sign at once as Bull had made a bad break & disgraced the Agency. I went up to the table & touched the pen,

& our boys at once began signing. I then went outside the platform & called to the Indians to halt & listen. They at once stopped. I then said what I had to our boys, & advised all to leave [Sitting] Bull & follow us, as the best thing they could do, & said that after such a break as [Sitting] Bull had made, we could not afford to wait for better terms, but must sign at once. The Indians remained quiet, & the advance to the tables of St. Joseph's boys on & outside of the platform, had the appearance of a very large crowd anxious to sign, & gave the necessary counter-stampede I wanted, & encouraged many of [Sitting] Bull's party to leave him & sign. He did not return. The signing began at 5 P.M. & lasted till about 8 P.M. In that time 279 signed, & the opposition was completely broken. I sent for [Sitting] Bull to come in & sign, & make amends, but though he promised, he didn't come.[9] I sent telegrams to F. Willard, F. Hopkins, & Rev. Sr. Hildegarde (about Rev. Sr. M. Christina (Emma Halsey) congratulating her on her vows, & saying her father would come soon.

Sunday, Aug. 4th

. . . Called on Crook. Wm. Halsey went to Bismarck with Sr. Gertrude. He will go to Zell. . . .

Monday, Aug. 5th

. . . Indians still signing. I got some to sign who had refused before. Agent [McLaughlin] was quite angry, & showed it as much as he dared, as also did Faribault (George). They give themselves away badly. Went with Mad Bear's family to get their photos taken for Gov. Foster. Telegraphed to F. Hopkins. Called on Crook, & kept him posted. Enough have now signed to ensure success of bill. F. Hopkins made me pay for telegrams I sent him.

Tuesday, Aug. 6th

. . . Last council at Agency, to take leave of Crook, etc. Commissioners visited the School. They paid my expenses at the rate

[9] For other accounts of this event, see McLaughlin, *My Friend the Indian*, 285; Schmitt, *General George Crook*, 288; and Kingsbury, *History of Dakota Territory*, 2:1279.

of $5.00 per day. I camped with Mad Bear & Antoine Clement. Crook thanked me for my aid & invited me to ride with him to Bismarck. I preferred to stay here awhile.

Wednesday, Aug. 7th

Commission left. I telegraphed to Globe (St. Paul) correcting statement in Pioneer press of August 2nd. Telegraphed to F. Willard, so he could first announce success to Government. Wired to Bishop at White Earth Agency. Went with Mad Bear's family to have their photos taken for Gov. Foster.

Thursday, Aug. 8th

. . . Paul came for me, but I waited for Sisters coming from Zell. F. Bede went to Cannonball. F. Martin still at Agency, where he staid during council.

Friday, Aug. 9th

. . . Good news from Zell. Sr. M. Josephine does well, & advises & consoles the rest, & is a perfect obedient religious. Thanks to the Sacred Heart. Sr. Gregory,[10] my cousin came.

Saturday, Aug. 10th

Went with Paul to Mission to stay for some days, & see our societies.

Sunday, Aug. 11th

. . . Preached at High Mass. Sisters came from Agency, with Sr. Gregory, O.S.B. She visited Augustina, her cousin, who wanted to see a Sioux sister before dying. Went to young men's & women's councils.

Monday, Aug. 12th

. . . Went to Emeran's at Grand River with Paul, Mary, & Father Bernard.

[10] Ellen Clark, the first Indian Benedictine sister.

Tuesday, Aug. 13th

Went with Paul, Mary, & Father Bernard to Jack Carignan's school. He was absent, & we returned to Emeran's. Visited Paul's sisters (they are mine too) on the way, & F. Bernard baptized a child—little Josephine.

Wednesday, Aug. 14th

Said mass at Emeran's, St. F. deSales' Mission, & F. Bernard sang High Mass. I preached in Sioux. We then returned to St. Benedict's with Paul's two sisters. F. Bernard is disgusted with Grand River. Flying By's camp, under Emeran's influence, is the only decent place on Grand River.

Thursday, Aug. 15th Feast of the Assumption

. . . My cousin Augustina Anaptapiwin died in school at 1 P.M. She died a very holy death. Council of Societies at the school & in the camp.

Friday, Aug. 16th

. . . Came to Agency, after burying Augustina, & preaching at her funeral. Telegraphed to Sr. Hildegarde.

Saturday, Aug. 17th

Said mass at School at 8 A.M., & returned to St. Benedict's. Stopped on the way to take medicine to F. Takukokipešni, & gave his daughter a note to go to the hospital for her eyes. Saw Placida Cinpi, & Rosa Bearface.

Sunday, August 18th

Said mass at 6:30, & preached at High Mass. Two Bulls came; he refuses to marry his dying wife. Last night I put out the candle, & laid down dressed, & went to sleep saying my beads. I woke suddenly; the room was lighted, & a Sister stood by the head of the bed. I recognized Rev. Sister Mary Christina, O.S.B. [Emma Halsey], my sister, now dying at Zell. I spoke to her, & she answered me, & then knelt at the side of the bed & said in English "Brother, please wash my face." She seemed pale & worn, & her face seemed stained as if with paint or medicine. Something seemed to tell me to give her my blessing & I did so. I got a wet towel & washed her face. She seemed much better & happier, & rose, saying: "Thank you, brother, I feel so much better. I feel quite well. I must go now. Good bye."

She disappeared, & the room was dark again. I looked for my beads, & could not find them. This morning the towel was wet. If it was a dream it was a strange one. I seemed to wake & see her near me. When she disappeared, I seemed not to wake, but to be still awake, & looked for my beads. Perhaps she wants me to pray for her. I at once wrote for her an intention in the list of the League, & remembered her at mass today. May the S.[acred] Heart aid her.

Monday, August 19th

. . . Two Bulls' wife died. (Augustina's sister) Wrote to Bishop, Mother, Claudia, Maj. Jones, & Mrs. Grady, & also to Rev. F. Bunning, suggesting that Sr. M. Josephine remain at Zell; sent love & best regards to my sister, Rev. Sister Mary Christina, O.S.B., & offered to take her purgatory for her. If she does not get the message on earth, she will know it &, I hope, avail herself of it when free from the body.

Tuesday, August 20th

Feast of St. Bernard. F. Bernard's Name's Day. . . . Preached at High Mass at 9 A.M. At mass I again remembered my sister Rev. Sister Mary Christina, O.S.B.

Wednesday, August 21st

. . . Rev. F. McNally[11] came with a letter from the Bishop. He is to go with me to Ft. Berthold. Went with him to Paul's. Telegram from Rev. Sr. Hildegarde. My dear sister in the Sacred Heart, Rev. Sister Mary Christina, O.S.B. passed to eternal rest on August 20th at 11:30 A.M. on the Feast of St. Bernard, within the Octave of the Assumption, as she desired. R.I.P.

[11] Father James McNally from Fort Yates, assigned by Bishop Marty to assist in establishing the new mission at Fort Berthold Reservation.

Thursday, August 22d

Said mass for my sister, Rev. Sister Mary Christina, O.S.B. at 6:30 A.M. As she was to be buried yesterday, the mass was "in die depositionis" [the Mass text on the day of burial]. I begged a mass from the other Fathers, so Sister had four masses today. I went with F. McNally to Crowfeather's & instructed the family, & also to Rosa Bearface's. At Crowfeather's, little Josephine, my little sister 1 year old was dying. I gave her my blessing & the blessing for the sick. She stopped her querulous wailing, stretched out her little hands to me, smiled, & opened her little mouth, & kissed me most affectionately. It was hard to get away from her. Her little eyes followed me, & I had to return again & again to kiss her goodbye, & the last I saw of little sister was the little face smiling her last farewell, & the little eyes watching me with more than natural intelligence, & sisterly love. May I have grace to meet her in heaven. I shall know her in the resurrection. That last look can never be forgotten.

Friday, August 23d

Said mass in black at 6:30 A.M. for Rev. Sister Mary Christina, O.S.B. My dear little sister Josephine died this morning. I placed her in the coffin. She will be buried tomorrow.

Saturday, August 24th

. . . Harry McLaughlin,[12] Frank Steinmetz, & two others came on horseback, on false report of a picnic & dance across the river, among the whites. Little sister Josephine was buried today.

Sunday, August 25th

. . . Was deacon & preached at Solemn High Mass at 10 A.M. in honor of S.[acred] Heart of Mary. Sent intentions for month to Rev. F. Dewey. H. McLaughlin, etc., went home. F. McNally, Martin, Bernard, & I went to Society meeting at High Eagle's.

Monday, August 26th

. . . Wrote to Bishop, but did not send the letter. Sisters from

[12] One of Agent McLaughlin's sons, about age 20 at the time.

Zell came via Eureka [in present-day South Dakota]. We hear that Rosa Bearface went to a dance of whites across the river, & F. Bernard & I started after her. Finding she had a place to stay if she wished, we returned, bringing back Mr. Wm. Halsey whom we met on the way. He was much edified by the novices at Zell. Their life was, he says, a new revelation to him. He says he never saw one die as holily & happily as Sister. In dying our dead sister Rev. Sister Mary Gertrude of the Sacred Heart, O.S.B. (Theodora Piicegewin) was with her, & Jesus seemed to come to her from the crucifix.

Tuesday, August 27th

. . . I found my beads. Mr. Halsey says they are the same as those sister used when dying. The night I saw her, he was with her. F. Bunning was absent on Mission. Mr. Halsey went home today. I wonder if Sister took my beads & returned them.

Wednesday, Aug. 28th

. . . Charging Eagle gave a "Ghost-feast" (Wanagi-glepe) & I find that several of the society attended it—against their rules. I went to Crowfeather's. Family all off cutting hay. Instructed Thunder Hawk. There is much hope for him. I met Rosa Bearface returning from Ghost-feast. I talked gently to her about it. She seemed sullen, & did not take the advice well, & walked off. She seemed to regret it, & would have returned, but I refused to talk further, & let her go. The society will advise her less gently. F. Martin & Sister M. Xavier returned.

Thursday, Aug. 29th

. . . Went with F. Bernard over river to get teams for Sisters going via Eureka to Zell.

Friday, Aug. 30th

Mass at 6:30. Went to Agency with Crowfeather. Looked for teams to bring Miss Lizzie Schoule's trunks to the Mission. Visited the school.

Saturday, Aug. 31st

. . . Enrolled in League of Sacred Heart Rev. Sisters Vincent, Gregory, & Stephen, O.S.B. Came with Emeran & Gertrude with Lizzie's trunks to Mission. Stopped at Halsey's & got lock of Rev. Sister M. Christina's hair. Doctor sick. Agent seems to be laying a trap for him.

Sunday, Sept. 1st

Mass at 6:30. (Mass of reparation to S. Heart). Preached at High Mass. Wind, smoke, & some rain. I will go with Sisters to Zell, & thence to Sioux Falls, to talk with Bishop about Berthold. Miss Lizzie & Sr. M. Adele came. Sr. Francis, Mrs. McLaughlin, & Sport went for John Grass, who is sick, yesterday, & will bring him to Agency.

Monday, Sept. 2d

. . . Went with F. Bernard over river & got teams. Corded & crossed the trunks over river, & will go tomorrow.

Editor's Summary: September 3–October 10, 1889

Father Craft reached the Benedictine Convent at Zell just as the sisters' corn crop was being harvested, but there were no volunteers among the local citizenry willing to help in the arduous task. As a few of the sisters were out cutting and stacking corn, he went into the field himself, cutting, carrying, and stacking corn all afternoon. "If it's good enough for the Brides of Jesus, it's good enough for me," he wrote. But he added, "If God don't punish these Zell people for their treatment of their Sisters and priests . . . I don't know who He will punish."[13] The next morning he sent out word to the community that there was an already-paid-for keg of beer waiting at the local tavern for those able-bodied men who would volunteer to bring in the corn. It cost him $2.75. Craft wrote, "They finished it [the harvest] before night,—thanks to the Sacred Heart, to whom

[13] Craft journal, 9 September 1889.

I had recommended it."[14] The local prohibitionists, though, were upset by the affair and invited Craft to one of their meetings, which he refused "without ceremony." The next day he described the prohibition meeting as having been a "fizzle."

After a few days counseling the novitiates at Zell, he went to Yankton, where he met with Bishop Marty to bolster the bishop's support for his postulants at Zell and Avoca and to report on progress at Fort Berthold Reservation. Together, they went to Sioux Falls. From there, Craft went on alone to Mankato, where he made an eight-day Ignatian Retreat, a customary practice secular clergy were required to make every three years. The eight-day format is designed to echo when the apostles withdrew to an upper room for eight days under the direction of the Holy Spirit.

On September 30, Craft went to the school operated by the Sisters of the Holy Child Jesus at Avoca, Minnesota, where he found that the nuns were less than enthusiastic in fostering the vocations of his Indian postulants. He wrote in his journal, "I find that the Sisters here, fearing that I will take children from their school to the Novitiate, are discouraging vocations. . . . To hold the children back, they told some to enter their congregation, while from the Sister's own talk to me it is plain they won't receive them."[15]

On October 3, he took a train to St. Paul, hoping to see Bishop John Ireland, who had sought his advice regarding candidates for the newly opened position of Indian Agent at Fort Berthold. He learned that John S. Murphy of Lisbon, DT, had been recommended for the assignment by Patrick Ford, editor of the *New York Freeman's Journal*, and that the bishop had already agreed to Murphy's assignment. Craft's response was that he "hope[d] Murphy won't be such a Catholic as McLaughlin."[16] On his return to Standing Rock, Craft again visited the schools at Avoca and Zell, then went to Yankton, where he met with Bishop Marty. The two of them then left for Standing Rock, via Jamestown and Bismarck.

[14] Craft journal, 10 September 1889.

[15] Craft journal, 1 October 1889.

[16] Craft journal, 3 October 1889.

AT STANDING ROCK RESERVATION, DT, 1889

Friday, Oct. 11th

Came on stage to [Fort] Yates with Bishop [Marty]. Crossed at Winona. Met Abbot Frowin[17] with John Pleets at landing. Sisters & children gave us a reception at the school. Put up at F. Bede's.

Saturday, Oct. 12th

. . . Heard confessions all day either of school girls in school chapel, or of society people in house & church, when school girls also came. F. Bede, Bernard, & McNally also heard confessions. Spoke with Abbot & Bishop about societies. In the morning before confessions, I took the Abbot to the beef killing, & introduced him to Indians.

Sunday, Oct. 13th

Said mass at 7 A.M. in church. Bishop said mass at 8. 2 Sisters professed at 7 in chapel. F. Bernard sang High Mass. Bishop preached & I interpreted. After Bishop's sermon (after mass), Bishop confirmed 76 Indians. In the afternoon went with Bishop to Society meeting in Agency Warehouse. Bishop spoke & I interpreted. Jos.[eph] Crowfeather met the Bishop at F. Bede's. Bishop confirmed Barbara Huhana in hospital, & told her she would soon die, & I gave her a badge, & received her in League.

Monday, Oct. 14th

. . . Spoke with the Bishop about my Indian relatives, & gave him account of my methods which he approved, only advising caution because of the foul minds & views of the surrounding whites. Went with F. Bernard to Mission. Got St. Joseph's boys mounted & went in wagon with them & met Bishop at Blackfoot creek where an arch of green branches was put over bridge. Got his blessing (he came with Abbot, F. McNally, & Agent), & escorted him to Mission under the arch over the gate. Introduced Societies, & heard confessions in church. Barbara Huhana died this morning in hospital. R.I.P.

[17] Frowin Conrad, OSB, first abbot of Conception Abbey, Conception, Mo.

Tuesday, Oct. 15th

Said mass at 7:30 (after Bishop's mass, which I served). Served the Abbot's mass with F. Bernard, at the Sister's profession. F. McNally sang High Mass at 10. Bishop preached after mass. I interpreted. Bishop confirmed 84 Indians. Society meeting after dinner in class room. They gave the Bishop a reception. Bishop spoke to them & I interpreted. Jos. Crowfeather & his wife Scholastica, were present with the Sisters.

I came with Bishop to [Fort] Yates. The Abbot remained to give the Russians across the river a mission, as the Bishop has to go again on the Chippewa Commission. A Presentation Sister came from Fargo to meet Bishop. Gave the Bishop message from Carrie Tazi, & recommended retreat for Giles & Indians. My mail came from Berthold. Showed Agent Jones' letter to Bishop. Letters from Mother, F. Bunning, F. Nilan,[18] Lexan, & Duffy.

Wednesday, Oct. 16th

Bishop said mass at 5:30 A.M. at school, & left, with Presentation Sister, at 6:30 A.M. I recommended Yankton instead of Avoca for Carrie & others who may have vocations. . . . Wrote F. Willard at Bishop's request to remind F. Stephan to attend to Bishop's orders for goods, etc. for Berthold.

Thursday, Oct. 17th

. . . Wrote to Maj. Jones, C. L. Lexan, & Mother, inviting Fanny [Craft's sister in Pennsylvania] to Berthold. Lexan wrote that men had nothing to eat, & would quit if I did not come this week. My letter will reach him before I can & will quiet him. He must deal with Stephan. . . . Lexan's letter came just as I was about to write to him, so I had time to answer it.

Friday, Oct. 18th

. . . Sent dispatch to F. Willard about my & Bishop's letters to F. Stephan & about Lexan's demand for money. I will wait for answer. Called again at school to see Louisa St. George, whom Sr.

[18] Father James Nilan of St. Peter's Church in Poughkeepsie, N.Y.

Gertrude asked me to see yesterday. Cramp in popliteal [the back part of the leg behind the knee] space. Somewhat better.

Saturday, Oct. 19th 1889

. . . Waited patiently for answer to telegram. None came. Will have to start Monday. Visited school. F. Bede went to Porcupine [DT].

Sunday, Oct. 20th

. . . Visited & marked graves of Rev. Sister Mary Aloysia of the Sacred Heart, O.S.B.,[19] & Rev. Sister Mary Gertrude of the Sacred Heart, O.S.B.,[20] my dear sisters. Visited & prayed at their graves at night. F. Bede returned from Porcupine. Fearing trouble, he did not bring back Julia. Got ½ fare ticket at Douglas'. Took leave of Sister Gertrude after Benediction.

Monday, Oct. 21st 1889

Woke this morning, but thinking it was too early, slept again. I wanted to rise at 4:30 A.M. At 4:30, some one knocked on the wall for some time till I woke & answered. Thinking it was F. Bede, I answered & dressed. F. Bede said when he came out that he did not knock, & woke after me. F. McNally from upstairs cried out "spook." I asked if he knocked. He said he did not. In fact, he could not, as it was on the wall near the head of my bed. Perhaps my dear sisters whose graves I visited last night wanted to help brother to start on time. Took breakfast at school, & went by stage to Mandan, & staid with F. Perreault. Visited White Horse in Mandan jail.

Editor's Summary: October 22, 1889–May 28, 1890

Father Craft faced an uncertain future as he returned to Fort Berthold, where Henry Lexan's construction team was building the two-story school for the Sacred Heart Mission. First of his priorities was to have Lexan build an altar in the school, where he would celebrate the mission's first Holy Mass on November 1, 1889, the

[19] Black Bear's daughter, Cunegunda, who died January 3, 1889.

[20] Theodora Piicegewin, who died June 14, 1889.

feast of All Saints. He often slept on borrowed bedding in the unheated school. Temperatures reached zero, and the Missouri River began to freeze over by mid-November.

Although Father Stephan ignored Craft's several letters to the BCIM, Craft did maintain a correspondence with Stephan's assistant, Father George L. Willard.

Most of the construction of the school was completed, but Lexan wanted to hold off painting until spring. In the meantime, the school had no desks, no school supplies, no stoves—nothing. Coal for heating would soon be frozen in the ground. Craft was dismayed by Stephan's silence. In a letter to Willard, Craft wrote, "I don't know what we will do if we don't soon get money to buy fuel. . . . One letter from F. Stephan saying that he would, or would not, or would be willing if possible, to send supplies & money, would have settled everything. . . ."[21]

Willard responded that Katharine Drexel would provide funds to complete the construction of the school, but that Bishop Shanley would have to fund the actual school operations. And in an aside, he advised that Father Stephan wanted the school to be named St. Edward's, after a member of the Drexel Family. Bishop John Shanley, though, had his own struggle to face as he established the new Diocese of Jamestown on November 10, 1889, in response to North Dakota's elevation to statehood on November 2, 1889. Bishop Marty, who had been the most supportive of Craft's plan to eventually move his novitiates from Zell and Avoca to Fort Berthold, was now seemingly out of the picture in South Dakota, where he was assigned to lead the new diocese of Sioux Falls.

Craft replied that they could name the school anything they wanted, but the mission he founded would remain Sacred Heart Mission. He also advised them that he was ordained by Bishop Marty for the agencies of South Dakota and was only on a temporary assignment in North Dakota. Marty finally agreed to support Craft by paying his monthly salary and providing funds for fuel during the winter.

---

[21] Craft to Father George L. Willard, 11 November 1889, Sacred Heart Priory Archives.

To complete the perfect storm of upheaval among competing Catholic Indian missionary interests in the Dakotas and political assignments in Washington, a new agent, John S. Murphy, was replacing Thomas H. B. Jones on the Fort Berthold Reservation in North Dakota. Through all this, Father Craft was able to sustain a rapport with the Three Tribes (Gross Ventres, Mandans, and Rees), even as he counseled the new agent: "Advis[ing] the limiting of dances, etc. & also the separation of the mixed-bloods from the Indians, as at [Fort] Yates. . . . These mixed-bloods differ from the Sioux métis, & are not so good."[22]

By mid-December, it was clear that Commissioner of Indian Affairs Morgan would not extend the contract school system to any new schools, and that another source of funds would have to be found if St. Edward's School was to survive. Craft determined to raise the funds himself.

First, however, he would have to ensure that his postulants at Zell and Avoca would be safe in their vocations. A journal entry on December 8, 1889, reflects the depth of his devotion and concern:

> In the memento for the dead, I remembered my Indian sisters, as I always do, especially my three Benedictine Sisters, Mary Aloysia of the Sacred Heart [Cunegunda], Mary Gertrude of the Sacred Heart [Theodora Piicegewin], & Mary Christina, O.S.B. [Emma Halsey]—also of the Sacred Heart, since she took her vows on the first Friday of the month. They seem to be with me yet.
>
> Whittier says truly of each of them, speaking of a dead sister—
>
> And she is with thee; in thy path of trial
> She walketh yet;
> Still in the baptism of thy self-denial
> Her locks are wet.[23]
>
> In view of their visits to me, & of my offering for them, how true it is of each of my dear Sisters in our holy Order. Tomorrow Sister Annie [Gaudreau] takes her vows, Sister Mary Josephine [Crowfeather] after

[22] Craft journal, 4 November 1889.

[23] John Greenleaf Whittier, "To My Friend on the Death of His Sister," st. 10. Craft substitutes "in" for "Still with the baptism . . ."

next Easter. May the Heart of Jesus keep her safe, & accept my offering for her, especially, & may it bring her happiness & final perseverance.

Remember me,—but not as I
On thee forever, ever dwell.
With anxious heart & drooping eye,
& doubts 'twould grieve thee should I tell.
But in thy calm unclouded heart,

Whence dark & gloomy visions flee,
Oh, there, my Sister, be my part,
& kindly there remember me.[24]

Edward Everett must have had a sister,—but none so holy as mine.

As word spread in Catholic circles concerning plans for Katharine Drexel's order of sisters, Craft heard rumors that she and Father Stephan intended to draw from other orders of sisters to fill theirs. He believed this to be "ruinous to vocations, and I don't intend to allow it."[25]

This called for redefining his current position in relation to Father Stephan, bishops, and Indian bureau figures like McLaughlin and Commissioner of Indian Affairs Morgan. In a letter to Father Willard, Craft wrote, "I wish to work in peace & harmony with F. Stephan, & it rests entirely with him to enable me to do so. . . . He will find it very unjust & imprudent, & productive of much shame, humiliation, & defeat to himself, to persecute me, & join such reprobates as those who, like McLaughlin & his corrupt & dishonest allies, have tried to overthrow my work and failed."[26] He had an inherent distrust of Catholic Indian agents "who might do much to aid us, but, practically, . . . won't, & we needn't expect it. McLaughlin passes for a 'very successful Agent.' He has been anything but successful in raising the standard of civilization & moral-

[24] This is the last of eight stanzas of Edward Everett's poem, "To a Sister," which first appeared in Horace Greeley's (ed.) *The New Yorker* 1 (Sept. 10, 1836): 399. The likely source of the poem for Father Craft was Rufus Wilmot Griswold's 1885 anthology, *The Poets and Poetry of America*, p. 202.

[25] Craft journal, 19 December 1889.

[26] Craft to Father George L. Willard, 15 November 1889, BCIM Records.

ity among the Indians and employees. In fact, he has been most successful in lowering it. Our success would have been much greater, had his been less."[27]

In Sioux Falls, South Dakota, on January 10, 1890, Craft received personal assurances from Bishop Marty that Craft's Indian sisters would not be transferred into any order founded by Father Stephan or Katharine Drexel. Marty also agreed to his recommendation that he (Craft) tour eastern cities to lecture and raise funds for the Indian missions. That part of Craft's plan in place, he next sent $200.00 to the sisters in Yankton as a "dowry" for Josephine Crowfeather's transition to a Benedictine order.

After also gaining the approval of Bishop Shanley for his tour of eastern cities, Craft returned for a final visit to the Rosebud Reservation, where his ministry among the Sioux had started almost seven years earlier. He collected Indian artifacts to use in his lectures and obtained photos and other memorabilia from his adopted family of Spotted Tail. On March 24, 1890, he described in his journal how he had confronted Crow Dog, Spotted Tail's assassin, and had given him "a blasting for killing my father."

On the train trip to New York City, Father Craft made a detour to the Shrine of Kateri Tekakwitha in Auriesville, New York, where he took cuttings from a nearby red willow bush. That evening, he wrote a letter of encouragement to each of his postulants at Zell and Avoca, enclosing a piece of the red willow. Three weeks later, as he worked on his lecture notes in Brooklyn, New York, he received a letter from Josephine Crowfeather saying that she had made her profession as a Benedictine religious, taking the name Sister Mary Catharine, OSB. "Thanks to the Sacred Heart of Jesus, our Divine Spouse," he wrote in his journal. "'Say to your sister, Thou hast obtained mercy.'"[28]

When Father Craft reached New York City on May 8, 1890, he had already developed and tested a two-hour lecture he planned as the centerpiece of his fund-raising efforts. A Poughkeepsie audi-

[27] Craft to Father George L. Willard, 15 June 1889, BCIM Records.

[28] Craft journal, 26 April 1890.

ence had netted a contribution of $62.58 for his cause.[29] In Brooklyn on May 10, however, Bishop John Loughlin rudely dismissed him, refusing him permission to lecture or collect funds in his diocese. Although Craft still had a measure of encouragement from his two bishops in the Dakotas, he had lost all support from Father Stephan, who had reached the Bishop of the Diocese of Brooklyn ahead of him. Undaunted, he called on Austin and Patrick Ford, owners of two of the more strident newspapers of the day. Patrick Ford was the firebrand publisher of the *Irish World*; Austin Ford published the *New York Freeman's Journal and Catholic Register*. Craft wrote extensive articles in both publications describing the wretched conditions on the country's Indian reservations, "facts disgraceful to us" that "make us see that all 'Indian Policy' has always been a policy of extermination, and it remains so today. Government civilization of the remnant of the tribes is merely an excuse for the existence of an Indian Department, with its officials and salaries, that politicians and not Indians may live."[30] He proposed that the federal government "do away with the Indian Department, with all its officials and useless expenses, and place the Indians under the care of the War Department."[31]

None of this set well with Father Stephan, who was desperately trying to fend off Commissioner Morgan's not so subtle assault on the contract school system. Nor was it well received by Commissioner Morgan. In August, Father Stephan wrote to Patrick Ford's editor, asking him to refrain from publishing Craft's ideas until he, Father Stephan, had a chance to "throw such additional light on the subject as will . . . induce him to change his views."[32]

Reports are mixed on the relative success of Father Craft's lecture tour. Bishop Shanley later wrote that it "failed signally. During his eight month sojourn in and around the populous Eastern cities he [Craft] succeeded in collecting $80.00 for missionary pur-

[29] Craft journal, 21 April 1890.

[30] "Catholic Indian Missions in America," *Irish World and American Industrial Liberator*, August 16, 1890.

[31] "The Poor Indians," *New York Freeman's Journal and Catholic Register*, June 21, 1890.

[32] Stephan to M. Farrell, 28 August 1890, BCIM Records.

poses."[33] Father Stephan, on the other hand, advised Bishop Shanley in August (in a letter written by Lusk) that Craft had collected as much as $7,000 or $8,000 and that it "would be well for you to look pretty closely into the matter."[34]

Temporarily blocked from the local press, Father Craft joined with Gen. James R. O'Beirne to finally end the outrageous practice of exhibiting Indians in "Wild West" shows.[35]

Exasperated with the notoriety that Craft was attracting, Father Stephan finally summoned him to Washington, D.C., where on December 4, 1890, he announced that Craft would be sent to the Navaho missions in the southwestern United States. Father Craft responded on Stephan's own letterhead: "Conditions for taking charge of the Navaho Indians in New Mexico & Arizona." First, he wrote, "the safety of the Indian Sisters must be assured." Second, his position "must be so fixed that I cannot be crowded out by incoming missionaries." Third, his "methods in Indian work must be thoroughly understood & approved by recognized Church authorities." Fourth, he "must have such an official position as will command the respect & silence the opposition of those who respect nothing but dignities." And fifth, "Church authorities must not be induced by the enemies of Christianity & civilization to do anything against me or my work, either by omission or commission." He concluded: "If this is done, I can guarantee the conversion & civilization of the Indians under my care within three years after I have mastered the language,—which will take about six months. If this is not done, let who will take the mission, for I will not."[36]

Yes, Father Craft could be just that arrogant. Besides, he had no intention of going among the Navaho in the southwest. He already had his ticket to the Dakota Reservations. He was returning to the Sioux.

---

[33] Bishop John Shanley, "The Catholic Indian Missions," *Irish World*, January 20, 1891.

[34] Charles S. Lusk, secretary of BCIM, to Bishop John Shanley, 28 August 1890, BCIM Records.

[35] "Stopping Indian Demoralization," *New York Freeman's Journal and Catholic Register*, November 15, 1890.

[36] Document in Craft's handwriting, 4 December 1890, BCIM Records.

Part IV
Wounded Knee Observations

Wounded Knee Observations

In the months that Father Craft spent lecturing and traveling in the East, the seeds of a great apocalyptic movement among the Indians of the West found fertile ground in the desperate conditions that beset the Dakota reservations. Wovoka, a Paiute holy man in Nevada who had been raised in a deeply religious white Christian family, experienced a vision during an eclipse of the sun on New Year's Day 1889. The Indians called it "the day the sun died." Wovoka, too, "died" and in the course of his vision learned that a second messiah would appear in the spring of 1891. This time, though, the Son of God would return as an Indian who would resurrect all the Indian dead, restore the buffalo and other game to the prairies, and cause the earth to swallow up the invading white man. Wovoka introduced the "Ghost Dance" to his followers as an outward sign of this new gospel, a petition to the Great Spirit for the fulfillment of his prophecy.

As word of Wovoka's vision spread eastward toward the Dakotas, tribes from Standing Rock, Cheyenne River, Rosebud, Pine Ridge, and other reservations sent delegates to investigate this new religion and learn its dance. Wovoka's blend of an Indian Christianity had peaceful origins. "Be a good behave always," [*sic*] he advised the delegates in Carlisle English. "Work for the white man, and do not make any trouble with them until you leave them."[1] The Miniconjou Sioux on Cheyenne River Reservation, however, became radically zealous believers after their representative, Kick-

[1] Smith, *Moon of Popping Trees*, 72.

ing Bear, returned to fill the role of the principal Lakota apostle for the new cause. Spotted Elk, called "Big Foot" by the whites, led a large Miniconjou encampment on Cheyenne River Reservation that eagerly embraced the Ghost Dance and its promise during the spring of 1890. So zealous had these dancers become that by April of that year, the military had established a so-called camp of observation at the fork of the Cheyenne River, where they kept watch on Hump—leader of about 600 Sioux on Cheyenne River Reservation—and Big Foot's activities throughout the summer.

Excitement spread among the tribes, and settlers, Indian agents, and U.S. authorities became increasingly concerned at the potential for a major uprising throughout the Dakota Reservations. Short Bull and Mash the Kettle had called councils to explore the movement on Rosebud Reservation in April, as did Good Thunder on Pine Ridge Reservation. Kicking Bear introduced the Ghost Dance itself on the Pine Ridge Reservation in August 1890, adding an eventually tragic element by promoting the same concept of invulnerability that caused Father Craft to challenge Frosted on Standing Rock back in August 1888. Kicking Bear's version, though, involved bulletproof "ghost shirts" that would cause bullets to sail over the wearer and fall harmlessly on the prairie. By September, the dance was in full swing on Rosebud.

On Standing Rock Reservation, Sitting Bull requested a pass to visit Hump and Big Foot in their off-the-reservation camp at the forks just west of the Cheyenne River Reservation. Agent McLaughlin, however, denied him that opportunity. Frustrated by the agent, Sitting Bull invited Kicking Bear to Standing Rock, where he arrived on October 9. And back in Washington, D.C., and other eastern metropolitan centers, garbled rumors of this Indian unrest only increased the level of anxiety.

Among the concerned citizens of New York City was General James R. O'Bierne, with whom Father Craft had recently collaborated to end exploitative displays of Indians in Wild West shows. O'Bierne, a Civil War veteran who had earned the Medal of Honor and who had powerful political and military connections, was in charge of the U.S. Department of Immigration's New York office. For Craft's trip to the capital (where Craft would reject Father Stephan's gambit to reassign him to the Navaho Reservation), the general had provided Craft with a letter of introduction to Secretary of War Redfield Proctor, suggesting that the priest be sent "on a quasi-official . . . confidential mission, under the secret service of the War Department" to quiet the resurgence of Indian unrest on the Dakota reservations.[2] On November 27, Proctor acknowledged O'Bierne's recommendation: "General Miles is expected here tonight and we shall have a full conference with him; and I will submit Father Craft's letter with yours to the President. I have no doubt there is much truth in his view."[3]

On December 3, Proctor wrote to Father Craft that he would be "pleased to see you any afternoon this week. . . . This letter will admit you after hours if necessary—show to watchman."[4] The next day, Craft met with Secretary Proctor, who then wrote to Interior Secretary John W. Noble: "General Schofield and myself have been conversing with him [Craft] this afternoon, and were much interested in his account of matters in Dakota, and [therefore] this letter to you, thinking you might like to talk with him."[5]

After meeting with these senior military and government officials, Craft returned to Pine Ridge Agency in South Dakota, arriving at Holy Rosary Mission on December 10, 1890. By now, most of the dancers, including Kicking Bear, were on the Pine Ridge Reservation, in an almost inaccessible part of the Cuny Table plateau called the Stronghold. Hump, beset with second thoughts about the movement, returned to Cheyenne River Agency on

---

[2] Gen. James R. O'Beirne to Redfield Proctor, 24 November 1890, RG 75, National Archives.

[3] Secretary Redfield Proctor to Gen. James R. O'Beirne, 27 November 1890, RG 75, National Archives.

[4] Secretary Redfield Proctor to Father Francis M. Craft, 3 December 1890, in author's possession.

[5] Secretary Redfield Proctor to Secretary John W. Noble, 4 December 1890, in author's possession.

December 9. Gen. John R. Brooke, directing the operation from Pine Ridge Agency, asked Father John Jutz, the Jesuit missionary at Holy Rosary Mission, to assist in negotiations with Two Strike and others in the Stronghold. By mid-December almost a thousand of his people had peaceably returned to the Agency. Big Foot's fanatical followers were the only major group still out and off their reservation.

Sporadic dances were occurring throughout the Sioux reservations, however, and when Craft first saw the dance performed in the Rosebud Indian camp on the evening of December 14, "He found it to be all right, quite Catholic and even edifying."[6] This is not at all a surprising judgment by Father Craft. He had long encouraged and defended various Indian dance expressions, such as the Omaha Dance "just as we ourselves have many different dances common to many nations."[7] Moreover, the concept of the resurrection of the body certainly introduced a Catholic doctrine he would endorse.

Additional federal troops simultaneously entered Pine Ridge and Rosebud reservations on November 20. Among the concerns of Gen. Nelson A. Miles was whether Sitting Bull, from his cabin on Grand River, would support the dancers or, worse yet, go to Pine Ridge himself. Initially, the plan called for Buffalo Bill Cody to interrupt any move by Sitting Bull to jump the reservation. Cody was one of the few white men who had established a rapport with the intransigent Hunkpapa leader during Sitting Bull's four-month stint with Buffalo Bill's Wild West Show in 1885. However, Agent McLaughlin, who had already denied Sitting Bull's request to visit Big Foot and Hump, was not inclined to allow Cody to usurp his authority on Standing Rock Reservation. Instead, he ordered his own Indian police to arrest the chief on the morning of December 15. Sitting Bull, Lt. Bull Head, and several others died in the bloody clash that followed.

Reports of the death of the great Sioux leader alarmed eastern populations. General O'Beirne wrote to Craft on December 17

[6] Emil Perrig, S.J, diary, 86–87, BCIM Records.

[7] "Craft Answer to Charges," 10 July 1884, RG 75, National Archives.

expressing concern that the killing of Sitting Bull would lead to a "genuine, full-fledged Indian War." He asked the priest to send written accounts, "about a column for each letter, sending the correspondence . . . in such a way they will not know it along the stations of the mail route, and closed with sealing wax; or, if you think better, put them under cover to me to be forwarded to the Herald."[8]

On December 20, Father Craft sent off a news dispatch blaming McLaughlin for Sitting Bull's death and made the following statement, which appeared in the *Freeman's Journal*:

> Just as the tree can be traced from its smallest branches to its root, just so all this Indian trouble can be traced through all its phases to its true cause, *starvation, abject misery, and despair*, the cause of which is the outrageous conduct of the Indian Department for many years, culminating in the later blunders and cruelties of the present Commissioner Morgan. You can see now how the prophesies of the Freeman's Journal have been verified. If the army had charge this never could have happened, and if it could be kept now in charge, the Indians will have some hope of life and civilization.[9]

After the death of Sitting Bull, several hundred frightened Standing Rock Hunkpapas fled toward Cheyenne River Reservation. Although most of them soon returned to Standing Rock Reservation, about a hundred continued south, where they joined up with Big Foot's Miniconjous as they made their escape toward Pine Ridge on December 23.

Troops of the Seventh Cavalry captured Big Foot's band on Sunday, December 28, and moved them into camp on Wounded Knee Creek, where Col. James W. Forsyth intended to disarm them. Both Brooke and Forsyth surmised that Father Craft might be as helpful at Wounded Knee as Father Jutz was in negotiations at the Stronghold.

Modern-day accounts would have us believe that Big Foot's band was composed of desperate "women, children and elderly" fleeing

---

[8] Gen. James R. O'Beirne to Craft, 17 December 1890, in author's possession.

[9] Craft, "Father Craft's Statement," *New York Freeman's Journal and Catholic Register*, January 3, 1891.

FIGURE 13. *Top*, Miniconjou Ghost Dancers of Big Foot's band with troops from the camp of observation in background, fall 1890; *bottom*, Big Foot's band of Miniconjou Sioux in costume at a dance in Cheyenne River, S.Dak., August 9, 1890. Photographs by John C. H. Grabill. *Library of Congress*, LC-USZ62-11567 (*top*) *and* LC-USZ62-22968 (*bottom*).

in panic after the death of Sitting Bull.[10] Contradicting these claims, however, are actual photographs and contemporary reports that Big Foot, "in council on November 25, 1890, urged his people to acquire all the guns and cartridges they could find and stay together in one camp. Two days later it was reported that white traders were furnishing the recalcitrants with rifles. . . . and that the dancers were spoiling for a fight and intended to have one soon."[11]

Most, perhaps all, of the young warriors and their families seated in the wagons behind them shown in the bottom photo of figure 13 died at Wounded Knee. There are about twenty young men in the bottom photo, perhaps one-sixth of the total number of warriors generally acknowledged to have been present at the impending tragedy on December 29, 1890. The official title assigned to this photograph by the Library of Congress refers to "Miniconjou Sioux in costume at a dance."

A reviewer of my biography of Father Craft, *Father Francis M. Craft, Missionary to the Sioux*, took me to task (along with Father Craft) for having described one of the priest's contemporary Indians as being in "full Indian costume." "Native Americans do not wear 'costumes,'"[12] he admonished. If such is the case, then the breechcloths worn by the young men in these photos may have been uniforms. Note that only one young man (center left) has the white stripe at his waist, whereas all the rest wear it at the bottom of the breechcloth. He may be the lead dancer, or he may also be the leader of a Miniconjou Akicita society. Although such societies served varying purposes in Lakota culture, "it is most probable that the original motive of the Akicita societies was directed to professionalism in war and only later shifted to partial control of civil matters."[13]

Suffice it to say that Big Foot's band was not a forlorn group of helpless innocents. Thousands of Indians had moved onto or through Pine Ridge Reservation to the Stronghold during the

---

[10] Fedarko, "Why We Must Return to Wounded Knee," 5.

[11] Utley, *Last Days of the Sioux Nation*, 131.

[12] Perez, "Father Craft."

[13] Hassrick, *Sioux: Life and Customs of a Warrior Society*, 20.

months leading up to Wounded Knee. Many of them were well armed. A news release dated December 11 from Pine Ridge Agency reported, "It was noticed yesterday by the Indian Police that 300 or 400 Indians were at the beef issue with guns who did not belong to the agency, and who took no part in the killing of cattle."[14] Yet it was Big Foot's band that General Miles gave the order to intercept and disarm. It was the uniformed warriors of Big Foot's band that attracted the attention of the camp of observation back in April and who posed for photographs that fall—a band that included about 120 "invulnerable," fanatical followers of an apocalyptic dream that promised the annihilation of the white man from the face of the earth. They were armed with Winchester repeating rifles, weapons that have been largely ignored or unnoticed in many accounts by those who assumed that Big Foot's band had already surrendered their guns before the first shot was fired.

It is not clear what model of Winchester rifles Big Foot's band may have used. Model 73 used.44-caliber cartridges; the standard model held 15 rounds, the musket model 17, and the carbine model 12. The model 76 used .45–.60- or .40–.60-caliber cartridges; the standard model held 12 rounds, the musket 13, and the carbine 9. Whatever the individual capacity may have been, 120 of these weapons were clearly capable of considerable firepower in a short time frame.

When Father Craft went to negotiate with Big Foot, he was accompanied by Colonel Forsyth as well as a few soldiers and other civilians. They arrived at Wounded Knee near midnight on December 28. In the morning, to facilitate the disarming of the Indians, Forsyth ordered that the Indian men be assembled on a council ground between the Indian camp on the south and the military camp to the north. Dismounted cavalry troopers surrounded the Indians on all sides, and mounted cavalry encircled the outer perimeter, which also included the Indian camp where the women and children remained. Following standard military field practice, a battery of four Hotchkiss guns was placed on a vantage point,

[14] Kelley, *Pine Ridge 1890*, 108.

Cemetery Hill, 200 yards to the west. Forsyth's command totaled about 500 soldiers armed with single-shot Remington rifles; some had Colt pistols as well.

According to differing accounts, at least 106 of the 120 Indian men were gathered in the center of this scene; perhaps 230–250 of the women and children watched the proceedings from the Indian encampment.

What happened next has been a subject of debate and controversy for much of the past century, leading to a current-day scholarly consensus that establishes Wounded Knee as a senseless massacre—a slaughter of unarmed Indian men, women, and children by drunken and vengeful white troops of the Seventh Cavalry. Today's consensus generally agrees that the troops and officers were still drunk, or at least hung over, from celebrating the capture of Big Foot and his band the night before. A local trader, James Asay, provided the keg of whiskey.

Indian accounts tell of the abuse their women and children suffered at the hands of soldiers as their camp was searched for weapons, how most of those weapons had been gathered and stacked near the council grounds, and how the first shot was fired inadvertently by a deaf Indian who was reluctant to give up his Winchester. These accounts state that this accidental firing was met immediately with a volley from the troops resembling a massive single shot, including the shelling of the camp by the Hotchkiss guns on Cemetery Hill. As those who survived this initial volley ran to the protection of a ravine beyond the Indian camp, mounted troopers and the Hotchkiss guns tracked them down in a dreadful slaughter. Bodies of women and children were found scattered for three miles from the camp. Blatant racism, mixed with a large measure of revenge stemming from the Custer defeat in 1876, explained this slaughter of women and children so far from the camp.[15] The number of Indian men, women, and children killed on that day numbered at least 170 and may have been more than 200.

---

[15] Hoxie, *Encyclopedia of North American Indians*, 694–7.

A thorough military investigation of the tragedy was promptly ordered by Gen. Nelson A Miles, who was furious both at reports indicating that Colonel Forsyth had placed the troops and Indians in such close proximity to each other as well as at the shockingly high number of women and children casualties. Miles had issued specific orders to his commanding generals, advising them that Big Foot's band was an especially treacherous group that must not be allowed to get mixed up with their troops. Forsyth had placed them all within a few feet of each other. One officer, twenty-six enlisted men, and one Indian Scout were killed; four officers and thirty enlisted men were wounded, several of them by the crossfire of their own bullets.[16]

The military's version of the event held that Forsyth's configuration of the troops surrounding the Indians in such close quarters resulted from a conviction that absolutely no trouble was anticipated. The Indians had already surrendered under a white flag of truce. However, as the search for arms proceeded, a medicine man began a harangue about the protection afforded by the invulnerable ghost shirts, and as he threw some dirt in the air as a signal, the warriors began to draw concealed Winchesters from beneath their blankets. As a soldier struggled to wrest a rifle from an Indian, the gun fired accidentally, precipitating a volley of shots from the Indians. Many shots that missed a trooper went directly into the Indian camp, where the women and children scattered for protection. Several of the casualties among the women and children may well have been the result of this crossfire. The military also contended that the Hotchkiss guns did not fire for some moments because of the hand-to-hand combat taking place on the council grounds but waited until the Indians had broken out and were running through their camp, with women and children, toward the ravine to the south. The warriors, still firing as they ran, were indistinguishable from the women and children as the Hotchkiss guns opened up on the Indian camp. Upon reaching the ravine, some Indians continued firing, drawing further response from the Hotchkiss guns.

[16] Scott, "Wounded Knee," n.p.

Father Craft's detailed eyewitness accounts of events on that fateful day have never been published. One such report was in a deposition submitted to the federal commission charged with investigating the tragic event:

> Rev. Francis M. J. Craft, Catholic Missionary priest, being duly sworn, deposes & says:
>
> I am a missionary priest of the Catholic Church, & have worked in that capacity among the Indians of the North West for the past ten years. I came to Pine Ridge Agency in December 1890 to visit the Catholic missions & schools as a representative of the Bureau of Catholic Indian Missions,[17] & also to render what service I could in the settlement of the Indian troubles. On Sunday, Dec. 28th I learned that Big Foot's band of Indians had been taken, & were in a camp near Wounded Knee Creek, & that Indians from Standing Rock whom I knew were with them. By permission of General Brooke I went out to see if I could be of any service. As malicious whites on & near all Agencies, during the present excitement, have, by misrepresenting the intentions of the army, caused such a state of alarm & suspicion among the Indians as to make it possible for the least excitement or misunderstanding to precipitate serious trouble, I hoped to be of some service by going among the Indians & reassuring them. I reached the military camp at Wounded Knee about 11:00 P.M.
>
> In the morning while the troops were preparing to disarm the Indians, I learned from several Indians with whom I spoke, that they had left their Agency alarmed by the reports of the Indians who escaped from Standing Rock after the death of Sitting Bull. The Standing Rock Indians were not with them, but, as they said, left them on the way down, & went towards the Missouri. I saw that the Indians with whom I was speaking were the worst element of their Agency, whose camp had for years been the rendezvous of all the worst characters on the Sioux Reservation.[18]

---

[17] A letter from Father Stephan to Craft, 5 January 1891 states, "On Dec. 6th, 1890, I authorized Rev. F. M. J. Craft to visit the Indian Cath. Missions at Rosebud and Pine Ridge, South Dakota and now I extend the above visits to Standing Rock & Crow Creek Missions and he shall report to me the standing of said schools" (in author's possession).

[18] Craft's description of Big Foot's band as the "worst element of their Agency" matches that of both William F. Kelley of the *Nebraska State Journal* (a "sullen and unwilling . . . band of savage fanatics") and Lt. John C. Gresham ("Big Foot's band was the worst of their race"), both of whom were also participants in the battle (Shaw, *Battle of Wounded Knee*, 69).

About 8:30 A.M., Genl. Forsythe [*sic*] called all the Indian men from the Indian camp to the point marked on the accompanying map P (page 303), in order to separate them from the women & children. This seemed to be a very necessary precaution although no trouble was apprehended.

Gen. Forsythe then spoke to the men through an interpreter, kindly & pleasantly, & explained the necessity of taking the arms, & assured them that they were now perfectly safe in the hands of their old friends the soldiers, & that starvation & other troubles were now happily at an end.

The Indians answered in a way that showed they were pleased. Big Foot & others, however, denied having any guns, saying they had all been burned up. Gen. Forsythe reminded them, however, that the day before every man was seen to have at least one gun. Gen. Forsythe then began sending the Indians in, a few at a time, to the camp to get their guns. They returned saying they had none. Gen. Forsythe then pointed out to the Indians how plain it was they were deceiving him, & begged them not to compel him to search for the guns, but to have confidence in him, & bring them, themselves

A Medicine Man [Yellow Bird] now began praying, singing, & walking around the circle of Indians, his words indicating that the Indians were afraid of what might happen to them, when their guns would be taken, & going through various ceremonies that the bullets might not hurt them. Gen. Forsythe told him he had nothing to fear & he was induced to sit down & be quiet.

As the Indians did not care to produce their guns, soldiers (E & F) were sent to search for them in the Indian camp, but returned with very few.

At this moment, a soldier saw guns under the Indians' blankets, & informed Gen. Forsythe & Maj. Whitside.[19] As quietly as possible they directed the Indians, to come forward one by one, from the location marked on the map P. to those marked S. & R. & throw aside their blankets & lay down their arms if they had any.

Col. Forsythe spoke very kindly to them, & said he did not wish, himself, to take their arms, but would rather they would come forward themselves like men & lay them down. The Indians began to come forward as directed one by one, to lay down their arms. Fifteen or

[19] Maj. Samuel M. Whitside, commander of Troops A, B, I, and K.

twenty guns had been thus collected, when I heard among the soldiers, in the positions marked Q. & V., some one cry out "Look out. Look at that" & saw them attempting to fall back to the square surrounding the Indians. I looked toward the Indians in the position marked P. & saw that some were taking their guns from under their blankets, & others were raising them ready to fire.

The Indians seemed agitated, & from my knowledge of their habits, & especially of the character of this particular band, probably affected by the misrepresentations of malicious whites, I am convinced that the movement came from their fear of what might happen, when the guns would be all surrendered as they saw them being given up one by one.

I went up to them & tried to reassure them, but very few listened to me. It is possible that nothing might have occurred had not one young man said to be the son of Big Foot suddenly fired. His shot was followed by many others from the Indians.

The soldiers did not fire until they were actually compelled to, & after the Indians had fired many shots.[20]

When the soldiers returned the fire, the Indians broke up into small parties, & charged back & forth across the square firing & trying to break through. Some broke through towards the southwest, & some I believe towards the southeast. As they passed the end of the camp a few women & children ran out & joined them. The hotchkiss battery opened on them as they crossed the Agency road. It is possible that by this fire some women & children were killed, if so the killing was unavoidable, as the soldiers could hardly have distinguished them from the men among whom they were, who were firing backwards as they ran. Many concealed themselves in the ravine B., & fired on the soldiers. The battery then shelled the ravine. This ended the main battle, which lasted from one-half to three-quarters of an hour. After all was over at least two shots were fired from the Indian camp C, but the soldiers did not reply to them.

I was wounded early in the fight, but kept up until everything was over, & attended to the dying. After I finally gave out & was carried to the field hospital, J., I heard a volley of rifle shots fired from the Indian camp, C.

---

[20] A major reason for the military's delayed response was that their ill-conceived formation had placed their comrades in their own line of fire Most of these Indians had repeating Winchester rifles, which were capable of producing a deadly fusillade of bullets before the first shot from a soldier's Remington rifle was heard.

No shots were fired by the soldiers for some minutes, but I heard some one shouting in Dakota as if an interpreter was speaking.

The rifle shots from the Camps continued & then the hotchkiss battery shelled the camp, & also the tents at K. & M., from which Indians were firing upon the soldiers.

I afterwards learned, that contrary to their usual custom of protecting their women & children from danger & respecting the white flag, which they had hoisted over their camp, these Indians had actually managed to get back to their camp & fired from it upon the soldiers.

If women & children were killed in the shelling of this camp, the Indians who caused it are alone to blame. I have heard this act of these Indians severely condemned, by Brules [*sic*] & Oglalas, who denounced them as the murderers of the women & children & exonerated the soldiers.[21]

The first news from the field at Wounded Knee reported that Craft had not survived: "Father Craft Killed," proclaimed the headline of the *New York Freeman's Journal* of Saturday, January 3, 1891. Subheadings in that article read "The Great Indian Missionary Shot Through the Lungs While Fulfilling His Mission of Peace," "A Noble Martyr," and "One of the Horrible Results of Morgan's Inane Indian Policy."

In March, still recovering from his wounds, Craft wrote to his artist friend James E. Kelly, who had already sketched his vision of the priest's heroic deeds at the scene of the battle.

I wrote to Mr. Drowne an account of the troubles here, & another one with a fuller account of the battle to Gen. O'Beirne. Your sketch of the battle was correct in all points, except that the two parts—the main battle, & my falling with the soldier, were not at the same time. I was with the Indians during the battle, & received the fire of cavalry & artillery, just as you have it.

When the firing ceased, & after I got through with the Indians, I attended to the soldiers. That Irish soldier was the pluckiest young fellow I ever had the good luck to meet. He came up with four balls

[21] Draft of Craft's affidavit, n.d., in author's possession. This is substantially the same as a typed copy in RG 75, National Archives, with the exception that Craft misspelled Forsyth's name by adding an "e" in his draft. "Deposes and says" was also changed to "testifies as follows." Some differences in punctuation also occur.

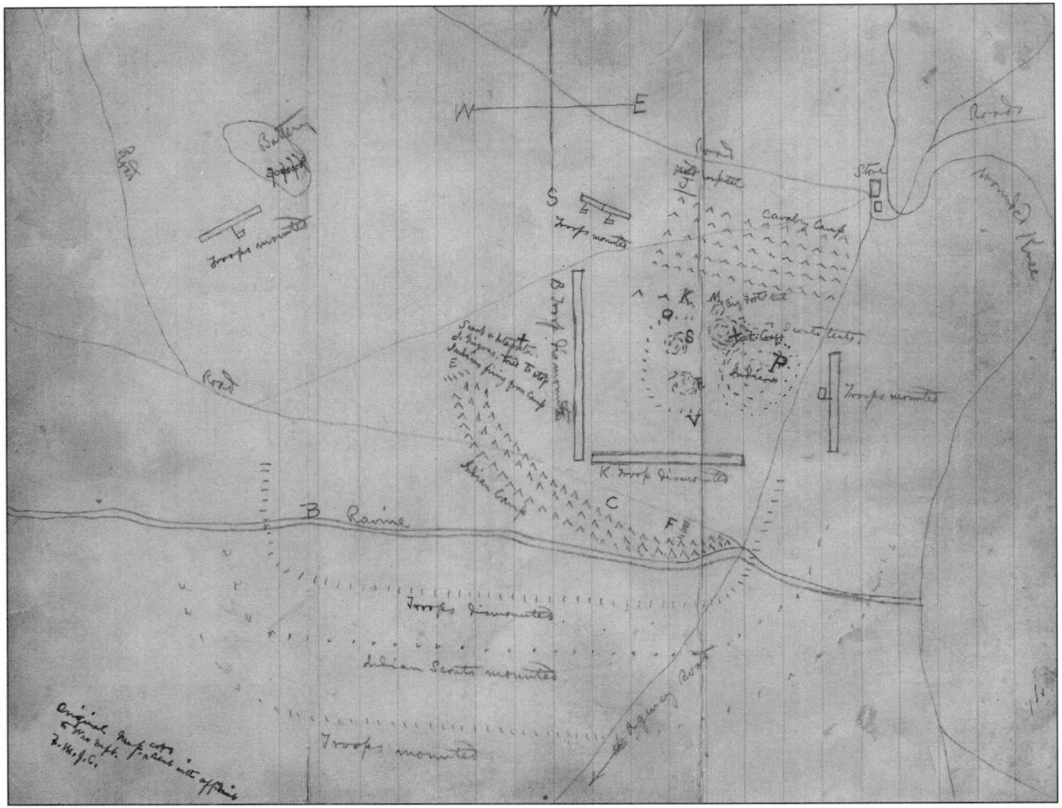

MAP 3. Father Craft's hand-drawn map of the field at Wounded Knee, keyed to his affidavit to the U.S. War Department dated January 7, 1891. *Foley/Craft Collection.*

Figure 14. James E. Kelly's sketch of Father Craft at Wounded Knee appeared in newspapers throughout the country in January 1891. *Courtesy of Marquette University Archives.*

through him, & the blood pouring like a pump, but smiling & saluting as coolly & politely as if in a ball room instead of a battle field. While I was giving him absolution, his hands slipped from my shoulder, & he fell, just as you have it. I caught him, but the blood was all out of me then, & I was too weak to hold him, & was carried down with him. I finished the absolution lying beside him. The Indian with me helped me up, & my strength & "yellowness" came back in a hurry when a party of soldiers, who naturally mistook the affair for a fight, aimed at the Indian, & I had a lively time keeping him behind me until I could quiet them. After we all had a good laugh at the mistake, the Indian & an officer started to help me to the place where the wounded were lying, but I went down again in a heap, like a wet rag, & had to be carried. However, I took my Indian along with me. I felt little pain, & never fainted once, but was as weak as a kitten. The insignia of the Sons of the Revolution got a thorough "baptism of fire." The ribbon was darkened by powder smoke, & the balls that cut the buttons from my cassock nearly touched it, but it "staid with me" all right.

There has been an effort to charge the soldiers with cruelty & slaughter, but it is a vile slander. They worked hard to stop the fight, & to save lives. After the battle, some of them had little Indian babies wrapped in their coats, carrying them off the field. The poor little ones crowed & laughed at their blue-coated "mothers," & the soldiers broke down & cried like babies, & cursed everything & everybody that caused the war,—in fact everything except the Indians.[22]

Among the papers of Father Craft is a second map of the Battle of Wounded Knee, which is keyed to a letter he wrote to James E. Kelly in February 1892. The letter (without the map) is in the collection of The New-York Historical Society:

I enclose a map of the field of Wounded Knee, giving my movements during the battle, as you requested. My personal movements & positions during the battle are marked by a "cross within a circle"—thus ⊕. I thought I sent you an account of the battle. I know I intended to, but perhaps I forgot it. It was a battle between the 7th Cavalry & about three hundred Miniconjou Dakota Indians under Chief Big Foot, from Cheyenne River Agency, one hundred & fourteen of whom were armed warriors. The cavalry numbered about eight hundred.

[22] Craft to James E. Kelly, 13 March 1891, Kelly Papers.

These Indians were quiet, until alarmed by the killing of Sitting Bull & others by the police at Standing Rock Agency, when they made an effort to escape & join the Indians in the Bad Lands near Pine Ridge, but were stopped and their fears relieved by the kindness of the officers at Cheyenne Agency. While the Indians in the Bad Lands were slowly moving in towards Pine Ridge Agency to surrender to Gen. Brook, & while it was necessary that they should not be alarmed & stampeded again, & while Big Foot's band were resting quietly in their homes at Cheyenne River Agency, a white man went into Big Foot's camp, & persuaded him & his band that the soldiers meant to disarm & kill them, & told his story so plausibly that Big Foot's band stampeded in fright, & hurried towards the Bad Lands.

If they reached there, they would alarm the Indians who were quietly leaving there, & the whole work of relieving their fears would have to be done over again, with greater difficulty. Gen. Brooke sent the 7th Cavalry to intercept them & bring them to Pine Ridge Agency by another road, so they would not frighten the other Indians by alarming reports. The first body of Cavalry, under Maj. Whiteside, met the Big Foot band on Porcupine Creek, quieted their fears, & brought them as far as the crossing of Wounded Knee Creek, where they were met by the second detachment of Cavalry under Gen. Forsythe, & all went into camp, as shown on the map. The Indians were to give up their guns in the morning to avoid the natural consequences of any panic that might arise, & all were to go together to Pine Ridge Agency eighteen miles from Wounded Knee Creek.

From what we heard of the false reports the Indians had received of the soldiers' intentions, & their consequent fears, it seemed probable that the least accident might precipitate a fight, & I therefore went out to Wounded Knee after talking the matter over with Gen. Brooke, & reached there about midnight. I spoke with Forsythe, & early in the morning went among the Indians, & found that they were getting alarmed again, & hesitated to give up the guns they had concealed under their blankets, but I did not know it at the time. They told me their fears, & I reassured them by telling them Gen. Brooke's intentions, & all seemed greatly relieved. I promised to stay with them to convince them there was no danger, & we had quite a pleasant time smoking & talking of old times.

About 8 A.M. Forsythe called all the men (114) to the point marked on the map, to separate them from the camp & women & children so as to avoid excitement & panic, & drew up K & B troops in the positions marked on the map to keep them separated. He then reminded them of their promise to give up the guns. They said they had none, though Forsythe had seen all armed the day before. Big Foot, who was sick, & under the care of the surgeons in the tent in the scout's camp, came out & told the Indians to give up the guns, & Forsythe sent them twenty at a time to their camp to get them, but they came back apparently without any.

He talked pleasantly & assuringly to them, & they answered in the same way but brought no guns. I spoke among them as Forsythe did, but they said they had none, though they seemed free from anxiety. The fact was, as we heard afterwards, they had the guns under their blankets, & kept them to use if attacked, as they still doubted a little, but hoped there would be no trouble.

A medicine man walked around the Indians praying, & preparing them for death if they should be attacked. Forsythe & I talked to him & to the others & reassured them. Forsythe then sent a few soldiers through the Indian camp at each end to look for guns, but they found only a few. It seemed evident the guns had been hidden, & as long as the Indians did not have them, Forsythe would have said nothing more, but all would have gone quietly to the Agency. Just then a soldier saw the guns under the blankets & told Forsythe, & I looked & saw all were armed, as they took less trouble to hide the guns when they saw it was useless.

Forsythe & everybody else, Indians & all, laughed, & Forsythe jokingly & laughingly tried to coax the Indians out of their fears, & asked them to come forward one by one, & give the guns up, saying he would not take them by force if he had to wait ten years.

I walked around among the Indians advising them to listen to him, & all agreed to, & we passed around cigarettes, of which I had a good supply, & had a good time over the absurd fears & concealment of the guns. We were all looking towards two young men in the position marked on the map "disarmed Indians," who were laying down their guns, when the few soldiers waiting to receive the guns ran back to their ranks, & I looked around to my Indians in time to see them throw away their blankets, raise their guns to heaven towards the west, & then level them at the lines of B & K Troops. The Indians acted as if a sudden panic had started, & we afterwards learned that it came from remembering the lies of the white man at Cheyenne River Agency, & the thought that they might be attacked when the guns would be all taken. I ran along the line of Indians & told them to stop & listen, & Lieut. Robinson rode up on the other side & spoke to them. They laughed & lowered their guns, & all would have been quiet in a few moments, when in the position marked on the map "First shot" +, a young man, (at first thought to be a relative of Big Foot, but afterwards found to be "Black Fox,"[23] a deaf man, who could not hear our words, & saw only the excitement) suddenly leveled his rifle on B Troop. I saw what was coming if a shot should be fired, & jumped to catch him, but I was too late. Before I could reach him the shot came, & the next second the Indians, excited by the shot, poured volley after volley into the lines of B & K Troops, their fire also mowing down like grass the crowd of their own women & children who stood in the camp looking on behind the soldiers.[24] I shouted to them to stop, that it was all a misunderstanding, & so did Lieut. Robinson, in English, as I did in Sioux, but they paid no attention, only answering that they would "die like men." After the first excitement they seemed cool enough, but continued their fire in spite of all our efforts. They started to charge the two troops, towards their camp, & Robinson, seeing all his efforts useless had to return to his troop. The soldiers kept cool & held their fire, until many had fallen, & then received the order of their officers to return the fire, when it was clear that the fight could not be stopped. I kept up my efforts to stop it, & when the soldiers fired a ball grazed my head & knocked me down. I rose at once, & was knocked over by another ball, rose again, & shouted to the Indians to cease firing & lie down; but all were charging then, & only eight obeyed me, & one caught hold of my coat & dodged behind me. I ordered the eight to run for the creek, which they did at once, the other would not leave but kept hold of my coat, & I had to tow him around with me. The charge on the lines was beaten back, but some broke through, & the artillery opened from the hill (4 cannon) with grape, canister, shell, & shrapnel, on two points where they broke through & turned to fight, & on the ravine where some fired from cover. I tried to get others out, but they would not go. A ball crushed a bone in my foot, & a small sliver of shell pierced my side. I saw an Indian driven back from the charge running & staggering towards

[23] The young man in question was actually Black Coyote, not Black Fox.

[24] "The warriors emptied their rifles at Troop K, and every shot that missed a soldier plowed into the village, where women and children scrambled in terrified confusion to get out of the way" (Utley, *Last Days of the Sioux Nation*, 213).

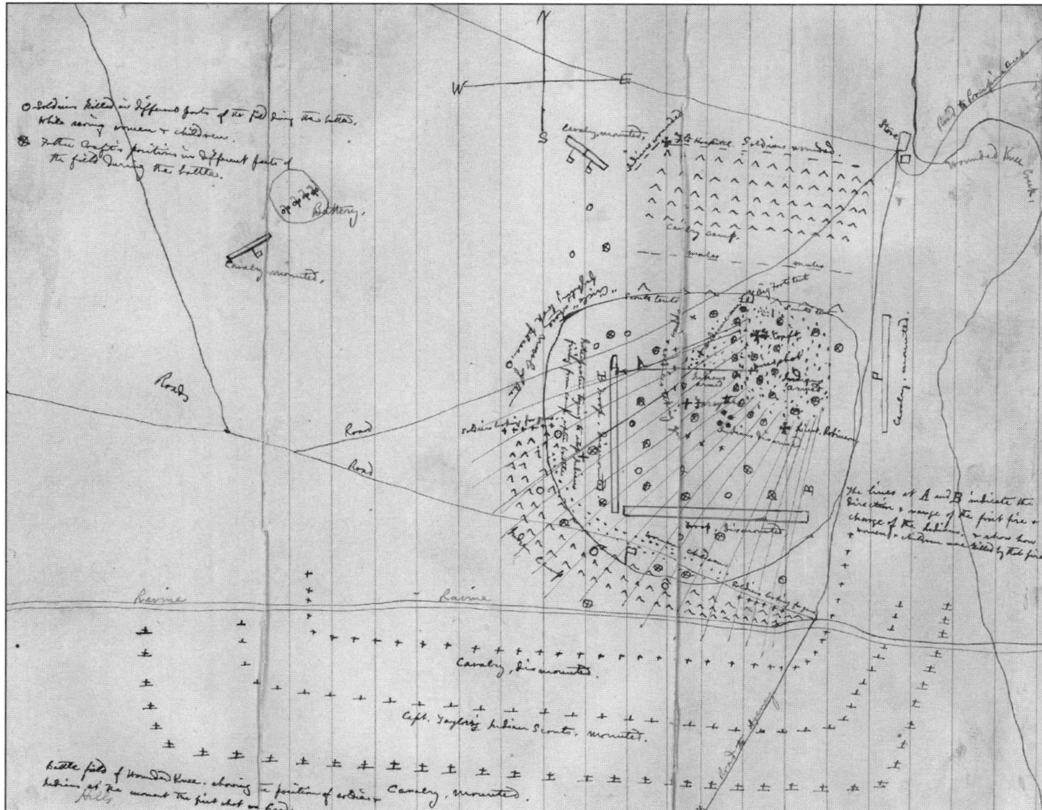

Map 4. Father Craft's hand-drawn map of the field at Wounded Knee, keyed to his letter to James E. Kelly, dated February 12, 1892. *Foley/Craft Collection.*

me, rifle & knife in hand, & shot through the breast. I called to him to lie down, but he did not hear, & seemed unable to see where he was going. He brushed against me in passing, & the next moment I felt a blow under the right shoulder blade & against the inside of the collar bone, followed almost instantly by another. (I was then facing towards the line of K Troop & the Indian camp.)

I supposed I was shot by balls from the camp (cavalry) where a troop had formed, & did not know that one was a knife wound until told afterwards by a soldier in the field hospital who saw the Indian strike back without looking as he passed me. It was afterwards found that the knife passed from back to breast, & swept across the lung in turning, but I did not bleed as much from the mouth as might have been expected from such a wound. The ball entered at the lower edge of the knife wound & lodged near the liver.

I really felt no pain, only the shock, & could scarcely distinguish what pierced the body from what merely grazed & tore the clothes. I could do nothing to stop the fight, & had to turn my attention to the dying, & that kept me busy till the fight ended. The scouts called to the women & children to lie down, but very few obeyed, & the soldiers had to catch them & put them behind whatever could shelter them, or take them over the hill by the cavalry camp. Many soldiers were shot down while doing this. As the battle ended, a few Indians who had reached the Indian camp, fired again. The Interpreter went to stop them, but was fired on, & the artillery shelled the camp, but the women & children had left it or been taken from it by the soldiers long before. One Indian got in a scout's tent & from there shot several soldiers, & was dislodged & the tent burned by shells. Another got on a hill, & stood off the soldiers. He could easily have been killed by shell, but as he did not fire unless an attempt was made to take him, & as it would have cost too many men to get him alive, the soldiers, not wishing to kill him, let him escape. When the battle was over I heard Kelly's confession, & kept my Indian from getting shot, when it looked very much as if he had killed Kelly,[25] & then I finally dropped, & had to be carried to the field hospital.

I think I have got down the main points of the battle, as far as I recall them. The worst fighting was done within what is called "the circle," (I don't see what gave the idea of a "circle") & there I got all my wounds & did most of my work. In the account of Kelly's death

[25] This is James E. Kelley (not to be confused with James E. Kelly, Craft's frequent correspondent), later identified as a mortally wounded soldier attended to by Craft.

in the Annual, I see the printer got "Indians" for "Indian" & "them" for "him." The one Indian hanging to my coat, was the one who helped me up, & the one the soldiers aimed at. The mistake of plural for singular makes no difference, as it changes nothing of the facts.

If the soldiers had been the bloodthirsty, excited savages they have been falsely described, I never could have managed to save that Indian, as I must admit his helping me to rise just then & just as he did, made it look very much as if he had killed Kelly & then grappled me,—at least it must have seemed so to that party of soldiers, who just came up returning from another part of the field, & had not seen the beginning of the affair. They all behaved well through the fight, & would not have lost half as many as they did if they had tried to kill instead of trying to save the Indians,—even the fighting men. One of the survivors called "Lip" as a nickname, (I forget his real name) told me that a soldier whom he charged on, fired his carbine in the air over his (Lip's) shoulder, & then laughingly pushed him back with his carbine, & pointed to the military camp where the women & children & wounded Indians were being taken. He says the soldier evidently did not want to kill him, but as he wanted to escape & make sure of his safety, he grappled with the soldier, & as they went down together a volley was fired, he don't know whether by Indians or soldiers, killing the soldier & wounding himself. There were many such instances. Some time, when I have leisure, I will write up all the incidents of the fight, that I think might be of interest. There was a great deal crowded into very short space, both as to place & time, as the fight was sudden, sharp, & at very close quarters.[26]

Two other items from Father Craft's papers on Wounded Knee are reproduced herein. One (figure 15) is a smaller map oriented from behind the cavalry camp (the larger maps are oriented from the Indian camp), and provides interesting insight into the dimensions of the scene. This was close-in combat, often measured in feet rather than yards. The notations on this map are not in Father Craft's handwriting, yet the comment on the right, at the site of the Hotchkiss battery, stating that the "H[otchkiss] Guns not used until Indians on retreat," is supportive of the priest's affidavit.[27]

[26] Craft to James E. Kelly, 12 February 1892, Kelly Papers.

[27] The comment on the left "(over)," leads to a few pencil scribbles and a brief indecipherable sentence of just a few words.

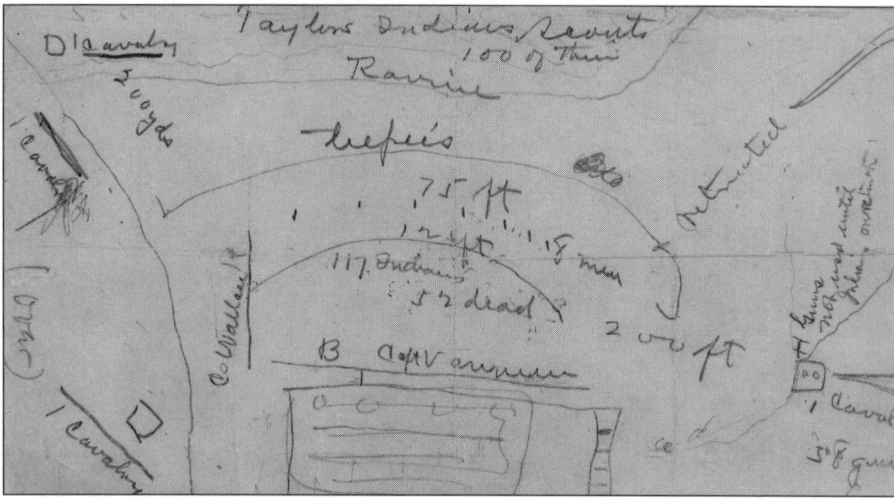

FIGURE 15. Wounded Knee notes from Father Craft's personal papers showing a sketch of the battlefield at Wounded Knee. *Foley/Craft Collection.*

The second item (figure 16) tells us that someone named Hawk Day knew the number of dead, and that Big Foot was buried with "one bullet" in the neck. As no mention is made to the mass burial on this note, it may have been written on or before January 1, 1891, the date on which the burial detail gathered up the dead for interment the next day in the mass grave on Cemetery Hill.[28]

Aside from raising a question as to the actual location of Big Foot's grave (why would someone comment on Big Foot's burial and not mention all the others presumed to be in the same grave?), the notation raises yet another question regarding the descriptions of Wounded Knee that have evolved through the years. Many current-day versions make reference to Big Foot's "bullet-riddled body,"[29] just as others strain to imply that Father Craft adminis-

[28] Eighty-four men, 44 women, and 18 children were buried in the grave. Capt. George Wallace was shot in the head early in the fight. No other reference to a "Little Dutchman" was found anywhere in the annals of Wounded Knee literature or records.

[29] For example, see Kelley, *Pine Ridge 1890*, 198; Mattes, "Enigma of Wounded Knee," 6; and Seymour, *Sitanka*, 172–73.

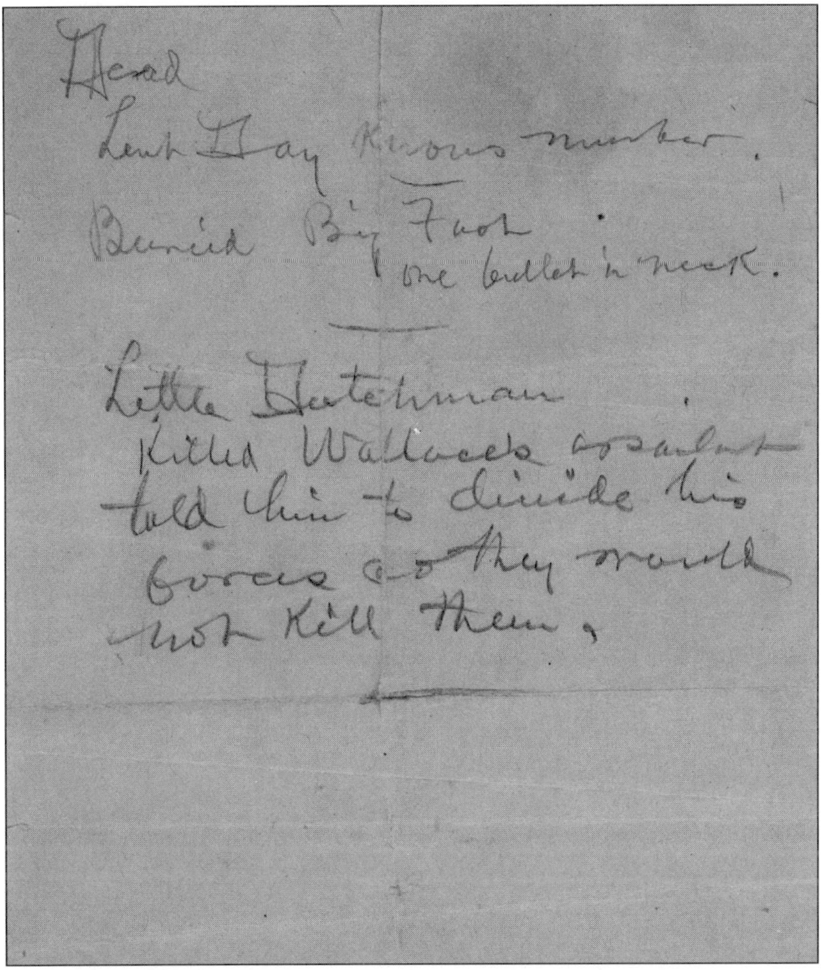
Dead
Lieut Day knows number.
Buried Big Foot.
one bullet in neck.
Little Dutchman.
Killed Wallace's assailant
told him to divide his
forces so they would
not kill them.

FIGURE 16. Wounded Knee notes from Father Craft's personal papers showing a list of the dead. *Foley/Craft Collection.*

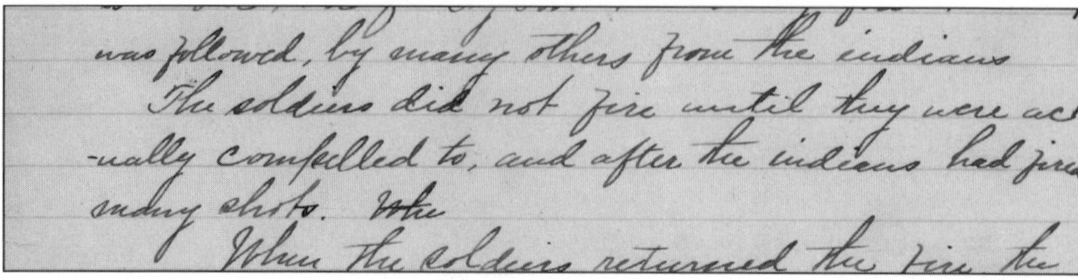

was followed, by many others from the indians
The soldiers did not fire until they were act-
-ually compelled to, and after the indians had fired
many shots. the
When the soldiers returned the fire the

FIGURE 17. Excerpt from Father Craft's handwritten affidavit submitted to the U.S. War Department, January 7, 1891. *Foley/Craft Collection.*

tered the last rites to a bewildered group of innocent, unarmed Indians before the command to "FIRE!" was given.

Father Craft's part in this tragic end to the Indian Wars in December 1890 has been little more than a footnote in the historical record. Most accounts make only passing reference to him; none provide any detailed information. The eyewitness documentation left by Father Craft has been largely ignored or is simply unknown to most historians. James M. Mooney, who presented the first detailed study of Wounded Knee and its causes in 1896, mentions Craft as a "heroic missionary priest," highly regarded by the Sioux, who was "stabbed through the lungs" in the conflict. No mention, however, of what Craft saw.[30]

James H. McGregor published the popular *Wounded Knee Massacre from the Viewpoint of the Sioux* in 1940, which included the eyewitness accounts of Dewey Beard (Iron Hail) and James Pipe-on-head, along with several hearsay versions by some who were not actually present at the encounter. The sole mention of Father Craft was that he "assured the Army officers that the Indians were not on the warpath" (p. 27).

Merill J. Mattes, in "The Enigma of Wounded Knee," published in the *Plains Anthropologist* in 1960, came closest to actually quoting

[30] Mooney, *Ghost-Dance Religion*, 872.

Father Craft but then adds a qualifier, writing that "Father Craft is alleged to testify that 'Indians fired first. The troops fired only when compelled to'" (p. 5).

Alleged? Well, no. As figure 17 shows, it is actually what he wrote in his affidavit to the War Department, submitted on January 7, 1891.

In Robert M. Utley's highly respected *Last Days of the Sioux Nation,* Utley describes Craft as an "extroverted Catholic missionary" who reassured the Indians "that they were perfectly safe in the hands of their old friends the soldiers" (pp. 199, 206). But again, there is no mention of what Craft saw.

Dee Brown stirred a global interest in Wounded Knee with the best selling classic, *Bury My Heart at Wounded Knee* in 1970. Brown never once mentions Father Craft.

Rex Allen Smith, in *Moon of Popping Trees*, published in 1975, recounts how "an Indian plunged a knife deep into [Craft's] back, collapsing a lung." (p. 191), but he gives no notice to the priest's affidavit submitted to the War Department.

More recently, Richard E. Jensen's collaborative work in *Eyewitness at Wounded Knee*, published in 1991,[31] presents a full page photo of Craft and quotes that section of Craft's testimony concerning the priest's hope "to be of some service by going among the Indians and reassuring them" (p. 36). In 1997, Jensen edited and wrote the introduction for Charles W. Allen's *From Fort Laramie to Wounded Knee.* In that introduction, Jensen notes that Craft "accompanied Forsyth's command to Wounded Knee on the evening of December 28 . . . to see if [he] could be of any service" (p. 136). Again, however, the crucially significant statements of Craft are nowhere to be found.

In 2004, Jeffrey Ostler's *The Plains Sioux and U.S. Colonialism from Lewis and Clark to Wounded Knee* became the most current exposé on Wounded Knee, finding the battle's origins to be deeply seated in 400 years of abuse, treachery, and deceit by white expansionists. Ostler notes that testimony from Craft is in the records but chooses not to quote it directly.

[31] Jensen, Paul, and Carter, *Eyewitness at Wounded Knee.*

Another account, published in 2004 in the popularly familiar *Parade Magazine,* states that Big Foot "led a band of 350 women, children and elderly more than 300 miles across South Dakota to seek refuge at the Pine Ridge Reservation."[32] Presumably, there were no young men among them.

Therein lies the uncertainty and controversy of Wounded Knee: all too often there is an agenda-driven effort to make Wounded Knee into something it may never have been. Craft's statements, for all their conflict with today's popular consensus, generally conform with contemporary accounts. His descriptions of the attempted disarming and the movements of the Indians can all be reconciled with other eyewitness reports. Troops on the east and west flanks withheld their fire for several minutes, as did the Hotchkiss guns, until the Indians who had crossed back into the camp began firing from there as well; even so, several soldiers died in the crossfire of their own bullets.[33] Today's scholarship, however, emphatically disagrees with the priest's conclusion that the Indians were responsible for the death of their own women and children. For the rest of his life Craft never varied from his position, always defending the military as public sentiment turned increasingly against it.

We are told today that there were no heroes at Wounded Knee, only murderous white soldiers and innocent Indian victims. Yet there is in the Denver Public Library a photograph of Father Craft bearing the legend "Hero of Wounded Knee" across his chest. He went to Wounded Knee to do what he had always considered his calling: to save the Indian. Had he died of the wounds he suffered there, he asked to be "buried in the trench with the Indian dead," preferring "the Indian to the white dead."[34] It would have been in keeping with Black Elk's later recollection of Father Craft: "He was a very good man, and not like the other Wasichus [white men]."[35]

---

[32] Fedarko, "Why We Must Return to Wounded Knee."

[33] For other descriptions of the encounter, see Jensen, Paul, and Carter, *Eyewitness at Wounded Knee*; Mooney, *Ghost-Dance Religion*; and Utley, *Last Days of the Sioux Nation.*

[34] *Milford, PA Dispatch*, "Correcting His Own Obituary," February 19, 1891. See also Emil Perrig diary, 11, BCIM Records.

[35] Neihardt, *Black Elk Speaks*, 252.

FIGURE 18. Father Craft wears a crucifix and medal of the Sons of the Revolution in this portrait taken by the Northwestern Photo Co., as he recovered from wounds received at Wounded Knee. *Denver Public Library, Western History Collection, Call No. X-31321.*

The 400-year history of conflict between Native Americans and Euro-American settlers from 1492 to 1890 was marked by a series of alternate massacres. In March 1622, Powhatans killed 237 English settlers at Jamestown, Virginia. In May 1637, English troops attacked a large Pequot village on the Mystic River, slaughtering over 700 men, women, and children. In 1757, an estimated 70 to 180 British and colonial prisoners were killed by Indian allies of the French after the fall of Fort William Henry. In 1778, Iroquois in the Wyoming Valley of Pennsylvania massacred 360 settlers. In January 1813, during the Black Hawk War, 850 Indian men, women, and children were slaughtered by white soldiers at Bad Ax, Wisconsin. In 1862, as many as 800 settlers were killed in the uprising of the Santee Sioux in Minnesota. In 1864, militiamen dispatched 160 Cheyenne men, women, and children at Sand Creek, Colorado. In 1876, the Sioux, Cheyenne, and Arapaho joined together to wipe out Custer and 260 officers and troopers of the Seventh Cavalry on the Little Big Horn in Montana. And for the past century, writers and historians have been trying to turn Wounded Knee into a butchery that avenges Custer's massacre.

Ironically, the American public generally remembers Custer and the Little Big Horn in heroic terms, despite the fact that it was arguably the U.S. Army's single greatest defeat of the later Indian Wars. Proponents who would enshrine Wounded Knee as the iconic epitome of Native American victimization diminish the heroic stand taken by Big Foot's warriors. A well-known painting from the 1960s, for example, shows soldiers lined up along a pit, shooting directly down into the writhing bodies of warriors, women, and children. And Johnny Cash, in his ballad "Big Foot," laments "the white flag is still waving today at Wounded Knee."

On one level, proponents are certainly free to choose their icons and provide their own interpretation of events. On a historical level, however, care should be taken that participants in those events are not slandered or scandalized. This applies not only to a missionary priest who almost sacrificed his life in their service, but also to the Sioux warriors of Big Foot's band, who sought to join up with Kicking Bear, Two Strike, and other Ghost Dancers. Many of them had gathered near Pine Ridge for hostile, yes even heroic, purposes. There is no shame to have fought and lost a battle at Wounded Knee. In fact, Wounded Knee may well have been one of the very few battles ever fought in the so-called Indian Wars. It was all the rest that were massacres. The ignominy lies in insisting that there were only victims at Wounded Knee—helpless, defeated, sickly, panicky, "women, children and elderly."

Alfred Lord Tennyson forever immortalized the charge of the Light Brigade at Balaclava in the Crimean War: "Into the valley of Death / Rode the six hundred."[36] Few returned, but all are remembered as heroes.

[36] Tennyson, "The Charge of the Light Brigade," stanzas 1 and 2.

Afterword

When he recovered from his wounds, Craft brought Sister Mary Catharine (Josephine), OSB, and five postulants from the Benedictine convent at Yankton, South Dakota, to St. Edward's School at Fort Berthold Reservation, North Dakota, where they would form the nucleus of his order of Indian sisters. Bishop Marty and Craft's new superior, Bishop John Shanley of Jamestown, North Dakota, both offered initial, albeit irresolute, support. Father Stephan, however, was enmeshed in a church and state struggle over Commissioner Thomas J. Morgan's threatened cessation of the contract school system and refused to support any mission that employed Father Craft. For his part, Commissioner Morgan, rankled by Craft's published allegations before Wounded Knee, would spend the rest of his term in office trying to expel Craft from Indian Country.

From the fall of 1891 until early in 1897, Father Craft's heroic efforts transformed Sacred Heart Mission from a boarding school to a medical clinic, staffed by a convent of a dozen Indian sisters. Even the tragic loss of his beloved Mother Mary Catharine Sacred White Buffalo (Josephine Crowfeather) failed to stem his determination to succeed. Cofounder and mother superior of the Congregation of American Sisters, Josephine succumbed to tuberculosis on April 30, 1893.[1] Despite being ostracized by Stephan, Craft never ceased in his efforts to persuade the BCIM to support and capitalize on the public relations potential afforded by his sisterhood, the Congregation of American Sisters. His attempts to solicit help from Bishop John Ireland of St. Paul, Minnesota, and Cardinal James

[1] For more information on the sisters, see Foley, *Faces of Faith*.

Gibbons of Baltimore, Maryland, were met with evasive platitudes; no one in the American Catholic hierarchy had the vision to support him or the courage to condemn him. But most of them worked to undermine him.

Emboldened by Craft's lack of support within his own ranks, the Indian agents at Standing Rock and Fort Berthold Reservations, in concert with Commissioner Morgan, began to question Craft's sanity. They not only eroded his standing with the tribes, but they also continually harassed the members of his sisterhood to return to their camps. Through Stephan's efforts, even the priest's Eastern supporters began to distance themselves.

Then, in the spring of 1897, scandalmongers on the agency "wishing to get rid of the Agent, chief clerk, &c . . . School Superintendent"[2] complained to Bishop Shanley of alleged sexual misconduct between the sisters and agency employees. The agent suspended four of his employees and was then himself dismissed by Commissioner Morgan. When neither Bishop Shanley nor a recently promoted Monsignor Stephan came to the defense of his sorely maligned sisters, Craft became increasingly critical of the Roman Catholic Church's hierarchy.

In the wake of the disastrous accusations, all but four of the Indian sisters returned to their tribal homes. Craft determined to take the remaining four back East, where they might serve among other minorities or the poor. They left Fort Berthold during the summer of 1897 and visited other reservation sites at Oak Creek, Standing Rock, and Cheyenne River. When they reached Cheyenne River Agency, Bishop Thomas O'Gorman (Marty's successor) of Sioux Falls, South Dakota, refused to grant priestly faculties to Craft. By June 1898, Secretary of Interior Cornelius N. Bliss served notice on Craft that he was banned from all Indian reservations, and by October, federal warrants were being readied for the priest's arrest, alleging that he was "living with four Indian girls in open adultery near Pierre [South Dakota]."[3]

[2] Craft to James Edward Kelly, 10 April 1897, Kelly Papers.

[3] James E. Jenkins, special Indian agent at Sisseton Indian Reservation, telegram to Commissioner of Indian Affairs, 10 October 1898.

However, while the Department of Interior was building the case for his arrest, Craft had been exploring opportunities presented by the outbreak of the Spanish–American War. Characteristically, when attacked by the Department of Interior, he sought refuge in the War Department. Probably before Special Agent Jenkins's scandalous accusations reached Cheyenne River or Washington, Father Craft and the sisters were already en route east and south.

Commissioned to serve as nurses in the Spanish–American War, the four sisters and Father Craft reached Camp Cuba Libre in Jacksonville, Florida, on October 21, 1897. For the next several weeks, they worked in military hospitals, first at Camp Cuba Libre, then, beginning in early December, in Camp Onward in Savannah, Georgia, and finally in Havana's Camp Columbia beginning on December 22. All the sisters served admirably and were awarded the silver crosses of the Order of Spanish–American War Nurses. Congressman John Francis Fitzgerald of Massachusetts introduced HR 379 on February 28, 1899, to convey the "thanks of Congress [to] the Sisters of American Congregation who, bravely and heroically, in the hospital and on the field, ministered to the wants of the soldiers in the Spanish–American War."[4]

Craft's reputation had preceded him to Cuba, however, and Archbishop Placide L. Chapelle, the apostolic delegate, expelled him and the sisters from the island. One of the sisters died and was buried there, and the other three eventually left the religious life and returned to their homes in the Dakotas. Through General O'Beirne, Craft tried to get an appointment as a chaplain with the 1st Infantry, which was then being reassigned to China. This attempt, however, was unsuccessful.

Early in 1901, Father Craft returned to his home in Milford, Pennsylvania. His clerical faculties were restored by Bishop M. J. Hoban of the Diocese of Scranton, who named him pastor of a new parish, St. Matthew's, in East Stroudsburg, Pennsylvania—a post he assumed on July 4, 1902. Perhaps it was this bucolic and invigorating environment that led Craft to spend the next eighteen years

[4] U.S. Congress, HR 379.

FIGURE 19. St. Matthew's Catholic Church (postcard view), ca. 1920, East Stroudsburg, Penn.

in relative anonymity as a parish priest; possibly he was squelched by the bishop as a condition of granting faculties; or maybe he was just burned out. He never returned to Indian Country, and he ceased writing for publication in any religious or secular press.

Poor health prevented him from visiting Gettyburg on the 50th anniversary (1913) of the epic battle, where he eagerly wished to meet with "old friends of both armies,"[5] but a few years later, he felt well enough to again volunteer his services as an Army chaplain in World War I. Father Craft never made it into what would

[5] Craft to James Edward Kelly, 5 July 1913, Kelly Papers.

have been his sixth war, though, as he was considered too old for service. However, St. Matthew's continued to grow and prosper under his pastorate. He passed away peacefully on a Saturday evening, September 11, 1920.

Bishop Hoban traveled from Scranton to deliver the eulogy in a service attended by priests from Pennsylvania and neighboring states. Craft was beloved by the congregation he had served for almost twenty years, as witnessed by the throng of mourners who filled St. Matthews. Reportedly, the overflow crowd extended down the entrance stairway and into the street, a verbal description that benefits from an actual view of St. Matthew's Church in Father Craft's time, as seen in figure 19.

The loss was felt far beyond the parochial bounds of the Catholic community. Soon after the funeral, a letter appeared in the local paper. In it, the author concluded that "Stroudsburg has lost a noble citizen, and his country a real patriot, and the church of God a superb Christian minister and priest. God give his soul rest and light and peace in Paradise, and may the same God send us in this time of great need many many more (in all parts of His church), of the same glorious type is the prayer of Reginald S. Radcliffe."[6] The author of this letter was not a member of the Catholic Church. Archdeacon Reginald S. Radcliffe, the author, was a prominent priest of the *Episcopal* Church.

Father Francis M. Craft was a complex, controversial figure on the Dakota reservations as the western frontier came to a close. In almost two decades in the Dakotas, he fought federal bureaucrats and church hierarchy alike as he strove to improve the wretched conditions that beset the Sioux. In the process, he earned the deep respect and admiration of the Indians and the enmity of Indian agents and his own Catholic hierarchy. Some even questioned his sanity in the 1890s but never in the next twenty years as St. Matthew's Catholic Church flourished under his leadership. His

[6] *Stroudsburg Record*, October 2, 1920.

severest critics were those who had most at stake in quieting him.[7] Perhaps the most fitting epitaph for Father Craft was that provided by Black Elk, who in the 1930s said, "He was a very good man, and not like the other Wasichus."[8]

[7] For a full discussion of allegations of insanity against Craft, see Foley, *Father Francis M. Craft*, 137–153.

[8] Neihardt, Black Elk Speaks, 252.

FIGURE 20.
Father Craft's coat of arms, from his personal stationery 1905–1920. Translation: "To be rather than to seem." *Foley/Craft Collection.*

Bibliography

Allen, Charles W. *From Fort Laramie to Wounded Knee.* Edited by Richard E. Jensen. Lincoln: University of Nebraska Press, 1997.

Bartlett, John. *Familiar Quotations.* 16th ed. Edited by Justin Kaplan. Boston: Little, Brown & Company, 1992.

Bland, Thomas A. *A Brief History of the Late Military Invasion of the Home of the Sioux.* Washington, D.C.: National Indian Defense Association, 1891.

———. *A History of the Sioux Agreement.* Washington, D.C.: Self-published pamphlet, n.d.

Bordeaux, William J. *Conquering the Mighty Sioux.* Sioux Falls, S.Dak., 1929.

Bower, Walter. *Scotichronicon.* 9 vols. Edited by D. E. R. Watt. Aberdeen: Aberdeen University Press, 1987–98.

Brown, Dee. *Bury My Heart at Wounded Knee.* New York: Holt Rinehart & Winston, 1970.

Buechel, Rev. Eugene. *A Dictionary—Oie Wowapi Wan of Teton Sioux.* Edited by Rev. Paul Manhart, SJ. Pine Ridge, S.Dak.: Red Cloud Indian School, 1983.

Catholic Directory, Almanac and Clergy List. Annual vols. Milwaukee, Wis.: Wiltzius, 1897–99.

Catlin, George. *North American Indians.* Edited by Peter Matthiessen. New York: Penguin Books, 1996.

Coleman, William. *Voices of Wounded Knee.* Lincoln: University of Nebraska Press, 2000.

Commissioner of Indian Affairs. *Annual Reports of the Commissioner of Indian Affairs.* 1881–1900. Available in the Congressional Serial Set, SuDocs Number I 20.1.

Cook, James H. *Fifty Years on the Old Frontier.* New Haven, Conn.: Yale University Press, 1923.

DeMallie, Raymond J., and Douglas R. Parks. *Sioux Indian Religion.* Norman: University of Oklahoma Press, 1987.

Dickens, Charles. *Pickwick Papers.* London: Chapman and Hall, 1929. First published in serial form 1836–37.

Duratscheck, Sister Mary Claudia. *Crusading Along Sioux Trails: A History of the Catholic Indian Missions of South Dakota.* St. Meinrad, Ind.: Grail Press, 1947.

Fedarko, Kevin. "Why We Must Return to Wounded Knee." *Parade Magazine*, May 16, 2004.

Finerty, John F. *War-Path and Bivouac, or the Conquest of the Sioux.* Norman: University of Oklahoma Press, 1961.

Foley, Thomas W. *Faces of Faith: A History of the First Order of Indian Sisters.* Baltimore: Cathedral Foundation Press, 2008.

———. *Father Francis M. Craft, Missionary to the Sioux.* Lincoln: University of Nebraska Press, 2002.

Hassrick, Royal B. *The Sioux: Life and Customs of a Warrior Society.* Norman: University of Oklahoma Press, 1964

Hinton, May E. *South of the Cannonball: A History of Sioux County, the War Bonnet County.* Grand Forks, N.Dak.: Washburn Printing Center, 1984.

Hoffman's Catholic Directory. Compiled by Rev. James Fagan. Annual vols. Milwaukee, Wis.: Hoffman Brothers, 1886–96.

Holley, Frances Chamberlain. *Once Their Home; or, Our Legacy from the Dahkotahs; Historical, Biographical, and Incidental, from Far-off Days, Down to the Present.* Chicago: Donohue and Henneberry, 1890.

Holy Bible. Chicago: Catholic Press, 1955.

Horace. *Ars Poetica.* Translated by H. Rushton Fairclough. Cambridge, Mass.: Harvard University Press, Loeb Classical Library, 1932.

Hoxie, Frederick E. *Encyclopedia of North American Indians: Native American History, Culture, and Life from Paleo-Indians to the Present.* Boston: Houghton Mifflin, 1996.

Hyde, George E. *Red Cloud's Folk: A History of the Oglala Sioux Indians.* Norman: University of Oklahoma Press, 1937.

———. *A Sioux Chronicle.* Norman: University of Oklahoma Press, 1956.

———. *Spotted Tail's Folk, A History of the Brulé Sioux.* Norman: University of Oklahoma Press, 1961.

Jensen, Richard E., R. Eli Paul, and John E. Carter. *Eyewitness at Wounded Knee.* Lincoln: University of Nebraska Press, 1991.

Karolevitz, Robert F. *Bishop Martin Marty, "The Black Robe Lean Chief."* Yankton, S.Dak.: Privately printed for the Benedictine Sisters of Sacred Heart Convent, 1980.

Kelley [*sic*], James Edward. "Rev. Francis J. [*sic*] Craft Served Many Countries." *Scranton (Pa.) Catholic Light*, Diocesan Historical Series, Dual Jubilee, vol. 3, no. 6 (October 6, 1921): 39–40.

Kelley, William Fitch. *Pine Ridge 1890: An Eye Witness Account of the Events Surrounding the Fighting at Wounded Knee.* Edited and compiled by Alexander Kelley and Pierre Bovis. San Francisco: Pierre Bovis, 1971.

Kingsbury, George W. *History of Dakota Territory, South Dakota, Its History and Its People.* Edited by George Martin Smith. 5 vols. Chicago: S. J. Clarke Publishing, 1915.

Kolbenschlag, George R. *A Whirlwind Passes: Newspaper Correspondents and the Sioux Indian Disturbances of 1890–1891.* Vermillion: University of South Dakota Press, 1990.

Koneberg, Hermann, OSB. *Blessed Ones of 1888.* Translated by Eliza A. Donnelly. New York: Benziger Brothers, 1888.

Marty, Bishop Martin. "The Indian Problem and the Catholic Church." *The Catholic World,* February 1889, 577–584.

Mattes, Merill J. "The Enigma of Wounded Knee." *Plains Anthropologist* 5, no. 9 (May 1960): 1–11.

McGinnis, Hugh. "The Wounded Knee Massacre." As told to O. M. Glasgow. *True West,* 8 (March–April, 1961): 6–9, 52–54.

McGregor, James H. *The Wounded Knee Massacre from the Viewpoint of the Sioux.* Rapid City, S.Dak.: Fenske, 1940.

McLaughlin, James. *My Friend the Indian.* Boston: Houghton Mifflin, 1910.

Miller, Nathan. *Ghost Dance.* Lincoln: University of Nebraska Press, 1959.

Mooney, James M. *The Ghost-Dance Religion and Wounded Knee.* New York: Dover Publications, 1973.

National Cyclopædia of American Biography. New York: James T. White & Co., 1930.

Neihardt, John G. *Black Elk Speaks.* Lincoln: University of Nebraska Press, 1979.

Ostler, Jeffrey. *The Plains Sioux and U. S. Colonialism from Lewis and Clark to Wounded Knee.* Cambridge, England: Cambridge University Press, 2004.

Perez, Benjamin L. "Father Craft, Late-Nineteenth-Century Catholic Missionary to the Sioux." Review of *Father Francis M. Craft, Missionary to the Sioux,* by Thomas W. Foley. *H-AmIndian, H-Net Reviews,* February 2003. http://www.h-net.org/reviews/showrev.cgi?

Pfaller, Louis L., OSB. *James McLaughlin: The Man with an Indian Heart.* New York: Vantage Press, 1978.

Powers, William K. *Oglala Religion.* Lincoln: University of Nebraska Press, 1977.

Robinson, Doane. *A History of the Dakota or Sioux Indians.* Minneapolis, Minn.: Ross and Haines, 1967.

Sadler's Catholic Almanac and Ordo. Edited and compiled by John Gilmary Shea. Annual volumes. New York: D & J Sadler and Company, 1888–90.

Schmitt, Martin F., ed. *General George Crook: His Autobiography.* Norman: University of Oklahoma Press, 1946.

Scott, Brig. Gen. E. D., Retired. "Wounded Knee—A Look at the Records." In *Winners of the West,* vol. 16, no. 5. St. Joseph, MO: May 1939.

Seymour, Forrest W. *Sitanka: The Full Story of Wounded Knee.* W. Hanover, Mass.: Christopher Publishing House, 1981.

Shakespeare, William. *The Riverside Shakespeare.* 2nd ed.. Edited by G. Blakemore Evans, with the assistance of J. J. M Tobin. Boston: Houghton Mifflin, 1997.

Shaw, Dennis E. *The Battle of Wounded Knee: Myth Versus Reality.* Coral Gables, Fla.: University of Miami, 1981.

Smith, Rex Alan. *Moon of Popping Trees.* New York: Reader's Digest Press, 1975.
Stevenson, Burton, ed. *The Home Book of Quotations.* 9th ed. New York: Dodd, Mead & Company, 1964.
Tilden, Anita S., and Eugenia Langford, comps. *Biographical and Historical Index of American Indians and Persons Involved in Indian Affairs.* 8 vols. Boston: G. K. Hall & Co., 1966.
U.S. Congress. H.R. 379. *Congressional Record.* 56th Cong., 1st sess., 1900. Vol. 33. Washington, D.C.
U. S. Senate. Committee on the Judiciary. *Wounded Knee Massacre: Hearing on S. 1147 and S. 2900.* 94th Cong., 2d sess., 1976.
Utley, Robert M. *The Last Days of the Sioux Nation.* New Haven, Conn.: Yale University Press, 1963.
Utley, Robert M., and Wilcomb E. Washburn. *Indian Wars.* Boston: Houghton Mifflin, 1977.
Utter, Jack. *Wounded Knee and the Ghost Dance Tragedy.* Lake Ann, Mich.: National Woodlands Publishing, 1991.
Vestal, Stanley. *Sitting Bull: Champion of the Sioux.* 3rd printing. Norman: University of Oklahoma Press, 1965. First published 1932 by Houghton Mifflin.

Archival Collections

Assumption Abbey Archives, Richardton, N.Dak.
Bureau of Catholic Indian Missions (BCIM) Records, Marquette University Archives, Milwaukee, Wis.
Catholic Diocese of Sioux Falls, S.Dak.
Foley/Craft Collection. In the author's possession.
Kelly, James Edward, Papers. New-York Historical Society.
Letters to and from Father Francis M. Craft. Sacred Heart Monastery Archives, Richardton, N.Dak.
National Archives Depository, Washington, D.C. Records of the Bureau of Indian Affairs. RG 75.
St. Meinrad Archabbey Archives, St. Meinrad, Ind.
Woodstock College Archives, Lauinger Library, Georgetown University Archives, Washington, D.C.

Index

References to illustrations are in italic type.
Craft's variant spellings are parenthetically noted.